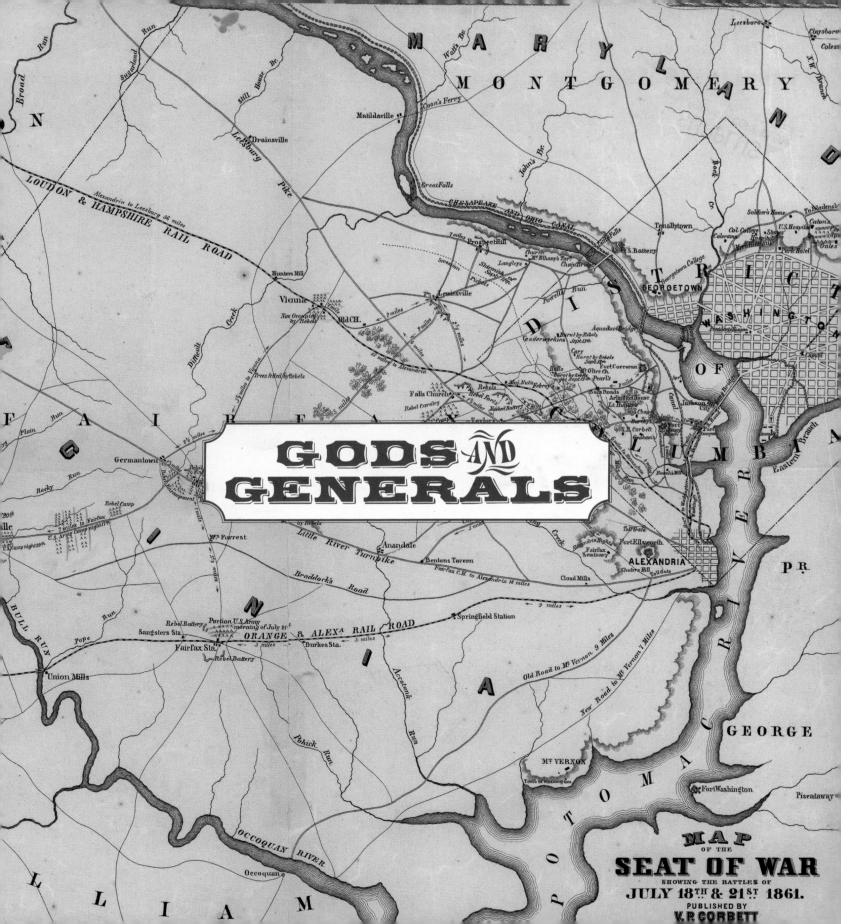

GODS AND GENERALS

MAP
OF THE
SEAT OF WAR
SHOWING THE BATTLES OF
JULY 18TH & 21ST 1861.
PUBLISHED BY
V. P. CORBETT

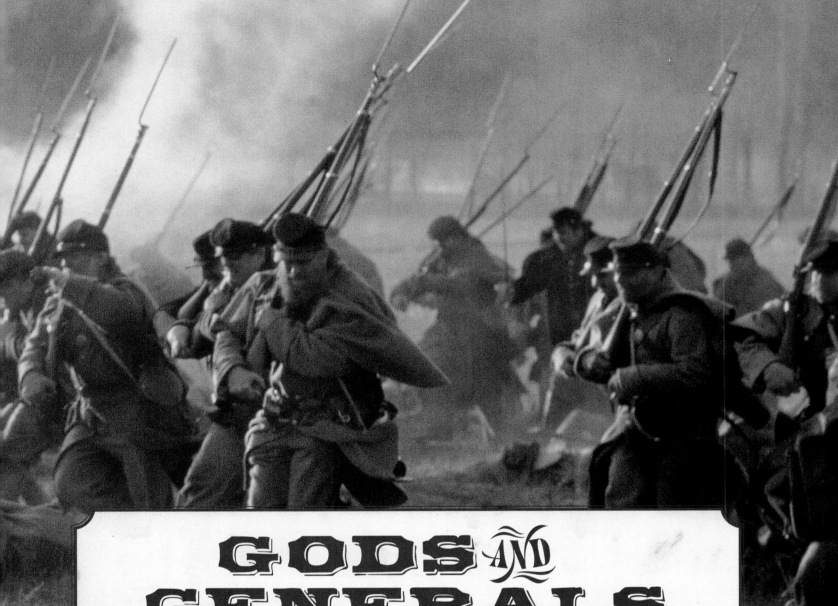

GODS AND GENERALS

The Illustrated Story of the Epic Civil War Film

Introduction and Screenplay by RONALD F MAXWELL

Foreword by JEFF SHAARA, author of the novel GODS AND GENERALS

Production photographs by VAN REDIN

Edited by DIANA LANDAU   Designed by TIMOTHY SHANER

With contributions by
JAMES I. ROBERTSON, JR., DENNIS E. FRYE, and FRANK A. O'REILLY

A NEWMARKET PICTORIAL MOVIEBOOK

NEWMARKET PRESS • NEW YORK

This book is published in the United States of America.

First Edition

10 9 8 7 6 5 4 3 2 1

Library of Congress Cataloging-in-Publication Data available upon request.

ISBN 1-55704-543-7

QUANTITY PURCHASES

Companies, professional groups, clubs, and other organizations may qualify for special terms when
ordering quantities of this title. For information, write Special Sales Department, Newmarket Press,
18 East 48th Street, New York, NY 10017; call (212) 832-3575; fax (212) 832-3629;
or e-mail mailbox@newmarketpress.com.
www.newmarketpress.com

Design by Timothy Shaner

Editorial services by Parlandau Communications

Manufactured in the United States of America.

CONTENTS

MARCH THROUGH A SETTING SUN
by Jeff Shaara

Above: *Novelist Jeff Shaara talks with Stephen Lang, who portrays General Stonewall Jackson, on the* Gods and Generals *set.* Right: *Jeff Shaara as photographed on the set in the costume of a Confederate Army officer by historical photographer Rob Gibson.*

It began with a shout. A vast line of Union soldiers rolled forward, a ragged formation, uneven steps; some already beginning to stumble and fall, the first to absorb the awful shock of the musket fire that ripped through their ranks. The shock was compounded now by the thunder of artillery shells, bursts of fire and smoke and black dirt, the impact throwing more men to the ground, many of them frozen and silent. In front of the wavering line, officers held their swords high and shouted through the chaos of sound, ordering or perhaps begging their men to continue the charge. The scene flowed past me, framed by the stunning backdrop of a fiery sunset, blinding me to the faces; the men now a wave of shadows still surging forward, their numbers growing smaller. And still they staggered on, closer to the guns of their enemy.

And then there was another shout, this one through a bullhorn: "Cut!"

As abruptly as it began, the wave of battered soldiers now drifted back to where they had started, to line up once more—the officers now calm, adjusting their uniforms or having their uniforms adjusted for them… by civilians.

Behind and beside me, dozens of film technicians moved into action, and behind them another hundred onlookers—reporters and actors—began to talk, breaking the reverent mood of the spectacle we had just witnessed. I was observing from inside a small tent, sitting next to the man who controlled the entire scene: director Ron Maxwell. There was no conversation, no idle chat; Ron was urgently focused on the setting sun, concerned not with the extraordinary beauty but with the loss of precious daylight. Although few observers were aware of it, Ron had seen something in the shot that detracted from the moment, some flaw that only the director sees—and so, before the daylight faded further, the scene would have to be replayed. The charge would begin again.

This scene portrayed one part of the Battle of Fredericksburg, the disastrous assault by the Union army against an impregnable Confederate defense: the stone wall that ran along the base of Marye's Heights. The history was familiar to me down to the last detail—the names and faces of the men who made the charge, what they saw and felt, and how those who survived that awful day would recall the experience. I had researched and gathered those experiences, reached as far as I could into the minds of those remarkable people. I'd been fortunate enough to bring a story to the printed page about that day and many others, about what it was like to march and charge and die in those fields.

The book was called *Gods and Generals*, a title given to me by my father, who thirty years ago had wanted that title for a book of his own. But he had decided instead on another title for that book: *The Killer Angels*. Thus was his legacy now a part of my own.

The scene I witnessed that day was the result of a filmmaker's dream, of Ron Maxwell's quest to bring my written words to life in a way few can duplicate. As the author of the book, my task was complete. Now I could only marvel at the attention and care, the expertise and talent that transformed the book to another form— Ron's screenplay—and from there to the action I was witnessing. Actors and technicians and men dressed as soldiers were living those words, creating the experience of men long dead by marching across a vast field framed by a setting sun. It is a moment I will remember the rest of my life.

BEYOND THE MYTHS
by Ronald F. Maxwell

The starry cross of the Confederacy is at the center of a roiling controversy. Protesting crowds want it removed from state capitols; vociferous groups insist on keeping the flag flying. The Saint Andrew's cross embedded in this emblem can be seen as a symbol for the crossroads and cross-currents of American history. To many Americans, black and white, the flag is like a dagger to the heart, a painful reminder of the worst of America's past injustices and persistent racial prejudices. To others—mostly but not all white—the flag inspires pride in a heroic past; it stirs, in Lincoln's phrase, the "mystic chords of memory" for gallant and fearless warriors fighting for their independence. Each side finds it difficult to appreciate the genuine feelings of their counterparts or to reconcile one viewpoint with the other. Few other icons inspire such passionate and mutually exclusive responses.

In this highly charged atmosphere, how can a filmmaker hope to make a serious film on the Civil War without inviting even more controversy? While cognizant of his fellow citizens' legitimate sensitivity, he must do his best to keep contemporary pressures out of his work. If not, the work risks being a sanitized, lame, and gratuitous exercise in political correctness, unworthy of its subject or of today's discerning audiences. And unworthy of future generations, who will not thank us for putting career aspirations ahead of the first duty of all artists and storytellers—to get to the truth of the matter, to the mysterious heart of the human condition with all its paradoxes, contradictions, and complexities.

There are more than a few in the academy, in the media, in politics, who want to reduce the fearful agony of the Civil War to simplistic jargon. They insist on seeing the war in terms of the good guys and bad guys. Since this is Hollywood's customary way of looking at all human history, it is particularly challenging to avoid taking this dramatic turn in a film on the Civil War.

In his insightful essay, "The Legacy of the Civil War," Robert Penn

Director Ron Maxwell guides Donzaleigh Abernathy, who plays Jane Beale's servant, Martha, through a scene around the Battle of Fredericksburg.

Warren posits the notions of two great myths persisting in the American consciousness: for the South "the Great Alibi" and for the North "the Treasury of Virtue." "Once the War was over," says Warren, "the Confederacy became a City of the Soul....[O]nly at the moment when Lee handed Grant his sword was the Confederacy born; or to state matters another way, in the moment of death the Confederacy entered upon its immortality." In the Great Alibi, the attempt to recall and enshrine the best motives for Southern independence, the most repugnant factor is often overlooked or de-emphasized—the issue of slavery.

"If the Southerner, with his Great Alibi, feels trapped by history, the Northerner, with his Treasury of Virtue, feels redeemed by history, automatically redeemed," Warren continues. Or, as Brook Adams once noted, "The Yankees went to war animated by the highest ideals of the nineteenth-century middle classes.... But what the Yankees achieved—for their generation at least—was a triumph not of middle-class ideals but of middle-class vices. The most striking products of their crusade were the shoddy aristocracy of the North and the ragged children of the South. Among the masses of Americans there were no victors, only the vanquished."

Warren offers a cautionary note to future novelists, historians, and yes, even filmmakers: "Moral narcissism is a peculiarly unlovely and unloveable trait. . . . [E]ven when the narcissist happens to possess the virtues which he devotes his time congratulating himself upon. . . ." It would be taking the easy path, seeking the approbation of those who guard the Treasury of Virtue, to present the Civil War as a contest between good and evil. Conversely, it would be all too tempting to strike the pose of the outrageous provocateur—to indulge in perpetuating the Great Alibi.

What interests me as a filmmaker and chronicler of the Civil War are the hard choices that real people had to make. Our film is populated by characters with divided loyalties and conflicting affections. Each character embodies his own internal struggle—his own personal civil war. The film begins with a quote from George Eliot's *Daniel Deronda*, referring to the importance of place—of the local, the particular. I included this quote because it sets up the central dilemma. Humans by nature are attached to

Cadets of the Virginia Military Institute open fire at the Battle of First Manassas, as portrayed by Civil War re-enactors in the film.

place and home. These attachments can be powerful in both constructive and destructive ways.

People are also attached to family and to group. They can also be motivated by ideas and ideals. The characters in *Gods and Generals* are not immune to these forces. They are all, to a man and woman, pulled and pushed by these conflicting allegiances. What may be novel in this film is how it reveals the complex ways in which African-Americans, like their white neighbors, were confronted with their own hard choices.

In this film "patriotism" metamorphoses from a philosophical abstraction to an organic life force. For many nineteenth-century Southern whites, patriotism expressed a love of state and locality that seems strange if not incomprehensible to inhabitants of the new global community. To nineteenth-century Unionists, who found themselves on both sides of the Mason-Dixon line, patriotism constituted a love of the entire country, from Penobscot Bay to the Gulf of Mexico. For African-Americans, patriotism could mean all of the above, further leavened with the group identity and group allegiance fostered by slavery in the South and prejudice in the North.

Martha, the domestic slave in the Beale family, has genuine affection for the white children she has helped rear alongside her own. She is also tied by emotion, tradition, and circumstance to the larger community of blacks, whose fate she shares. When Yankee looters come to ransack her home in Fredericksburg, she will not let them pass. A few days later, when Yankee soldiers seek to requisition the same home as a hospital, she opens the door and attends to the wounded.

Historians write about the forces of history, about ideology and determinism. Whatever truth lies in such analysis, it is not the place where individuals live out their lives. Ordinary people like you and me and the characters who inhabit this film live their lives day by day, hoping to make the best of it with dignity, hoping to get by—in the context of this film, hoping to survive. They in their time, like us today, have bonds of affection across racial, religious, sexual, and political divides. "To experience the full imaginative appeal of the Civil War," says Robert Penn Warren, "…may be, in fact, the very ritual of being American."

Gods and Generals is only the first part of a trilogy of films on the Civil War, the second being the already produced *Gettysburg*, and the third the yet to be made *The Last Full Measure*. Even a trilogy can provide little more than a glimpse of the epochal event at the center of our national consciousness. We are with Jackson as he steels the First Virginia Brigade at Manassas, with Lee as he declines the command of the Union army, with

Chamberlain as he tells his wife Fanny he is going off to war, and later, in his defense of Little Round Top. Across more than four years, across the countryside and cityscapes of America, we are with these men and others wearing the Blue and the Gray as they write in their own blood the destiny of America—our destiny.

Warren provides a kind of credo for the filmmaker with the audacity to venture into these waters:

"Historians, and readers of history too, should look twice at themselves when the [Civil War] is mentioned. It means that we should seek to end the obscene gratifications of history, and try to learn what the contemplation of the past, conducted with psychological depth and humane breadth, can do for us. What happens if, by the act of historical imagination—the historian's and our own—we are transported into the documented, re-created moment of the past and, in a double vision, see the problems and values of that moment and those of our own, set against each other in mutual criticism and clarification? What happens if, in innocence, we can accept this process without trying to justify the present by the past or the past by the present? . . . [T]here is a discipline of the mind and heart, a discipline both humbling and enlarging, in the imaginative consideration of possibilities in the face of the unique facts of the irrevocable past. . . . History cannot give us a program for the future, but it can give us a fuller understanding of ourselves, and of our common humanity, so that we can better face the future."

Ron Maxwell evaluates a shot.

Can any filmmaker attempt a film on the Civil War without a sense of humility and a willingness to listen—not to the discordant voices of the here and now, but to the thousands of real-life people whose testimony has been recorded for posterity in diaries, letters, and memoirs; to the hundreds of scholars who have studied the War over the decades? Would there be something innately authentic in availing oneself of this kind of knowledge, in submitting to this kind of discipline, in modestly accepting one's valid place in the collective effort of generations seeking illumination and truth? In such an organic context, could a filmmaker make a lasting contribution to our understanding and continuing fascination with the American Civil War?

The Way to War

FATHERS AND SONS
Jeff Shaara's Literary Legacy

"The fact that I'm carrying on my father's legacy is not something I take lightly," says *Gods and Generals* author Jeff Shaara. "I will never take it for granted."

It's a large legacy—and not one that Jeff Shaara had ever expected to inherit. At the time of his father Michael Shaara's death in 1988 at age fifty-nine, Jeff was a successful rare coin dealer in Tampa, Florida. His father's career had been markedly less stellar. A prolific and determined writer of short stories and novels, Michael had had to take teaching jobs to support his family. Although his magnum opus, *The Killer Angels*—which had taken him seven years to write—won the Pulitzer Prize for fiction in 1975, it had been rejected by fifteen publishers before being bought by a small independent publishing company. It never achieved commercial success during Michael Shaara's lifetime.

Jeff sold his coin business to take over management of his father's estate, and he strongly supported Ron Maxwell's effort to transform *The Killer Angels* into the critically and commercially successful film *Gettysburg*, released in 1993. A year after that film's release, Maxwell suggested that Jeff continue the story that Michael had begun.

"The idea was to create a story that Ron could turn into a film," Shaara recalls. "I had no expectation of actually writing a book. And perhaps because I had no expectations, I had no fear. I just sat down and wrote." In the autumn of 1994 he sent the completed manuscript to an editor at Ballantine Books, who immediately recognized its potential. The novel, which interweaves the stories of Generals Lee, Chamberlain, Hancock, and Jackson in the years leading up to Gettysburg, spent fifteen weeks on the *New York Times* national bestseller list.

Look closer at Jeff Shaara's life, and you see that he may have been predestined to follow this path. The grandson of Italian immigrants named Sciarra, Jeff had been a Civil War buff since early childhood. It was mostly for his benefit that his family made a side trip to Gettysburg on their way home from the 1964 World's Fair in New York. "I was twelve years old, playing with the little soldiers and bayonets," he recalls. "I made my family stop at the souvenir stand so I could buy a hat and a rubber sword."

Above: *David Carpenter as the Rev. Beverly Tucker Lacy (General Jackson's chaplain) and Jeff Shaara as an officer in the Confederate encampment, winter 1863. Opposite: General Thomas J. (Stonewall) Jackson, played by Stephen Lang, and General John Bell Hood, played by Patrick Gorman, approaching Fredericksburg, Virginia, December 1862.*

More fathers and sons: Left to right, *stunt coordinator Chris Howell, his son C. Thomas Howell (as Tom Chamberlain), Jonathan Maxwell (as Captain Ellis Spear), and his father, director Ron Maxwell, on* the Gods and Generals *set.*

To the surprise of his family—and himself—Michael Shaara, who'd never considered himself a historian, was equally transfixed by the century-old battleground. "He became obsessed," says Jeff. "For the next seven years the Civil War took over his life. And it was really from standing there and walking in the footsteps of those historical characters."

It's a lesson that impressed him deeply, Jeff says. "My research has been much the same: You have to walk in the footsteps."

Jeff Shaara's second novel, *The Last Full Measure*, is a sequel to *Gettysburg*; published in 1998, it too is being adapted by Ron Maxwell into a feature film. *Gone for Soldiers*, published in 2000, takes a step backward, following the protagonists of the Civil War through their formative experiences in the Mexican-American War of the 1840s. Shaara's most recent novels, *Rise to Rebellion* and *The Glorious Cause*, go back farther still, to the Revolutionary War.

"Someone once asked me if all I'm ever going to write is war stories," Shaara says. "That's not really the point. The point is that during the most terrible periods in our history, some people have risen to the occasion. That's what interests me—whether it's the eighteenth, nineteenth, or twentieth century. That's what I want to write about. Those are the stories I want to tell."

Shaara finds deep satisfaction in seeing his stories take life on the screen. "It's wonderful to hear dialogue and realize that it's mine—I wrote that, it's on page 250. And there are certain scenes that work better on the screen than they do on the page. It's Ron Maxwell's genius to recognize what will work and what won't. I've learned a lot. It's been a wonderful experience."

Wonderful—yet bittersweet. "This is what my father never saw," Jeff Shaara acknowledges with a trace of sadness. "He had a very difficult writing career and never got the recognition he deserved. He never got the emotional support I've gotten from readers, or from the cast and crew of *Gods and Generals.*

"So I'm carrying a mantle of responsibility. I want to make my father proud. If he were alive, I'd want him to look at my work and say 'Good job.' That's what drives me."

Director Ron Maxwell on the Guiney Station set with (left to right): Jackson aides James Power Smith (Stephen Spacek) and Joseph Morrison (Scott Cooper), Hattie (Rosemary Meacham), Anna Morrison Jackson (Kali Rocha), and Dr. Hunter McGuire, Jackson's personal physician (Sean Pratt).

TED TURNER PICTURES
Presents...

Alifelong student of history with an avid interest in the Civil War, media entrepreneur and philanthropist Ted Turner has frequently translated that interest into television and film projects—including *Gettysburg*, which he helped produce through Turner Pictures and in which he has an uncredited role as Colonel Waller T. Patton. With *Gods and Generals*, Turner not only reprised that cameo—this time as a speaking role—but also took on full financing of the film through his new, independently owned movie production company, Ted Turner Pictures.

Turner may be best known for CNN and his other cable television ventures, but his interest in the big screen goes back nearly two decades. He acquired MGM Studios in 1985; when he later sold it he retained the famed MGM/United Artists library, which became the foundation of the Turner Classic Movies cable channel. Through Turner Pictures, now a subsidiary of AOL Time Warner, he produced eight made-for-TV movies about the Civil War, including *Andersonville* and *The Monitor and the Merrimack*.

Turner conceived of Ted Turner Pictures in 1999, almost a year before *Gods and Generals* began taking shape. To head the new enterprise he tapped Robert Wussler, a TV industry veteran who had been a co-founder of CNN and an executive at Turner Broadcasting. By late 2000 Wussler was meeting regularly with Ron Maxwell about the *Gods and Generals* project; production began in February 2001.

Born in Cincinnati in 1938, Turner is a longtime resident of Atlanta with a broad perspective on American culture. "The Civil War was one of the most important parts of our history," he says. "I believe it's important to show people that history. *Gettysburg* did that, *Gods and Generals* will do that, and hopefully I'll get a chance to complete the trilogy by bringing *The Last Full Measure* to the screen."

In the meantime, Ted Turner Pictures is taking a look at a much more recent slice of American—and world—history. Its new documentary, *Avoiding Armageddon*, is an eight-hour examination of weapons of mass destruction. It's scheduled to be broadcast on the Public Broadcasting System in April 2003.

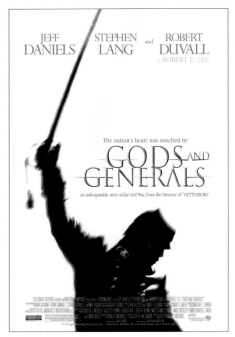

Above: *Poster for the theatrical release of* Gods and Generals. *Opposite: Ted Turner, in his uniform as Confederate Colonel Waller Tazewell Patton, as photographed on the set by Rob Gibson.*

18

THE BLUE AND THE GRAY
in Black and White (and Living Color)

Since the dawn of the silent era, filmmakers have found in the Civil War a nearly bottomless well of dramatic material. From early classics such as *The Birth of a Nation* to literary adaptations such as *Gone with the Wind*; from documentaries like Ken Burns's twelve-hour *Civil War* to fact-based dramas like *Andersonville* and *Glory*, movies and TV series have given generations of Americans born long after Appomattox their vision—skewed or accurate—of the War between the States.

In the hands of skilled and sensitive directors, the central theme of brother against brother has taken on a classic, even biblical resonance. Other filmmakers have turned a wide-angle lens on the epic military campaigns; still others turned the war into a backdrop for bosom-heaving romance (preferably draped in magnolias and Spanish moss). And in some movies—the thoughtful *Friendly Persuasion* (1956), with Gary Cooper as an Indiana Quaker patriarch; *Dances with Wolves* (1990); the several versions of *Little Women*—the war remains in the background, casting a long and meaningful shadow over the plot.

The earliest Civil War epic, D. W. Griffith's 1915 *Birth of a Nation*, remains one of the most ambitious and controversial. Born in Kentucky, Griffith grew up on firsthand stories of the lost Confederacy and channeled his towering energies into this four-and-a-half-hour adaptation of a successful novel and play, *The Clansman*. Technically far ahead of its time, the film was derided even by Griffith's contemporaries for its demeaning depiction of African-Americans and its glorification of the Ku Klux Klan.

In fact, few Civil War movies have provided a realistic view of slavery or African-Americans' role in the conflict: For many years, the subject was virtually taboo. A notable exception is *Glory*, the story of the U.S. Army's first all-black volunteer company, based on the correspondence of the white commander.

Above: *Howard Gaye and Donald Crisp as Generals Robert E. Lee and Ulysses S. Grant in D. W. Griffith's* Birth of a Nation, *1915.* Right: *Shirley Temple and Bill "Bojangles" Robinson in* The Littlest Rebel, *1935.* Opposite: *A scene from 1989's* Glory.

A Selective Civil War Filmography

ANDERSONVILLE (1996) Grim four-hour saga, made for TV, of the horrific Confederate POW camp where 13,000 prisoners died in 1864.

THE BIRTH OF A NATION (1915) D. W. Griffith's silent epic of war and Reconstruction, told through the stories of two families from North and South, is a film landmark, lauded for its innovative technique and deplored for its overt racism.

THE CIVIL WAR (1990) Ken and Ric Burns's PBS series blended inventive use of still photographs, period music, and distinguished voiceovers, reinventing the documentary form and kindling a worldwide revival of interest in the period.

THE GENERAL (1927) Buster Keaton directed himself in this classic silent comedy of Union spies and a stolen train. Based on true events, it was remade in Cinemascope by Disney in 1956 as *The Great Locomotive Chase* (aka *Andrews' Raiders*).

GETTYSBURG (1993) Written and directed by Ron Maxwell and based on the Pulitzer Prize–winning novel by Michael Shaara, this re-creation of the Civil War's most famous battle features outstanding performances by Martin Sheen, Tom Berenger, Jeff Daniels, and Richard Jordan (who died before the film's release) as General Armistead.

GLORY (1989) Skillful, moving drama about the U.S. Army's first all-black volunteer company. Based on the letters of Colonel Robert Gould Shaw (portrayed by Matthew Broderick), the film won

Oscars for best cinematography, sound, and supporting actor (Denzel Washington).

GONE WITH THE WIND (1939) Famous even before its release and is probably the grandest soap opera ever filmed. The Scarlett O'Hara–Rhett Butler love story plays more prominently than the war, but who could ever forget the stunning panorama of the Confederate dead?

THE HORSE SOLDIERS (1959) Drawn from historical events, director John Ford's only full-length Civil War feature casts John Wayne as a Union colonel (based on Benjamin H. Grierson), whose troops sabotage Confederate rail supply lines.

HOW THE WEST WAS WON (1962) Sprawling, all-star epic was filmed in Cinerama by three directors; John Ford directed the Civil War section. Narrated by Spencer Tracy; stars include John Wayne (as Sherman), Henry Fonda, Gregory Peck. Outstanding score by Alfred Newman.

THE LITTLEST REBEL (1935) Shirley Temple sings, dances (with Bill "Bojangles" Robinson), and charms President Lincoln into sparing her Confederate officer father. Available in a colorized version. Previously filmed in 1914.

THE RED BADGE OF COURAGE (1951) World War II hero Audie Murphy is cast memorably against type as the frightened recruit in this adaptation of Stephen Crane's 1899 novel. Directed by John Huston, it features cameos by comedic actor Andy Devine and war cartoonist Bill Mauldin.

RIDE WITH THE DEVIL (1999) Taiwanese director Ang Lee's foray into American history focuses on the Bushwhackers, Southern guerrillas who raided Union farms and towns along the Kansas–Missouri border. With Tobey Maguire, Skeet Ulrich, and teen singing star Jewel.

SHENANDOAH (1965) Set in 1863, with James Stewart as a Virginia widower trying to protect his six sons and one daughter from the conflict raging around them, the movie was the basis for a Broadway musical.

Most Civil War movies have stuck to conventional Hollywood themes of romance and adventure, with the war more or less an excuse for fabulous period costumes and opulent plantation settings. Nearly seven decades after its premiere, *Gone with the Wind* still moves audiences more for its love story than for its historic significance. *Raintree County* tried and failed to duplicate *GWTW*'s success despite the star power of Elizabeth Taylor as a Scarlett-ish spoiled Southern belle. *Quantrill's Raiders* (1958) and *The Great Locomotive Chase* (1956) are essentially caper movies with a wartime setting.

And a whole subgenre of Civil War movies simply ignores history in favor of light—even silly—entertainment. Consider Elvis Presley as an anachronistically crooning and hip-swiveling son of the South in *Love Me Tender*; Shirley Temple tap-dancing with Bill "Bojangles" Robinson in *The Littlest Rebel*; Marion Davies (in blackface) as a Union spy in *Operator 13*; or even the Three Stooges impersonating Union spies in a 1935 short subject, *Uncivil Warriors*.

Surprisingly, one of the most striking conflicts of the Civil War has until now been overlooked on film. Robert E. Lee's choice between commanding the Union Army and defending what he considered his "country"—Virginia— is as compelling as any crisis in classical tragedy. *Gods and Generals* is the first major motion picture to give this conflict its cinematic due.

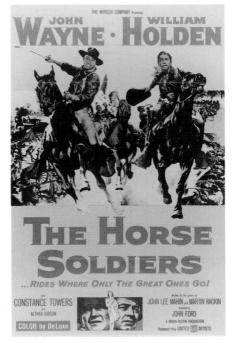

Opposite: *Scarlett O'Hara (Vivian Leigh) and Rhett Butler (Clark Gable) flee the advancing Union army in 1939's* Gone with the Wind; *inset: Soldiers lie wounded and dying in the streets of Atlanta in* GWTW. *Above, left:* The four sisters of the 1933 version of Little Women. *Left and above: Poster art for* The Horse Soldiers, 1959, *and* Love Me Tender, 1956.

PAINTING THE SCENE
The Parallel Visions of Artist and Director

When director Ron Maxwell sought ideas for staging several key scenes in *Gods and Generals*, he went to a reliable source: the highly detailed and evocative Civil War paintings of artist Mort Künstler. Renowned for his renderings of subjects from American history, Künstler has focused on Civil War imagery since the early 1980s. Maxwell knew that the paintings were carefully researched for historical fidelity—a quality both artists insisted on.

Künstler and Maxwell met in 1992 when the Gettysburg film was in progress, and Turner Publishing issued a book of the artist's prints in conjunction with that film's release. They discovered they shared a passion for Civil War history and have kept in touch ever since. "Ron told me that he was planning to film the prequel to *Gettysburg* eventually," says Künstler, "so I wasn't surprised to hear from him about *Gods and Generals*."

The illustrations on this page reveal the cross-fertilization of these collaborators' visions. Künstler's 1995 painting "War Is So Terrible" depicts the victorious Generals Lee and Longstreet overlooking the devastation of the Fredericksburg battlefield on the morning of December 13, 1862, after the failed Union assault on Marye's Heights. Production stills from the film show the two mounted generals in virtually the same pose, with background figures also arranged much as in the painting.

Similarly, Maxwell's shot of Generals Lee and Jackson riding through cheering troops after their triumph at Chancellorsville in May 1863, with the still-burning Chancellor house in the background, drew inspiration from Künstler's 2001 painting "His Supreme Moment." Again Künstler tracked down the telling details: the house is based on pre-war drawings and the flags are those of the regiments present that day.

Turnabout is fair play, and Künstler was given an early look at still photos from *Gods and Generals*—which he used as inspiration to create some of his most recent paintings. Along with historian James I. Robertson, Jr., who has consulted on many of Künstler's works, he saw an early cut of the film and provided feedback at the director's request.

Opposite: *"His Supreme Moment"* by Mort Künstler and the inset production photo both depict victorious Confederate soldiers cheering General Lee at Chancellorsville. Above and below: *The filmed scene echoes Künstler's painting "War Is So Terrible."*

SKETCHING THE SCRIPT
The Story Behind the Storyboards

Top: Bot Roda's panel showing Confederate troops defending the stone wall at Fredericksburg, and above, how the scene looks on film.

Bot Roda brought a valuable set of credentials to his role as sole storyboard artist for the *Gods and Generals* production. Not only does the Lancaster, Pennsylvania, illustrator have a background in advertising and design—disciplines that require quick visualization, as does storyboarding—but he also spent twelve years as a Civil War re-enactor, from 1980 to 1992. Those years "in the hobby," as Roda puts it, allowed him to accurately render complex action scenes "right out of my head."

Roda had first met director Ron Maxwell during the pre-production phase of *Gettysburg*, Maxwell's first Civil War epic. Rumors had been circulating in the re-enactor community about a new movie based on Michael Shaara's novel *The Killer Angels*. Roda had read the novel, and on an impulse—he'd never worked on a movie production—he created some color renderings of battle scenes and sent them to Maxwell. In a cover letter, he mentioned his re-enacting experience and the fact that he lives just 50 miles from Gettysburg and had participated in living history events there. Within a week he was hired as one of two artists for the film.

Maxwell contacted Roda again when he finished writing the *Gods and Generals* screenplay. Between January and June of 2001, Roda created nearly 400 charcoal-pencil drawings of battle scenes and special effects for the movie.

Storyboards are generally used for action scenes with little or no dialogue; they help the director and cinematographer choose effective camera angles and allocate resources economically. Because *Gods and Generals* is about three-quarters battle sequences, Roda's job was both essential and intense.

He began with a close reading of the script—especially the descriptive sections. "Ron's screenplay was very rich in detail," says Roda. "As I read it, I tried to think like a director looking through a viewfinder: Where would a wide shot work? A tracking shot? A closeup? Since I have no budget to consider, I'm free to play with the possibilities."

One of Roda's most challenging tasks was rendering the attack on

Marye's Heights during the battle of Fredericksburg. His illustrations segue dramatically from a low-angle foreground view of soldiers' boots on wooden planks, to a medium shot of men running, to a high crane perspective of the action below—all envisioned through a barrage of artillery fire.

Roda's years as a re-enactor heightened his appreciation for the historical accuracy Maxwell wanted to capture, he says. As a private in the 53rd Pennsylvania Volunteers he built his own weapon—an 1863 Springfield musket—from a kit and slept in the open on gum blankets. "Once, during a wintertime re-enactment, we woke up to find the water in our canteens had frozen," he says. With rewards like that, why did he quit? "As I approached forty, it got harder to portray a nineteen-year-old," Roda admits. With re-enacting as with storyboarding, Roda's commitment to authenticity won the day.

Storyboard panels by Bot Roda depict Federal troops crossing the Rappahannock River to occupy Fredericksburg on December 11, 1862.

PREPARING THE GROUND

Central to Ron Maxwell's conception of rendering *Gods and Generals* on film were the people who would take part in its sweeping battles and the places where those struggles were staged. His production shoot took place largely in the rolling hills and beautiful valleys of Virginia, West Virginia and Maryland, where many of the Civil War's defining events occurred. In some cases, the shooting locations were historic parks and battlefields themselves.

"There's a particular resonance to being on real ground," Maxwell comments. "I think a couple of things happen. First of all, the look is exactly right. Second, the participants are imbued with a sense of place, and it influences their performances. All of this translates onto the screen."

The authentic quality of the performances was paramount to the director—not just in featured roles but in every soldier or civilian who appeared on camera. To that end, *Gods and Generals* made use of thousands of experienced Civil War "re-enactors" on a scale unprecedented in filmmaking. The film contains an estimated 20,000 appearances by such re-enactors. (See page 73 for a detailed account of the re-enactor phenomenon and its role in the production.)

The formidable task of coordinating thousands of non-professional extras and arranging for the film company to shoot in historically sensitive locations fell to Dennis E. Frye, who is listed in the credits as associate producer for "military and civilian activities."

Until *Gods and Generals*, Frye had had no movie experience, but his qualifications for the job were second to none. A native of Washington County, Maryland, Frye grew up surrounded by battle sites and steeped in Civil War lore. He led his first Civil War tour at age eleven; as an adult, he turned his passion into his vocation, writing articles about Civil War history and working for twenty years at Harpers Ferry National Historical Park, where he eventually held the title of chief historian.

In 1997, Frye invited director Ron Maxwell and author Jeff Shaara to

Opposite: *The 1st Virginia Brigade in the Shenandoah Valley, en route to Manassas Junction, July 1862; the scene was filmed in the Shenandoah Valley in 2001. (Early in the war, many Virginia militia still wore blue-and-white uniforms, as they do here.)* Above: *The Antietam battlefield, September 1862 (seen in the DVD version of the film).*

"The land is a character in this movie."
—DIRECTOR RON MAXWELL

the Association for the Preservation of Civil War Sites' annual conference in Hagerstown, Maryland. "I think they were impressed with the interest here in the Civil War and in the preservation of battlefields in the area," says Frye. "That and the fact that we're a movie-friendly community enticed them to consider this their new home."

When production started in January 2001, Maxwell tapped Frye to manage a wide range of responsibilities under the loose rubric of "verisimilitude." Among those tasks: scouting locations that looked historically correct ("the right terrain: no wires or other modern developments"); working closely with Harpers Ferry National Historical Park Superintendent Don Campbell to ensure that location filming wouldn't destroy the park ("on the contrary, it would benefit the park"); and coordinating the more than 3,000 civilian and military re-enactors—all nonprofessional actors—who would add vital authenticity to battle and street scenes.

To production executives, the last undertaking was the most worrisome. Would enough re-enactors show up? Would *any* of them show up? Would their performances be of a high enough caliber?

To allay those fears, Frye and his team—including Dana Heim, a re-enactor himself—combed through thousands of photographs and letters to winnow out the best candidates. "We used more than 3,000 re-enactors in this film," Frye says, "and their love for and interest in history show in scene after scene."

Frye describes himself as "not very emotional" by nature, but he says the production of *Gods and Generals* moved him profoundly. "This is more than a movie and certainly more than 'a war movie,'" he says. "It's about people—about the relationships people have, the dangers people face, and

Preceding pages: *This scene of the 1st Virginia Brigade crossing the Shenandoah River (July 1861) was filmed on a private farm very near where the historical crossing would have taken place; there are only a few locations where the river can be forded. At right, signal corpsmen are sending a semaphore message to compatriots on a Blue Ridge mountain in the distance.* Above: *The set for Camp Mason (where the 20th Maine Regiment trained) in winter, during location scouting.*

the horror people experience in war. And when audiences see this film, they will relate to real people. Stonewall Jackson will no longer be a name on a page in a book—he'll be a real man. Every theater that shows *Gods and Generals* will become a classroom. And the best part is, audiences will learn without even realizing they're being taught."

Below: *Federal troops at the Camp Mason set in summer, with set dressing in place during the shoot.*

BUILDING THE CONFLICT
Sets and Locations

Creating 150 sets for a single movie is always daunting. Creating 150 sets on locations that spanned three states and comprised historically protected sites, battlefields, towns, bridges, railroad stations, colleges, and private homes was nothing short of prodigious. Then there were the locations themselves—as large as 600 acres, far in excess of the contained spaces that moviemakers customarily shoot in. And then there was the schedule: just ten weeks for preparing sets that normally would require six months' preparation.

To meet the challenge, Michael Z. Hanan, production designer for *Gods and Generals*, and his team of nearly eighty construction crew members and fifteen set designers combined rigorous research with a judicious helping of invention. Hanan knew something about Civil War set design from his experience on a made-for television Civil War movie, *Andersonville*. But that film had been shot on a single 30-acre set. For *Gods and Generals*, "historical authenticity was important, of course," says Hanan. "But we had other considerations as well. Would the shooting crew have a clear path in which to work? Would the actors feel comfortable on the set? Will the set stand up to the demands of the action? Could I fit two or three sets into the same location and not have one be seen from the other's vantage point?"

The production crew got a huge helping hand from the weather. The autumn and early winter of 2001, when most of the location shooting occurred, were unusually mild on the East Coast. "We shot up to mid-December and lost only half a day due to weather," notes line producer Ron Smith. "On a 71-day shooting schedule, that's remarkable."

Harpers Ferry

Some of the most striking sets were created at Harpers Ferry, West Virginia; shooting there, says Hanan, constituted "the most difficult work I've ever done." The site is a national historical park, which means it can't be altered in any way. "We couldn't touch any of the buildings," says Hanan. "Every bit of mortar, every fastener, every inch of ground is impor-

Above: *Harpers Ferry in 1859, before it was largely destroyed by bombardment during the War. Located at the confluence of the Potomac and Shenandoah rivers, the town was strategically important to both sides. It's now a national historic park, and the* Gods and Generals *production won special permission to film there.* Opposite: *Generals Lee, Longstreet, and Jackson lead Confederate troops through the streets of Fredericksburg, December 1862; Harpers Ferry stands in for Fredericksburg.*

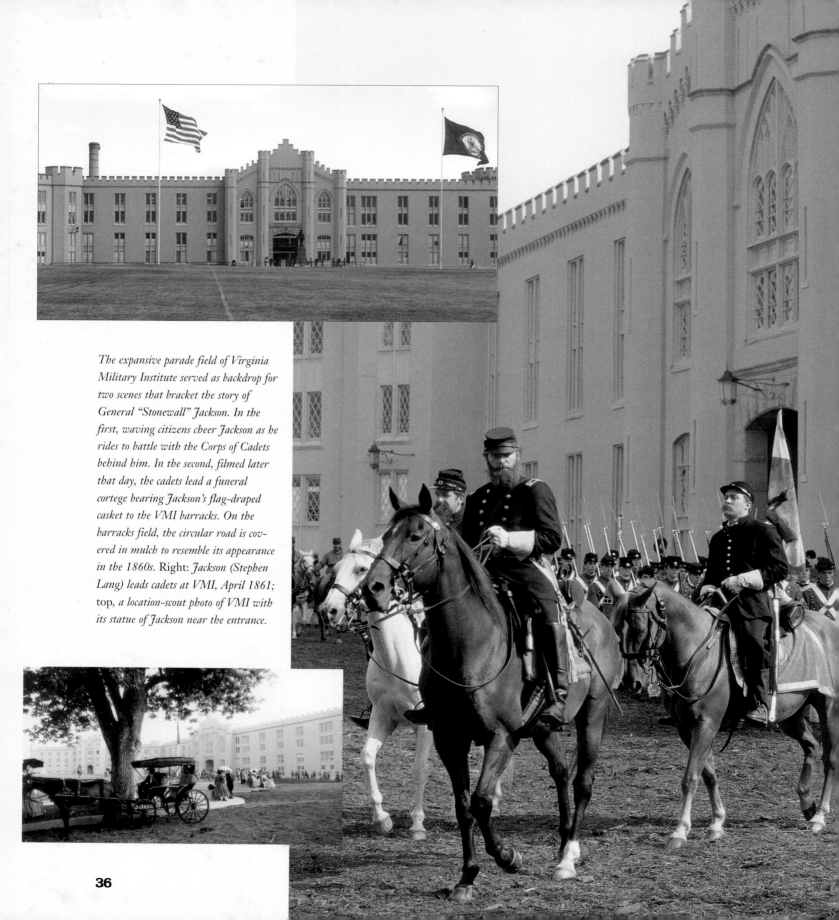

The expansive parade field of Virginia Military Institute served as backdrop for two scenes that bracket the story of General "Stonewall" Jackson. In the first, waving citizens cheer Jackson as he rides to battle with the Corps of Cadets behind him. In the second, filmed later that day, the cadets lead a funeral cortege bearing Jackson's flag-draped casket to the VMI barracks. On the barracks field, the circular road is covered in mulch to resemble its appearance in the 1860s. Right: Jackson (Stephen Lang) leads cadets at VMI, April 1861; top, a location-scout photo of VMI with its statue of Jackson near the entrance.

tant. And yet we had to find ways to add buildings for historical accuracy and for filming logistics, and we had to mask some of the modern infrastructure—wires, the bus terminal, and so on."

The site was used for tight shots of the historical Harpers Ferry, where Jackson made his headquarters in the spring of 1861, and for scenes of the historical Fredericksburg, Virginia, where one of the film's key battles takes place. Fredericksburg was a rarity in the first two years of the war in that significant house-to-house fighting took place in the streets of the town; in fact, it saw the first urban warfare ever to take place in North America.

Hanan researched every aspect of historical Fredericksburg—from street construction to building design to signage—but, in the end, was forced to rely on his imaginative skills. The Beale family house, for example—the setting for several key interior scenes and a dramatic basement scene—had been extensively remodeled in the 1880s. Hanan did some on-site sketches of the house as it appears today, then "redesigned" it, changing the structure and furnishings back to their 1862 appearance.

One of the biggest challenges of shooting at Harpers Ferry was geographic. The park sits in a canyon at the confluence of the Shenandoah and Potomac rivers—a virtual wind tunnel. "Some of the façades we built were 30, 40, 50 feet tall," says Hanan. "They were like big sails in that wind."

Normally, production crews tie their sets to telephone poles driven deep into the ground for stability. Because of Harpers Ferry's historical sensitivity, that wasn't an option. "There are artifacts within the soil that either need to remain there or that will be carefully excavated in the future," Hanan says. Instead, Hanan's crew used large containers to support and weight the sets. "It worked really nicely," he recalls. "As a bonus, the containers gave us a place to safely store equipment." In fact, the solution was so successful that Hanan predicts it will become standard on other film sets.

The Colleges

The contrasting personalities of Thomas Jackson and Joshua Chamberlain—both men were professors-turned-generals—are mirrored in their respective academic institutions. Virginia Military Institute, where Jackson taught, is built in the Gothic Revival style; Bowdoin College, in Maine, is Greek Revival. Hanan used the actual exteriors, then mirrored them, with true-to-period details, in his classroom sets. "We wanted VMI to be a little more austere than Bowdoin," he says. "But mostly I was paying attention to the scene and what the scene dictated."

"Sometimes the scene tells you what your sets should be; sometimes history does."

—Production designer
Michael Hanan

Below: *Professor Joshua Lawrence Chamberlain (Jeff Daniels) teaching at Bowdoin College, fall 1861. The blackboard writing reflects his post as a professor of religious philosophy. Six interior sets—including Jackson's and Chamberlain's classrooms and the room where Jackson died—were painstakingly re-created in an empty warehouse in Hagerstown, Maryland.*

The Trains

The Civil War was the first major conflict anywhere in the world in which railroads played an important role. Hanan felt it was critical that trains and train stations be depicted accurately in *Gods and Generals*—especially, he says, because "they're usually not done right in motion pictures." So he had them built as scenery—of wood, fiberglass, and plastic—right down to the water towers and part of the Harpers Ferry arsenal.

For the Baltimore train station, where Thomas and Anna Jackson are reunited after a long separation, Hanan found an authentic period train at the B&O Railroad Museum that he modified slightly. He also located a portion of some historical track in the middle of downtown Baltimore. The downside: the modern Baltimore skyline. Hanan started from a Mort Küntsler drawing of Guiney Station circa 1863, and designed the set to mask the contemporary skyline. The result looks so authentic that most viewers will assume it's an actual train station. And that's the way it should be, says Hanan. "Our job is to support the actors in the picture. If we do our job seamlessly, no one notices what we've done."

Top: *Production photo of the Guiney Station set, with a camera dolly paralleling the railroad tracks.*
Above: *Production drawing of the station by Tim Braniff, from a drawing by Mort Künstler.*

The Battlefields

Conveying the staggering scope of Civil War battles was one of the biggest challenges of Hanan's job. Visual and digital effects enhanced some scenes, "but if you used visual effects for every scene, you could never afford the movie," says Hanan. Instead, he took time-honored art direction tricks "to the limit" to maximize the depth of each set, "so that fewer than a thousand tents look like tens of thousands." Constructions were designed to appear thicker and denser than they actually were, fooling the eye into perceiving greater depth and perspective.

For the Chancellorsville battle, a night scene in which General Jackson is shot by his own men, the problem was reversed. This wilderness area had to appear densely overgrown to the point of confusion. Yet for practical purposes, the area had to be accessible to a large film crew that included cameras, lights, and sound equipment. To resolve the conflict, Hanan found a location that mimicked the historical setting, "and then we worked on it, opening up some spaces and camouflaging others."

The 1st Virginia Brigade sweeps past Rickett's Federal battery, Battle of First Manassas, September 1862.

The Theaters

The six-hour DVD version of the film includes a subplot about John Wilkes Booth, the actor who in 1865 would shoot President Lincoln; scenes from several plays-within-the-movie build toward the climax. Hanan's crew was charged with re-creating four historical theaters in Chicago and Washington—and then staging the plays as they would have been presented in the 1860s.

Instead of building a theater set from scratch, Hanan was able to use an existing "hemphouse" theater in Martinsburg, West Virginia, that had changed very little from the Civil War era. (Hemphouse theaters, which

Top: *John Wilkes Booth, center (played by Chris Conner), as Brutus in* Julius Caesar, *a play-within-the movie (seen in the DVD version).* Inset: *Production drawing of President and Mrs. Lincoln attending a performance of* Macbeth *starring John Wilkes Booth, April 1863.* Right: *Joshua and Fanny Chamberlain visit a Washington, D.C. theater (DVD version). Drawings by Tim Braniff.*

used hanging hemp ropes like ship's riggings for scenery changes, were the state of the art in the mid-nineteenth century; Ford's Theater, where Lincoln was shot, was a hemphouse theater.) The authentic look of the theater scenes owes much to nineteenth-century limelights used at the foot of the stage, which cast a distinctive glow on the actors.

The Colors

The look of *Gods and Generals* is the result of extensive research and careful planning. "We were working with a fairly compressed color scheme," Hanan says. "People in the 1860s couldn't go down to the paint store and choose from thousands of colors. In addition, we were very careful about how we used blue and gray—for obvious thematic reasons—and red, which we reserved for the emotional impact of blood. I used certain types of colors for Maine, and certain colors for the South. And I used color to suggest themes that tie characters, ideas, and situations together."

Finally, Hanan worked with the director of photography, Kees van Ostrum, to plan how the colors would look after they were lit. "Colors change under the intense lighting of a film set," Hanan points out.

Above: *Generals Thomas Jackson and John Bell Hood (Patrick Gorman) in a shot from the Fredericksburg battlefield.* Below: *Director Ron Maxwell looks at footage with director of photography Kees van Ostrum, center, and production designer Michael Hanan, right.*

The complete version of *Gods and Generals* to be released on DVD runs six hours, and Hanan says that designing such a big project to director Ron Maxwell's high standards of authenticity was a huge challenge. Why did he take it on? Hanan doesn't hesitate in responding.

"A lot of movies, including a lot of very expensive movies, will essentially be forgotten within two years of their release. *Gods and Generals* was an opportunity to create something that audiences would respond to and learn from. It tells an important story about a tragic episode in American history, and you do whatever you can to be involved in a project like that. It's why you do the work."

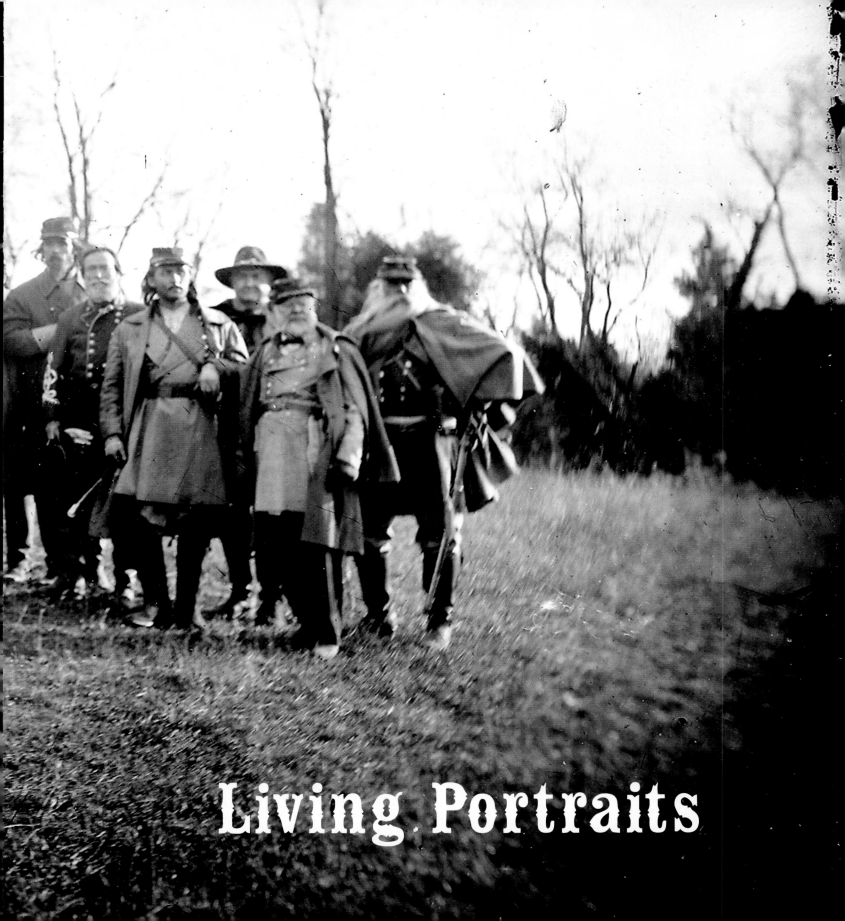

Living Portraits

CASTING AND COACHING

"If you make a mistake in casting, it's irreparable. I always tell myself, Go for the actor. Don't be seduced by marquee names."

— Director Ron Maxwell

With only one exception, all the characters in *Gods and Generals* are based on historical figures. (The Irish-American sergeant Buster Kilrain was created by Michael Shaara in his novel *The Killer Angels* and adapted by Ron Maxwell to give added dimension to the screenplay.) Casting those roles and preparing the actors to play them required unusual attention to historical and regional authenticity.

"If you make a mistake in casting, it's irreparable," says Maxwell. "I always tell myself, Go for the actor. Don't be seduced by marquee names or the flavor of the month."

As he had with *Gettysburg*, Maxwell enlisted veteran casting agent Joy Todd, who calls her work on *Gods and Generals* "a labor of love." She does not downplay the labor. "This was the biggest cast I've ever put together— more than 150 roles," she says. "At no point could I throw up my hands and say, 'Oh, he'll be fine.' Each character had to be perfectly cast."

Robert Duvall "looks just like Robert E. Lee did," Todd says, "and he brings a tremendous amount to the character." Other parts required agonizing choices. "I received nearly 5,000 letters from actors, casting agents, managers—even from Civil War re-enactors. More than a year before production started, there was tremendous interest in this project."

For bit players, Todd often turned to one of the film's several historical consultants. "If I was casting an adjutant, I might ask the consultant how old or how tall the man was—whatever would help me find the right actor," she says.

Todd met with dozens of child actors to cast the small but important part of Jane Corbin, the little girl who steals Stonewall Jackson's heart. She chose a six-year-old New Yorker, Lydia Jordan, "because she looked like a real little girl, not a theatrical child. And yet she was tremendously professional—always patient, always prepared. And she learned the Southern accent she needed."

John Janney (played by actor and dialect coach Robert Easton), Speaker of the Virginia House of Delegates, makes the case for secession.

For actors whose native accents did not match their characters', dialect coach Robert Easton provided invaluable support. Easton—known as "the American Henry Higgins" for his ability to shape actors' speech—coached 42 actors in what he calls "a multiplicity of regional accents" from backwoods Appalachia to Southern black to genteel New England.

"Everyone knows that dialects vary within linguistic groups—by region, by ethnicity, by education and by distinct localized influences," notes director Maxwell. "This was no different at the time of the American Civil War." Maxwell's screenplay carefully reproduces the rural patois of both blacks and whites and contrasts it with the more educated speech of the better educated, such as Joshua Lawrence Chamberlain and his wife, Fanny. "But Robert Easton's work with the actors transformed my written words, which can seem heavyhanded on the page, into invisible, organic touches of character."

Some of the distinctions are very subtle and nuanced. Robert E. Lee, for example, spoke in a Tidewater Virginia accent—"not dissimilar to a Canadian accent," says Easton, with "about" sounding like "aboot." Stonewall Jackson came from the opposite end of the state, from the mountains of western Virginia; speech patterns there, says Easton, "were less pleasant and drawling than on the coast." New England speech resembles the accent of plantation Georgia, he notes—both say "flo-ah" for "floor"—"but in New England the intonation is more staccato, while in the South it's more legato." Some of the Irish soldiers in the film betray their northern, Ulster origins, while others—the most recent immigrants to America—have southern Irish accents.

While researching the speech patterns of Robert E. Lee, Easton (himself an actor who can be spotted in an early scene as Virginia House of Delegates President John Janney) had a stroke of good fortune. "Bob Duvall and I had dinner with Taylor Sanders, a professor at Washington and Lee University," says Easton. "I mentioned to him that I'd never been able to find *The Word Book of Virginia Folk Speech*, published in 1899 and still the best reference for nineteenth-century Virginia accents. Not only did Professor Sanders have the book in his personal library, he offered to photocopy the entire volume for me. It was a tremendously helpful resource for which I'm extremely grateful."

Young Jane Corbin (Lydia Jordan) charms General Jackson during a winter interlude at the Corbin home, Moss Neck Manor, 1863.

THROUGH THE LENS OF TIME

Of all the state-of-the-art photographic equipment on the set of *Gods and Generals*, the camera that attracted the most attention was a simple, box-like contraption. This was a genuine wet-plate camera of a type dating back to the Civil War era. Through its ancient glass lens—once owned by a Civil War photographer named Walzl, who photographed Jefferson Davis and John Mosby, among others—photographer Rob Gibson captured memorable portraits of costumed cast members in the stiff, formal poses typical of the medium's earliest days.

Gibson works both at his studio—Gibson's Gallery in historic Gettysburg, where clients are authentically costumed and photographed with period props and lighting—and in the field, from his nineteenth-century portable darkroom. He is perhaps the world's foremost practitioner of wet-plate photography—the same delicate, time-consuming technique used by Civil War photographers such as Matthew Brady and Alexander Gardner. His work is well known to the Civil War community and has been featured at the Smithsonian's National Portrait Gallery, the National Archives, and the White House Press Photographers Association.

Gibson knew that he could add another dimension to the *Gods and Generals* production, but he had to show up at the Hagerstown, Maryland, production office in person to convince the filmmakers. "Once I was on the set," he recalls, "the more they saw, the more they liked."

Gibson's portraits became much sought after by the performers as keepsakes of their movie experience, from the re-enactors to the senators and congressmen who appear in cameo roles. "When an actor is photographed this way," Gibson explains, "he doesn't see an actor in costume but rather an image of the historical figure he portrays." Notes Ron Maxwell, "Our film strives for authenticity, and looking through his lens we can see how close we came to the real thing."

Those portraits look at if they should be hanging on the walls of 1860s rooms, and some do appear in the set decoration. Gibson himself found a place on the screen—he plays both a Northern and a Southern photographer in different scenes. One of his greatest accolades came from Robert Duvall, who told Gibson the portrait of himself as Robert E. Lee helped reinforce his transformation into the character. "I don't usually hang up pictures of myself," the actor said, "but I'll hang up this one."

Above: *Historical photographer Rob Gibson.* Below: *Taking photographs of enlisting troops, Camp Mason, Maine.* Opposite: *Rob Gibson portrait of Stephen Lang, Robert Duvall, Patrick Gorman, and Bruce Boxleitner as Generals Jackson, Lee, Hood, and Longstreet.*

Thomas Jonathan "Stonewall" Jackson

"Unpromising" may be the kindest way to describe the origins of the man who would become one of the Confederacy's most celebrated generals. Born in 1824 in what is now West Virginia, Jackson was a poor country boy when he arrived at West Point, the number-two pick of his congressman (the first-choice cadet dropped out after one day of classes). Through determination and hard work, Jackson graduated in the top third of his class, then served as an artillery officer in the Mexican-American War, where he proved his zest for battle. Promoted three times—more than anyone in the army—he returned home a major. He soon wearied of peacetime life and took a job at the Virginia Military Institute, where he taught natural and experimental philosophy (a discipline that encompassed physics, astronomy, acoustics, optics, and other scientific courses).

Meanwhile, Jackson had become a devout Presbyterian with some decidedly eccentric habits that included holding one hand high in the air—to balance his energies, he claimed—and sucking on lemons. In 1853, he married Elinor Junkin, who died a year later in childbirth, as did their baby. Jackson was devastated. After a long European tour, he married again in 1857, to Mary Anna Morrison, a minister's daughter. Their first (and unnamed) child survived only a month. Rather than embittering him, these tragedies convinced Jackson of God's omnipotence.

In November 1859, Jackson was among the VMI officers who stood guard at the execution of the abolitionist John Brown at Harpers Ferry. By July 1861, following the bombardment of Fort Sumter and Virginia's secession, Jackson had been promoted to brigadier general. At the battle of First Manassas (Bull Run), the tenacity of his troops earned him and his brigade the nickname of "Stonewall." His later successes in the Shenandoah Valley Campaign and at Second Manassas and Antietam made him General Robert E. Lee's most trusted general.

On May 2, 1863, the second day of the Battle of Chancellorsville, Jackson was accidentally fired on by his own troops during nighttime maneuvers. Struck by three .57-caliber bullets, he was taken to a field hospital, where his left arm was amputated. He was transported to a nearby farmhouse, where he developed pneumonia and died on May 10. His famous last words were, "Let us cross over the river and rest under the shade of the trees."

Above: *Daguerreotype attributed to H. B. Hull of Thomas Jackson made in 1855, while he was an instructor at Virginia Military Institute and after the death of his first wife, Ellie.*
Opposite: *Jackson's final portrait, made in 1863 two weeks before his death at the battle of Chancellorsville.*

Late in the afternoon of First Manassas, Confederate General Barnard E. Bee was trying to rally his broken ranks when he saw fresh soldiers advance to the hilltop. "Look, men!" Bee shouted as he pointed upward. "There stands Jackson like a stone wall! Rally behind the Virginians!" Bee fell mortally wounded a few moments later, but he had given American military history its most famous nickname.

— HISTORIAN JAMES I. ROBERTSON, JR.

Meeting General Jackson

Richard Taylor, who commanded a Louisiana brigade, tells of meeting Jackson for the first time in the spring of 1862 during the Shenandoah Valley campaign:

After attending to necessary camp details, I sought Jackson, whom I had never met.. . . The mounted officer who been sent on in advance pointed out a figure perched on the topmost rail of a fence overlooking the road and field, and said it was Jackson. Approaching, I saluted and declared my name and rank, then waited for a response. Before this came I had time to see a pair of cavalry boots covering feet of gigantic size, a mangy cap with visor drawn low, a heavy, dark beard, and weary eyes—eyes I afterward saw filled with intense but never brilliant light. A low, gentle voice inquired the road and distance marched that day.

"Keazletown road, six and twenty miles."

"You seem to have no stragglers."

"Never allow straggling."

"You must teach my people; they straggle badly." A bow in reply. Just then my creoles started their band and a waltz. After a contemplative suck at a lemon, "Thoughtless fellows for serious work" came forth. I expressed the hope that the work would not be less well done because of the gayety. A return to the lemon gave me the opportunity to retire.

—From *Deconstruction and Reconstruction: Personal Experiences of the Late War,* by Richard Taylor

Stephen Lang

For the pivotal role of Confederate General "Stonewall" Jackson, Ron Maxwell chose a versatile and distinguished veteran of stage, television, recording, and film—including Maxwell's own film *Gettysburg*. In that movie, Stephen Lang portrayed a relatively minor character, General George E. Pickett. In *Gods and Generals*, he steps into the spotlight.

Casting Lang instead of a big-name star was "a chance we took," Maxwell acknowledges. "But as soon as we began filming, I could see that he was delivering. He *is* Stonewall Jackson."

Lang dove into the part of Stonewall Jackson with characteristic thoughtfulness and commitment, inspired by the challenge of portraying this complicated, contradictory man. "It's a role that captures your soul," he says. "Jackson's legacy and reputation are in a sense as mysterious and elusive as some of the hidden glens of the Shenandoah Valley where he fought. It was a joy and an honor to play him."

To create the role, Lang researched Jackson's life and times, reading James I. Robertson's 950-page biography of Jackson and retracing the general's footsteps. He visited curator Keith Gibson at the museum at the Virginia Military Institute, where Jackson taught, and was shown Jackson's bullet-pierced raincoat. Lang came away with a picture of Jackson that went much deeper than the general's vaunted eccentricities—the hypochondria, the religious fervor, the odd physical habits.

"The real key to Jackson is that he was a self-improver," Lang says. "Teaching didn't come naturally to him, so he constantly worked at becoming better. He was by nature a taciturn man, but when the spirit moved him, he was capable of great flights of inspirational oratory. He also became a deacon in the Presbyterian Church and was involved in several successful business ventures."

Gods and Generals was "the most rewarding shoot I've ever been on," Lang says. He was particularly impressed by the civilian and military re-enactors who threw themselves into their roles as extras. "My debt to them is extreme," he says. "They allowed me to be Jackson—it's that simple."

Although he's not a Southerner—he was born in New York City and still lives there—Lang came away with an appreciation of Jackson as "a real American hero." *Gods and Generals*, he says, celebrates "a deep kind of patriotism—not merely flag waving but an ongoing process, a discussion about freedom. It's one of the things about the film that I'm proudest of."

Above: *Stephen Lang as General Thomas "Stonewall" Jackson.*
Opposite: *Rob Gibson's portrait of Lang as Jackson.*

Michael Shaara on Joshua Chamberlain

In his novel *The Killer Angels*, Shaara paints a scene of Colonel Chamberlain addressing a group of reluctant new recruits to his regiment on the road to Gettysburg:

They were silent, watching him. Chamberlain began to relax. He had made many speeches and he had a gift for it. He did not know what it was, but when he spoke most men stopped to listen. Fanny said it was something in his voice. He hoped it was there now.

"I've been ordered to take you men with me. I've been told that if you don't come I can shoot you. Well, you know I won't do that. Not Maine men. I won't shoot any man who doesn't want this fight. Maybe someone else will, but I won't. So that's that."

He paused again. There was nothing in their faces to lead him.

"Here's the situation. I've been ordered to take you along, and that's what I'm going to do. Under guard if necessary. But you can have your rifles if you want them. The whole Reb army is up the road a ways waiting for us and this is no time for an argument like this. I tell you this: we sure can use you. We're down below half strength and we need you, no doubt of that. But whether you fight or not is up to you. Whether you come along, well, you're coming." . . .

"Well, I don't want to preach to you. You know who we are and what we're doing here. But if you're going to fight alongside us there's a few things I want you to know."

He bowed his head, not looking at eyes. He folded his hands together.

"This Regiment was formed last fall, back in Maine. There were a thousand of us then. There's not three hundred of us now." He glanced up briefly. "But what is left is choice."

He was embarrassed. He spoke very slowly, staring at the ground.

"Some of us volunteered to fight for Union. Some came in mainly because we were bored at home and this looked like it might be fun. Some came because we were ashamed not to. Many of us came . . . because it was the right thing to do. All of us have seen men die. Most of us never saw a black man back home. We think on that, too. But freedom . . . is not just a word."

He looked up in to the sky, over silent faces.

"This is a different kind of army. If you look at history, you'll see men fight for pay, or women, or some other kind of loot. They fight for land, or because a king makes them, or just because they like killing. But we're here for something new. I don't . . . this hasn't happened much in the history of the world. We're an army going out to set other men free."

Joshua Lawrence Chamberlain

The hero of Gettysburg's Little Round Top was a citizen-soldier born in 1828 in Brewer, Maine, a small farming and shipbuilding community across the Penobscot River from Bangor. He was a brilliant student at Bowdoin College, where he became acquainted with Professor Calvin Stowe and his wife, Harriet Beecher Stowe, who at the time was writing *Uncle Tom's Cabin*. The book profoundly impressed Chamberlain, a serious-minded and devout young man who attended Bangor Theological Seminary for three years and who for a while considered entering the ministry. Instead, he accepted a post at Bowdoin as professor of "natural and revealed religion." In 1855, he married Fanny Adams, the adopted daughter of a local minister.

Although not a soldier by training, Chamberlain had strong family ties to the military: His grandfather had fought in the War of 1812, and his great-grandfathers served during the Revolution. When Bowdoin refused his request for a leave of absence to join the army, he applied for a sabbatical and then volunteered. He was soon made lieutenant colonel of the 20th Maine Volunteer Infantry Regiment.

Despite his inexperience, Chamberlain proved to be a brave and inspirational leader of men. Beginning with Antietam, he fought in twenty-four battles in the East, was wounded six times, and had six horses shot from under him. At Appomattox, Ulysses S. Grant chose Chamberlain to receive the Confederacy's formal surrender of weapons and colors. He insisted that his men salute the defeated soldiers as they marched by.

Chamberlain lived a long and productive life after the war. He was elected to four terms as governor of Maine and later served as president of his alma mater, Bowdoin. In 1893, he belatedly received the Congressional Medal of Honor for his valor at Gettysburg. During the last three decades of his life he invested in business ventures, served as surveyor of the port of Portland, and wrote his memoirs of the Civil War. Combat was "a test of character," he declared: "It makes bad men worse and good men better."

Above: *Portrait of Joshua Lawrence Chamberlain, c. 1861.* Opposite: *Lieutenant Tom Chamberlain (C. Thomas Howell) and his brother, Colonel Joshua Chamberlain (Jeff Daniels). Photo by Rob Gibson.*

> *"The inspiration of a noble cause involving human interest wide and far, enables men to do things they did not dream themselves capable of before, and which they were not capable of alone."*
>
> —Joshua Lawrence Chamberlain

Jeff Daniels

In *Gods and Generals*, Jeff Daniels reprises the role he played in Ron Maxwell's *Gettysburg*. To return to the part after eight years—and to reunite with several key cast members—was "a thrill," says Daniels. "There's Tommy Howell as Tom Chamberlain again. There's Kevin Conway as Buster Kilrain. It was strange yet familiar. It just felt right."

When Daniels originally signed on to portray Chamberlain, "I researched, researched, researched. I went to Maine. I visited with the people who had studied him their whole lives, including the historian Tom Desjardins. He told me, 'If you do nothing else, show Chamberlain's ability to think on his feet.'

"When we finally went to Gettysburg for rehearsals, I went to Little Round Top early in the morning. I was alone, it was raining, and it was like being in a cathedral. I remember promising Chamberlain's spirit that I would do the very best I could."

In *Gods and Generals*, viewers will see a new side to Chamberlain. "He's not just a military strategist," says Daniels. "He's a professor, a husband, a brother, a friend. He was passionate about learning and teaching, he was devoted to the religious life, and he was completely infatuated with his wife Fanny. And yet he gave it all up—his family, work at Bowdoin College—to join the Union Army. To fight for what he felt was right."

Biographers have puzzled over the fact that Chamberlain didn't tell his wife he planned to enlist in the army. As an actor, Daniels decided that Chamberlain "wanted to prove something to her—that he could be brave and courageous and a real man. He would suffer whatever she flung at him, but his sense of what was right outweighed any argument she might make."

Despite the earnestness with which he approached the part, Daniels earned a reputation on the *Gods and Generals* set as "the fun general." Chuckling, he acknowledges that "there was a bit of competition between the Blue and the Gray. We'd get to the hotel at the end of a day of shooting and the guys playing Confederates would ask how our day had been, and we'd say, 'We're the Blues—we're a done deal. *You* guys are the problem!'"

Daniels's career has alternated between laughter and seriousness as well. His film credits have spanned romantic drama (*Terms of Endearment*), raucous farce (*Dumb and Dumber*), and the Woody Allen comedy *The Purple Rose of Cairo*. Daniels founded, and continues to direct, the Purple Rose Theater Company in his home town of Chelsea, Michigan, near Ann Arbor; many of his own plays have premiered there.

Above: Jeff Daniels as Colonel Joshua Lawrence Chamberlain. Chamberlain was still a colonel at the time of the events depicted in Gods and Generals, *but had risen to the rank of major general by the war's end. Opposite: Rob Gibson portrait of Daniels as Chamberlain.*

Robert E. Lee

Heir to a lustrous pedigree—the Lees were related to most of Virginia's first families— Robert Edward Lee was born in Virginia in 1807, the fourth child of Revolutionary War hero Henry "Light Horse Harry" Lee, whose subsequent failed business ventures led the family into financial ruin. The younger Lee finished second in his West Point class and holds the still-unequaled distinction of graduating without a single demerit during his four years as a cadet. His marriage to Mary Anne Randolph Custis, the granddaughter of George and Martha Washington, was as close to a royal union as is conceivable in a democracy.

Lee served in the Mexican-American War as an engineer, and in one case led troops into battle. He worked with, and came to know, many of the officers who would fight alongside and against him during the Civil War, among them Ulysses S. Grant, James Longstreet, George Pickett, and Thomas "Stonewall" Jackson.

Returning to the United States as a colonel, Lee moved into the Custis mansion near Arlington, Virginia. When radical abolitionist John Brown seized the U.S. arsenal at Harpers Ferry in October 1859, Lee was rushed there by train, where he captured Brown.

After Lincoln's election and the secession of seven Southern states, General Winfield Scott asked Lee to head the United States Army to put down the rebellion. Instead, Lee offered his service to Jefferson Davis, the new president of the Confederacy. "I did only what my duty demanded," he later said. "I could have taken no other course without dishonor."

Honor and duty were central to Lee's character: He neither drank nor smoked, and in the middle of the war he freed the slaves that had belonged to his wife's father. Yet he was also relentless in battle, winning decisive victories at Second Manassas, Fredericksburg, and Chancellorsville. Stonewall Jackson said he was willing "to follow him blindfolded."

Defeated at Gettysburg, Lee fought on for two more years. After the surrender at Appomattox, his civil rights were suspended. He served as president of Washington University (now Washington and Lee), and died—revered almost as a deity among his fellow Southerners—in 1870. More than a century later, President Gerald Ford had his citizenship restored.

"Duty then is the sublimest word in our language. Do your duty in all things. You can not do more. You should never wish to do less."

— ROBERT E. LEE

Above: *Portrait of Robert E. Lee by Edward Caledon Bruce, 1864–1865.*
Right: *Mathew Brady photograph taken in May, 1865.*

Robert Duvall

"You can read fifty books on the man," says Robert Duvall of the character he portrays in *Gods and Generals*, "but in the end, it all goes back to blood." Blood as in kinship: Though Duvall was born in San Diego, his family had lived in northern Virginia for generations, and he traces a direct relationship to Robert E. Lee on his mother's side. And that, says Duvall, "is the equivalent of reading fifty books."

Duvall's striking resemblance to photographs of the Confederate general may owe something to genetics, but Duvall himself credits Manlio Rocchetti, the gifted makeup artist with whom he'd worked on *Lonesome Dove*. "He's so masterful—he puts you in a comfort zone," says Duvall. When in the days after September 11, 2001, Rocchetti couldn't fly back to the United States from Italy, where he'd been working, Duvall insisted on waiting for him.

Duvall felt a strong responsibility to be as authentic as possible in the role. "Lee was a godlike figure to many in the South," says Duvall. "He was held in complete awe by many Southerners—and not just the rich planters but small farmers as well. He was a gentleman, he was a soldier, he was a cultured man, and he was brilliant. When he served in the Mexican-American War, General Winfield Scott called him the greatest American soldier."

An intense, hard-working actor known for his interesting role choices, Duvall began his forty-year film career as Boo Radley in *To Kill a Mockingbird*. He delivered memorable performances in *The Godfather*, *Apocalypse Now*, *The Great Santini*, and many other films, and he has produced seven movies, including *Tender Mercies* and 2002's *Assassination Tango*.

The role of Robert E. Lee was "a special challenge," says Duvall. "Playing historical figures can be difficult—sometimes you feel you're imparting so much data that you can't simply play a scene with the other actors. With Lee, I wanted to convey what an exemplary person, what a special man, he was. And it was a great honor to do that." He smiles, his Virginia heritage summoning a mischievous twinkle. "I don't care what people above the Mason-Dixon Line say!"

Rob Gibson portrait of Robert Duvall as General Robert E. Lee.

Mary Anna Morrison Jackson

Born in Charlotte, North Carolina, in 1831, Mary Anna Morrison, known as Anna, became Thomas "Stonewall" Jackson's second wife in 1857. (Jackson's first wife, Elinor Junkin, had died in childbirth.) Their only surviving child, Julia, was born in 1863, just a few months before Jackson's death.

The newly widowed Mrs. Jackson returned to her native state with her infant daughter. She never remarried, but reared her two grandchildren after Julia's untimely death in her late twenties. Her second mission was perpetuating General Jackson's memory and legacy. Known as the "Widow of the Confederacy," she was a fixture at Confederate reunions after the war, and in 1898 she founded the Stonewall Jackson Chapter #220 of the United Daughters of the Confederacy in Charlotte, of which she was elected president for life. Failing health eventually forced her to step down, but she retained the title of honorary president until her death in 1915.

Anna Jackson Remembers

Anna Jackson left this account of one of her brief wartime visits with her husband, which took place just weeks before he was fatally shot at Chancellorsville. The photographic session she describes is depicted in the DVD version of *Gods and Generals*:

On the 23rd of April (the day she was five months old) General Jackson had little Julia baptized. He brought his chaplain, the Rev. Mr. Lacy, to Mr. Yerby's, in whose parlor the sacred rite was performed, in the presence of the family, and a number of the staff-officers. The child behaved beautifully and was the object of great interest to her father's friends and soldiers. . . .

It was during these happy days that he sat for the last picture that was taken of him—the three-quarters view of his face and head—the favorite picture with his old soldiers, as it is the most soldierly-looking; but, to my mind, not so pleasing as the full-face view which was taken in the spring of 1862, at Winchester, and which has more of the beaming sun-light of his *home-look*. The last picture was taken by an artist who came to Mr. Yerby's and asked permission to photograph him, which he at first declined; but as he never presented a finer appearance in health and dress (wearing the handsome suit given him by General Stuart), I persuaded him to sit for his picture. After arranging his hair myself, which was unusually long for him, and curled in large ringlets, he sat in the hall of the house, where a strong wind blew in his face, causing him to frown, and giving a sternness to his countenance that was not natural. . . .

Kali Rocha

The script of *Gods and Generals* wasn't available when Kali Rocha auditioned for the role of Anna Morrison Jackson. But casting director Joy Todd *had* given each actor a photograph of the historical character he or she would portray. When Rocha saw Anna Jackson's image, "I got chills. The resemblance is uncanny." She brought the picture with her into the audition, held it up to her face, "and everyone gasped. It was like an omen."

Rocha's looks may have helped her win the part, but her luminous performance is the result of diligent research. "I read the novel *Gods and Generals*—its characterizations of Thomas and Anna Jackson are so rich," she says. "I read the letters Anna and Thomas Jackson wrote to each other, which beautifully document their relationship. I got a personal tour of the Jackson house in Lexington, Virginia, which is so well preserved that every room feels as though Anna Jackson still inhabits it." She created her accent, a blend of Anna's native North Carolina and her adopted Virginia, with the help of dialect coach Robert Easton, whom she calls "fantastic." And, she says, "I kept the script by my bed and read my scenes over and over, letting them wash over me." At times, reading the screenplay, "I just wept."

Before making *Gods and Generals*, Rocha was probably best known to audiences for her recurring role as Hallie/Halfrek on television's *Buffy the Vampire Slayer* and for her comic turn as a flight attendant in *Meet the Parents*. But her early career had been spent in the theater, where she gravitated toward period roles. "I love the corsets and ringlets," she says, laughing. Born in Tennessee and reared in Rhode Island, she attended acting school at Carnegie Mellon University. "Because I didn't get a liberal arts education, I decided that every acting job would be a liberal arts course," she says. "I read voraciously for every part I got."

Stonewall Jackson's death scene, near the end of *Gods and Generals*, was "out of my realm," Rocha admits. "I've never been married, never been religious, never been with someone I loved as he died. My job was to trust the words in the script. The language was so true, I knew I could convey that truth if I simply tried to speak the words honestly."

Opposite: *Mary Anna Morrison Jackson in a photograph taken in 1857.* Below: *Rob Gibson's portrait of Kali Rocha as Anna Jackson.*

Fanny Chamberlain

Above: *Fanny Chamberlain, photographed c. 1860.* Opposite top: *Rob Gibson portrait of Mira Sorvino as Fanny Chamberlain.* Bottom: *Fanny and Joshua on the eve of his departure to take up his command.*

Frances Caroline Adams Chamberlain, known as Fanny, was an unusual woman for her time and place: educated, independent, and feminist in many of her views, including her opposition to early childbearing. She was born in Boston in 1825 but reared in Brunswick, Maine, by her "adoptive" parents, George E. Adams (who was also her cousin) and his wife, Sarah. George Adams, the pastor of the local Congregational church, kept a strictly religious home and saw that young Fanny received a good education.

Fanny first met Joshua Lawrence Chamberlain in church, where she accompanied the choir that he led. Their romance bloomed during Joshua's junior and senior years at Bowdoin College, but poverty and Joshua's seminary plans postponed their marriage. Instead, Fanny went to New York in 1852 to study music, and later taught music at a girls' school in Georgia. For two and half years the couple did not see each other at all. They finally married in 1855, when Fanny was 30 and Joshua was 27. Their daughter Grace was born the following year; their son Harold Willys was born in 1858.

After the children were born, Fanny traveled frequently to Boston and New York; during the Civil War she visited Joshua in Washington, D.C., and toured the Gettysburg battlefield. When Joshua was badly wounded at Petersburg, she went to Annapolis to help take care of him.

Frequent leavetakings were the rule after the war as well. When Joshua was elected governor of Maine, he moved to the capital, Augusta, while Fanny remained in Brunswick. In 1868, frustrated by the chronic separations, Fanny considered filing for divorce.

The marriage survived, and in the 1880s and 1890s the Chamberlains traveled together in Florida and New York, where Joshua had business dealings. But Fanny's worsening health—she suffered all her life from eye trouble and later became blind—forced her to return to Brunswick. She died there on October 18, 1905, a little more than eight years before her husband. Their correspondence during the courtship and marriage is the basis of a recent dual biography, *Fanny and Joshua: The Enigmatic Lives of Frances Caroline Adams and Joshua Lawrence Chamberlain* by Diane Monroe Smith.

"The brave wife of Lieut Col. Chamberlain of the 20th Reg. Me. Vol. is very anxious to visit her husband at the Camp near Stoneman's station and he as earnestly desires to see her."

—LETTER ACCOMPANYING FANNY'S REQUEST FOR A PASS TO VISIT JOSHUA AT HIS CAMP IN VIRGINIA, 9 APRIL 1863

Mira Sorvino

A Harvard graduate and the winner of multiple awards—including an Oscar—for her role in Woody Allen's *Mighty Aphrodite*, Mira Sorvino is an actress of impressive range whose credits span every genre from eighteenth-century French farce to contemporary drama. To her role as Fanny Chamberlain, wife of Union Colonel Joshua Lawrence Chamberlain, she brings both intelligence and surprising warmth—surprising because history has been less than generous to the woman Jeff Shaara describes in his novel *Gods and Generals* as "complex and difficult."

Sorvino came to see a more rounded personality. "Ron Maxwell gave me a biography, *Fanny and Joshua*, based on the correspondence between the Chamberlains," she says. "I learned that Fanny was artistic, that she was very independent for her time, and that she loved poetry—poetry was a part of the Chamberlains' daily life."

In their scenes together, Sorvino and Jeff Daniels, who plays General Chamberlain, make it clear that the couple were mutually devoted. "Mira is one of those actresses with whom you can establish years of a relationship with just one look," says Daniels. "They call it chemistry, but it's really about listening to each other as actors. The more time we spent together, the better it was, and it's apparent on the screen."

Sorvino originally met director Ron Maxwell when he cast her—after a 27-month search—to play Joan of Arc in a still-unproduced historical epic. "She auditioned for the part, and I knew right away she was the one. It's a combination of soulfulness, charisma, and appearance—not to mention her formidable talents as an actor. When we started to work on *Gods and Generals*, she came to mind right away.

"Fanny Chamberlain is a small role, a cameo really. But Mira makes a very big impact."

Jane Beale

Born in 1815 into a prominent Fredericksburg, Virginia, family, Jane Howison Beale is remembered today as one of the foremost civilian diarists of the Civil War era.

Beale married at 19 and was widowed at 35. She used the money her husband left her to pay off her home, and established a girls' school on the premises. She remained in the house until her death in 1882.

During the war, Fredericksburg was occupied on three separate occasions by Union forces. Beale's diary reflects the anguish felt by citizens during these invasions, their grief at their losses (Beale's own son, Corporal Charles D. Beale, was killed near Williamsburg in 1862), and their elation at Confederate victories.

On April 27, 1862, Beale wrote: "…[I]t is painfully humiliating to feel one's self a captive, but all sorrow for self is now lost in the deeper feeling of anxiety for our army, for our cause, we have lost every thing, regained nothing, our army has fallen back before the superior forces of the enemy until but a small strip of our dear Old Dominion is left to us.…"

The Journal of Jane Howison Beale was published by the Historic Fredericksburg Foundation and has been an invaluable resource for historians and Civil War buffs alike.

Since the battles in *Gods and Generals* span two years, from April 1861 to May 1863, Ron Maxwell thought it imperative to include the story of the women and children left behind as their husbands, sons, and fathers went off to war. The character of Jane Beale does not appear in Jeff Shaara's novel; in the film she provides a glimpse into the civilian wartime experience. Jane Beale, her sons, and daughter Lucy are introduced in April 1861, just at the moment of secession. Jane was later caught in the battle of Fredericksburg, and by her account (and others) we know what happened to civilians trapped there.

Most Southern women, like their menfolk, supported the war effort. In fact, contemporary accounts are rife with reports of slackers and malingerers who were shamed into the fighting ranks by their female relations. The war lasted longer and grew ever harsher than anyone on either side anticipated, and women were compelled to take on many chores and responsibilities formerly reserved for males. "Although they didn't consciously think of it as such, a kind of de facto women's liberation took place," says Maxwell. "At war's end, the social structures for women North and South had significantly changed. After the abolition of slavery, women's suffrage became the next great social reform in America."

"I love my servants, they are part of my family and their happiness has been my care as well as that of my own children. I can but hope that no evil influences will be brought to bear upon their minds . . ."

—JANE BEALE, *JOURNAL*, MAY 14, 1862

Mia Dillon

The skilled and versatile Broadway actress Mia Dillon portrays the widow Jane Beale of Fredericksburg, Virginia, in *Gods and Generals.* Dillon's scenes were filmed in mid-November, 2001, just two months after the September 11 attacks. She drew on her own fear and confusion for the harrowing, close-quarters scene in the Beale basement during the bombardment of Fredericksburg. "Bombs were going off, glass was flying everywhere," she recalls. "The fact that they were fake bombs and fake glass didn't make the experience any less terrifying." Yet Dillon found the filming strangely therapeutic. "I knew that we actors were going to get up and walk away," she says. "That was very consoling. And I also knew that my character was going to survive—she lived another 20 years."

Gods and Generals was a sort of reunion for Dillon, who had previously done stage work with Stephen Lang (General Jackson) and Malachy McCourt (Francis Preston Blair). "The entire company was an extraordinarily warm, generous group of people," she says. "Ron Maxwell set the tone—his passion for this project was infectious. You wanted to do your best because he wanted to do his best."

Above: *Mia Dillon as Jane Beale, left, and Karen Goberman as her daughter, Lucy Beale. Rob Gibson photo.* Left: *The Confederate command—Lee, Jackson, Longstreet, Stuart—spent Christmas day at Moss Neck Manor, Roberta Corbin's home on the Rappahannock just a few miles south of Fredericksburg. It was here that Jackson befriended little Jane Corbin and his adjutant, Sandie Pendleton, met his future wife, Catherine (Roberta's cousin). Shown here, sewing the new flag of the Confederacy, are Christie Lynn Smith, left, as Catherine Corbin, Karen Hochstetter as Roberta Corbin, center, and Mia Dillon as Jane Beale, right.*

John Wilkes Booth

Born in Maryland in 1838, Booth was the ninth of ten children of America's most distinguished Shakespearean actor, Junius Brutus Booth. Two of his brothers, Junius Brutus, Jr., and Edwin, were also famous actors. By the time he was 24, John Wilkes Booth was being called "the greatest tragedian in the country." Handsome, wealthy, always elegantly dressed, he had a galvanic effect on audiences. Women literally threw themselves at him, pressing in throngs at his dressing room door after performances.

His brother Edwin was a Union sympathizer, but Booth considered himself a Southerner. When his sister asked him why he did not join the Confederate Army, Booth replied: "I have only an arm to give; my brains are worth twenty men, my money worth a hundred. My profession, my name, is my passport. My knowledge of drugs is valuable, my beloved, precious money—oh, never beloved 'til now!—is the means by which I serve the South."

Booth maintained a busy acting schedule during the war years, playing in theaters from Buffalo to New Orleans, often for as little as a night or two. He used his mobility to smuggle quinine and other drugs across the lines to the Confederacy. And he began plotting with other Confederate sympathizers to kidnap or assassinate Union leaders.

"Booth was the box-office idol of his day," says Ron Maxwell. "But he was also a Marylander hostile toward the military occupation of his home state. And what's really fascinating is the acting roles he chose. He played regicides over and over again."

On April 14, 1865, during a performance of *Our American Cousin* at Ford's Theater in Washington, Booth shot President Lincoln—"He became the regicide in his own play," notes Maxwell—and then leapt onto the stage and cried, "Sic semper tyrannus"— "Thus always to tyrants." (The Latin phrase is Virginia's state motto.) Despite a broken leg, Booth escaped. On April 26 a search party cornered him in a burning barn near Bowling Green, Virginia, where he was fatally shot.

Above: John Wilkes Booth. Right: Brooke Riley and Olivia Maxwell as stage-door belles who admire the dashing Booth. Opposite: Chris Connor as John Wilkes Booth in the role of Macbeth, Washington Theatre, April 1963. (Both, DVD version.)

Chris Connor

"**I**n school, you're given the perception that John Wilkes Booth was simply a madman who killed the president," says Chris Conner. On the contrary, the young actor's research revealed "a definitely sane individual—a passionate young man who saw himself as an avenging angel.

"Booth is just 23 years old when the war begins," Conner notes. "He's already famous and wealthy, but he's trying to figure out where he stands on important topics of his times. For that reason, I play him boyishly—charming, yes, but also trying to answer those big questions."

Conner, a relative newcomer who has several small TV and film roles to his credit, had read Jeff Shaara's novel a few years before being called in to audition for *Gods and Generals*. Asked to perform "something Shakespearean," he delivered Hamlet's famous "to be or not to be" soliloquy during the audition. It was an appropriate choice: In 1862, the *Indianapolis Sentinel* had called Booth's Hamlet "a masterpiece of acting" that "held the audience spellbound."

Conner relished playing the part of Booth, one of only a few characters in the movie who do not appear in Shaara's novel. "It really doesn't get any better for an actor than to play a character whose arc progresses to a full climax," he says. "And when the character is well rounded and full of life, it's the greatest opportunity in the world."

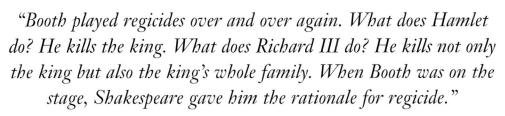

"Booth played regicides over and over again. What does Hamlet do? He kills the king. What does Richard III do? He kills not only the king but also the king's whole family. When Booth was on the stage, Shakespeare gave him the rationale for regicide."

— Director Ron Maxwell

SUPPORTING GENERALS

Several members of the Confederate and Union high command appear in *Gods and Generals*, including:

These pages: *Rob Gibson portraits of the generals, as portrayed in the film by the actors named in the text. Page 68: Photos of Alex Hyde White as Burnside and Les Kinsolving as Barksdale, with his son Tom, by Van Redin.*

James Longstreet (Confederate; 1821–1904)

A graduate of West Point and veteran of the Mexican War, Longstreet rose in rank from a brigadier general to lieutenant general during the Civil War. His record shows that Lee's "Old War Horse" was more capable as a supporting officer than as a commander of independent campaigns. Longstreet disagreed with Lee's strategy to attack Gettysburg and recommended maneuvering the federal troops out of position instead—and the Confederate failure proved him right. Badly wounded by friendly fire in a chaotic skirmish during the Battle of Wilderness, he recovered and stayed with Lee through the rest of the war. Later he shifted his allegiance to his longtime friend Ulysses S. Grant, who when president appointed him U.S. minister to Turkey. Longstreet is played in the film by Bruce Boxleitner, a self-described Civil War buff. "My great-grandfather on my mother's side was a little Irish cavalryman for the Union," he says, "and in fact he was captured by Jeb Stuart's troops and returned in a prisoner exchange. After that he'd had enough and went back to Illinois."

Ambrose Powell Hill (Confederate; 1825–1865)

Handsome, courageous, and often rebellious toward his superiors, A. P. Hill earned fame as the leader of the Light Division in the summer of 1862 and distinguished himself with powerful, well-timed attacks at Antietam and Fredericksburg. Wearing his trademark red shirt into battle, Hill took over the command at Chancellorsville after Stonewall Jackson was wounded. The illness Hill contracted during his college days (now believed to be a venereal disease) took a severe toll on his health; at times he traveled with his own ambulance because he could not ride a horse. Even so, by the time of the siege of Petersburg in early 1865, Hill had proven himself Lee's most dependable general. In a letter to President Davis, Lee wrote that Hill was "the best soldier of his grade with me." While defending Petersburg, he beat heavy odds to drive back every Federal effort to break through the Confederate lines. During his defense of a vulnerable line on April 2, Hill was shot and killed by a small band of Union soldiers. Actor William Sanderson depicts Hill in *Gods and Generals*.

George Edward Pickett (Confederate; 1825–1875)

A native of Richmond, Virginia, Pickett served as a brigadier general under Longstreet during the Seven Days' battles surrounding his home city. He is best known for his attack, under Lee's orders, on the third day of battle at Gettysburg. Pickett began the afternoon assault in high spirits and with his troops dressed smartly as if on parade. But the overpowering federal troops forced Pickett to command his troops to withdraw. He was relieved of his command just days before Lee's surrender at Appomattox, and after the war he worked as an insurance salesman in Richmond. TV star Billy Campbell, in a radical departure from his sensitive architect of *Once and Again*, is the film's General Pickett.

William Nelson Pendleton (Confederate; 1808–1883)

Before the war "Old Penn" had taught mathematics at West Point and was ordained an Episcopal minister. Entering the war as a captain, he was promoted to colonel and chief of artillery for the army. The names of the four cannons in Pendleton's battery—Matthew, Mark, Luke, and John—reflect his clerical background, as do his solemn words before commencing the artillery attack at the First Bull Run: "Lord, have mercy on their souls." After that battle he was made a brigadier general, and at the war's end he organized the army's surrender with Generals Longstreet and Gordon. Pendleton later resumed his position as rector of Grace Episcopal Church in Lexington, Virginia, where General Lee was a parish member and a longtime friend. His son, Alexander Swift Pendleton, served as an aide to Stonewall Jackson. Old Penn is played in the film by John Castle.

Winfield Scott Hancock (Union; 1824–1886)

Hancock's early efforts in the war included dissuading the secessionist movement in California. After going east he took on several commands in the Army of the Potomac and became one of the Union's most renowned commanders. Hancock led the Union division holding the center position on the second and third days at Gettysburg. During that campaign he was shot in the thigh and suffered for months from nail and wood fragments that entered the wound from his saddle. After his strong performance at Spotsylvania, Hancock was promoted to major general, but in 1864 his old wound broke open and he was forced to take an extended leave. After the war, Hancock nearly became the Democratic presidential candidate in 1880, narrowly losing the primary to James Garfield. Brian Mallon, who played Hancock in the *Gettysburg* film, reprises the role here.

James Ewell Brown Stuart (Confederate; 1833–1864)

"Jeb" Stuart, one of the Confederacy's most renowned cavalry officers, was considered a cavalier knight of the South. In June of 1862 he brought General Lee crucial intelligence following a four-day ride around McClellan's army. His cavalry then scouted, led the infantry, and raided Union supplies during the Seven Days battle, after which Stuart was promoted to major general. At Chancellorsville, he was asked to take over the command of the 2nd Corps after both Jackson and Hill left the field wounded. Stuart lost contact with the army during the Pennsylvania Campaign as he was bogged down with more than 100 captured Union supply wagons. He caught up with the army again at Gettysburg, fought at the Battle of the Wilderness, and was mortally wounded by gunshot at the Battle of Yellow Tavern on May 11, 1864. He is depicted in the film by Joseph Fuqua, reprising his role in *Gettysburg*.

Ambrose Everett Burnside (Union; 1824–1881)

A railroad worker in Illinois before the war, Burnside was the son of a South Carolina slaveholder who had moved North and freed his slaves. He began his service as a colonel in the 1st Rhode Island Infantry, and after capturing four prominent sites in North Carolina in early 1862 he was promoted to major general. Burnside suffered an embarrassing defeat to A. P. Hill at Antietam, however, and was also defeated at Fredericksburg. In his new command of the Department of the Ohio, he defeated Longstreet at the Battle of Knoxville in November 1863, and later returned to his command with the Army of the Potomac—from which he was relieved after the Battle of the Crater, in which many of his men were killed. After the war he served three terms as governor of Rhode Island and was elected to the U.S. Senate in 1874. Burnside is played by Alex Hyde White.

William Barksdale (Confederate; 1821-1865)

Before becoming a colonel in the 13th Mississippi Infantry, Barksdale had been a congressman from that state in the U.S. House of Representatives. He was promoted to brigadier general after his leadership in the Seven Days Campaign, and he routed federal troops at the Battle of Sharpsburg and drove back enemy bridge builders in Fredericksburg. He was shot in the chest and left leg at Gettysburg and died from his wounds on July 3, 1863. Radio personality Les Kinsolving portrays Barksdale, from whom he is directly descended.

LUXURIANT GROWTHS

The art of facial hair reached its apogee in the Civil War era, when mustaches and beards of every magnitude bloomed on men's faces. Muttonchops and sideburns—named after the Union general Ambrose Burnside—"imperials" and goatees, "walruses" and handlebars: Men had a seemingly limitless range of options for facial adornment.

To replicate this hirsute cornucopia, makeup department head Patty Androff did intensive research and drew on her experience with previous Civil War–era productions, including *Dances with Wolves*, *Glory*, and *Andersonville*. One of her crew members, Leslie Devlin, then interpreted the distinctive facial stylings, as well as the female characters' hair. "Our goal was not just historical correctness but also suitability to the character," she says. "Sometimes if you're too correct the effect is cartoonish."

Beards for each of the 25 principal male characters began with a form of the actor's face fashioned out of Saran Wrap and tape. Androff used yak hair imported from Italy—"it's coarser than human hair and stands up to humid weather"—and permanent-waved some of it to create curls. Actors were asked to grow a "foundation" beard of about half an inch so the makeup artists would have a natural beardline to follow. Stephen Lang, as General Jackson, had his own beard colored and a false beard added every single day for 62 days of shooting. "He was a real trouper," Androff says admiringly.

Androff's favorite creation? That would be Brigadier General James Ewell Brown "Jeb" Stuart, who was renowned for his showmanship, daring, and personal flair. "That was one beautiful beard—long and curly," says Androff.

Above: *Actors C. Thomas Howell, Jeff Daniels, and Jonathan Maxwell sport distinctive varieties of beards, mustaches, and sideburns, as does former Texas senator Phil Gramm in his cameo role, below.* Left: *Confederate General J.E.B. Stuart, in an oil portrait owned by the Virginia Military Institute, artist unknown.*

THE "JACKSON FIVE"

The historical Thomas "Stonewall" Jackson enjoyed an unusual rapport with his closest aides, a group of young men who largely shared his devout Presbyterian faith. (Nearly a third of Jackson's staff were ministers or seminary students.) Art imitated life during the production of *Gods and Generals*: the relationship among the men who played those roles was as close as that of the real-life officers. In fact, the four actors who played Jackson's support staff—Stephen Spacek, Jeremy London, Sean Pratt, Scott Cooper—along with Stephen Lang himself—came to be known as "the Jackson Five."

"Stephen Lang, as General Jackson, set the tone," recalls director Ron Maxwell. "From the first day of shooting, he established himself as their commander." Lang immediately issued three "orders": Never be late. Know your lines. Don't allow your hat to fall off your head while you're on horseback. The four actors willingly obeyed.

Lang's distinguished reputation as an actor was partially responsible for the bond among the men. "Stephen is incredibly respected in our industry," says Jeremy London (Sandie Pendleton), who had worked with Lang on a television movie some eight years before *Gods and Generals*. "He demands respect and he deserves it."

The younger actors also knew that the historical Jackson, who had experienced the tragic loss of two children, treated his men as though they were his sons. "Jackson and my character, James Power Smith, had a very close, father-son relationship," notes Stephen Spacek (the real-life nephew of actress Sissy Spacek). "Smith was in awe of Jackson's power and presence. And after Jackson died, it was Smith who marked the spots where Jackson had been shot, where his arm was amputated, and where he died. Without Smith, we probably would have lost all that."

For his part, Lang was inspired by the camaraderie among the "Jackson Five." "They were so present, so committed to their roles. It was extremely moving."

Above: *The "Jackson Five": left to right, Jeremy London as Sandie Pendleton, Sean Pratt as Dr. Hunter McGuire, Scott Cooper at Lt. Joseph Morrison, Stephen Spacek as Capt. James Power Smith, and Stephen Lang, seated, as General Jackson. Opposite: Jackson exhorts the 1st Virginia Brigade.*

THE TROOPS
Living Historians Bring Battles to Life
by Dennis E. Frye

Why would you dress in a wool uniform coat and pants and march around in a field in 90-degree temperatures on a weekend afternoon?

Why would you carry a ten-pound rifle or musket that loads from the front of the barrel, fires only after your teeth have ripped opened the ammunition, and blinds you with smoke that smells like rotten eggs?

Why would you rise at 4:00 a.m. to the sound of drums and bugles, march through darkness into a wet cornfield, then kneel for an hour on the muddy earth?

Ask any Civil War re-enactor these questions, and he will tell you why. He does it because he believes in America and the story of America. He wears the uniform because it enables him to become a teacher of our history. He carries the rifle not to glorify war but to remind us of the tragedy of war—especially the Civil War, where the unthinkable occurred: Americans killing Americans on American battlefields. He marches to the drum and bugle because it honors the memory of the men of Blue and Gray. He answers the call because he is preserving our heritage, ensuring that the battlefields of North and South remain testaments to courage, honor, pride, and patriotism.

"It is a chance to be part of a fraternal organization with a purpose," remarks John Bert, who typically portrays a Union soldier from his native Pennsylvania. "Remembrance and the preservation of a historical moment seem to be the base reasons" that motivate re-enactors.

Chris Caveness of Roanoke, Virginia, offers a philosophical perspective. "Living history programs and battlefield re-enactments are a profound way to provoke thought about this tragic period in American history." Caveness, who represents a soldier in the 28th Virginia Infantry, observes that "America is a multicultural and multiracial society that is constantly evolving while struggling with the issues of how we came to be. . . . [B]y donning the uniforms, accoutrements, and weapons of the Civil War, Union and Confederate re-enactors create an atmosphere whereby Americans are learning to appreciate the viewpoints of both sides."

> *"By donning the uniforms, accoutrements, and weapons of the Civil War, Union and Confederate re-enactors create an atmosphere whereby Americans are learning to appreciate the viewpoints of both sides."*
>
> — CHRIS CAVENESS, WHO REPRESENTS A SOLDIER IN THE 28TH VIRGINIA INFANTRY

Opposite: *Re-enactors filming the Battle of Chancellorsville.*

The History "Hobby"

Nearly 30,000 Civil War re-enactors reside in the United States. Many also hail from England, Ireland, Germany, Austria, Canada, and Australia. The "hobby," which first became popular during the 1960s Civil War Centennial, has grown into a worldwide phenomenon.

Edwin C. Bearss, Chief Historian Emeritus of the National Park Service, has witnessed the re-enactor hobby mature over the past 40 years. "When it first began, the research was inadequate and many impressions were bad. But today re-enactors pride themselves on authenticity." Bearss concludes: "No academic in any classroom can match the reality of the authentic re-enactor."

Those qualities of reality and authenticity attracted *Gods and Generals* producer, writer, and director Ron Maxwell to the re-enactors. "They know the ethos and moral universe of the people in the nineteenth century," Maxwell marvels. "They are, in essence, living historians. We can move the camera across them, and you're in the 1860s."

Cobb's Brigade at the wall on Marye's Heights, Battle of Fredericksburg, December 1862.

Maxwell's first experience with re-enactors occurred during the production of *Gettysburg* in 1992. In fact, *Gettysburg* was the first major film to use Civil War re-enactors extensively. Re-enactors had participated in 1980s television miniseries such as *North and South* and *Blue and Gray*, but not on the same scale as *Gettysburg*, where more than 5,000 re-enactors took part in Pickett's Charge.

Gods and Generals, however, is dramatically different from *Gettysburg*. Whereas *Gettysburg* features one battle; *Gods and Generals* mounts four. *Gettysburg* depicts the events of three days; *Gods and Generals* spans two years and all four seasons. *Gettysburg* is virtually all military action, while *Gods and Generals* requires both military and civilian re-enactors.

The General Staff

To assist in meeting these new challenges, Maxwell hired me as his associate producer. Ron and I had met in 1991 at Harpers Ferry National Historical Park, where I was serving as chief historian. I had long experience with living history and good connections with re-enactors; in 1997, I coordinated the 135th anniversary of the Battle of Antietam, which attracted over 12,000 re-enactors to Hagerstown, Maryland. I also had led the effort to obtain initial funding from Washington County, Maryland, for the *Gods and Generals* venture. Maxwell charged me with recruiting the thousands of re-enactors his new film required.

It was clear I couldn't do this alone—I needed a respected team to attract re-enactors in both quality and quantity. My first recruit was Don Warlick, a Georgian with a southern-accented baritone who entered the hobby as a cavalry private. A former high school history teacher, Don began organizing re-enactments in the mid-1990s and served as re-enactor coordinator for the 135th Antietam event. His expertise was mechanics and logistics: roads, waters supplies, camp layouts, directional signage, firewood, parking, security, and communications. In essence, Don became responsible for building and tearing down temporary "cities" at filming locations.

Next, I needed a re-enactor commander—actually two commanders, Union and Confederate. Dana Heim, a former Marine Corps drill instructor and retired veteran of "Desert Storm," was my choice as the U.S. "general." Dana's living history résumé included commanding nearly 7,000 Federals at the 1997 Antietam re-enactment and more than 10,000 Yankees at Gettysburg the next year. He was, without question, the most experienced Civil War re-enactor general—and the most respected. He also was

"They know the ethos of the people in the nineteenth century. They are, in essence, living historians. We can move the camera across them, and you're in the 1860s."

— DIRECTOR RON MAXWELL

Above: *Dennis E. Frye and Ron Maxwell instruct the troops.* Overleaf: *Jackson's 1st Virginia Brigade.*

the elected leader of the U.S. Volunteers, the nation's largest Civil War re-enactor organization.

For the Confederate chieftain I tapped Jim Maupin, commander of the re-created Longstreet's Corps. I had never worked with Jim, but he bore an outstanding reputation as a fair and congenial man able to work with the numerous Confederate re-enactor factions. I had the chance to meet Jim and his staff at the 2001 Gettysburg re-enactment, where he commanded the Rebels. Observing his calm and sturdy leadership throughout the weekend, and the admiration shown by his troops, I became convinced that Jim was our Confederate general.

Much More than Extras

Our team began the task of recruitment in early 2001. Fortunately, re-enactors publish specialized newspapers, which tracked the *Gods and Generals* project and advertised our needs. We also established recruiting tents at two large re-enactments (1st Manassas and Gettysburg) during the summer of 2001. And we developed our own Web page, becoming the first movie to recruit re-enactors through the Internet.

We targeted our message to the individual re-enactor rather than his unit, because we wanted each re-enactor to determine when he could participate, for how long, and what scenes or battles he desired. This represented a drastic departure from the Gettysburg formula, in which re-enactors were recruited by unit—a method that often created last-minute chaos, with

Confederate advance at the Battle of First Manassas.

fewer members of a unit showing than promised, or none at all. By recruiting individuals we secured personal commitments, which greatly enhanced our planning and turnout.

We did not, however, accept any and all individuals. We needed an army—actually two armies—that looked as soldiers would have in the 1860s. We needed men whose age ranged from 18 to 30 and whose weight averaged about 160 pounds. Since many of today's re-enactors are in their mid-40s, with a waist size in the same numbers, our search was difficult. Complicating matters, we had little time—just 70 days to select, schedule, and deliver two armies.

Every re-enactor had to submit a detailed application with a full-length photograph of himself in his Civil War uniform. Each submission was reviewed by a jury of three to determine authenticity and appropriateness. This tedious process took hundreds of hours and many bloodshot eyes, but it winnowed 2,200 quality re-enactors from an applicant pool of 7,500. Of these 2,200, about ten percent were selected for the "Core Company"— those who could portray both Union and Confederate soldiers, and who could devote the most time to the project.

Nearly 800 more re-enactors were chosen for civilian roles in the film. They included women, children, and men who applied as civilians or who didn't meet the soldier qualifications and chose to participate as civilians. Differing again from *Gettysburg*, where the civilian presence was slight,

> *"The re-enactors bring the picture much, much more than mere extras could. Not just because they have proper uniforms and weapons but because they know how 19th-century American soldiers fought."*
>
> — DIRECTOR RON MAXWELL

Making History by Saving History

As you watch the "background artists" in *Gods and Generals*, both military and civilian, keep in mind that virtually all of them are volunteers. How did the film company attract nearly 3,000 volunteers to the set?

Among other things, money. But not money for the individual re-enactor. Money, instead, earmarked to preserve Civil War battlefields. The "promise of funds toward preservation was a rallying cry throughout the re-enactor community," remarks John Bert, who served as a re-enactor liaison for the film. By volunteering for *Gods and Generals*, individual re-enactors were making history by saving history.

The bulldozer spurred this motivation. During the past two decades, thousands of acres of Civil War battlefield land have been raped and carried to the dump, unceremoniously replaced by commercial and residential development. Re-enactors have witnessed battlefields stained with American blood paved into parking lots—the ultimate insult to our heritage.

The response of the *Gods and Generals* production was to establish a nonprofit organization on behalf of the participating re-enactors, and managed by re-enactors, for the purpose of preserving the Civil War heritage they passionately defend. Contributions as of the film's opening have reached $500,000.

Gods and Generals needed civilians for significant background roles: in early-war recruiting scenes, on various theater and tavern sets, and in the evacuation of Fredericksburg. In fact, civilians fleeing through the Fredericksburg streets under Union artillery bombardment provided some of the movie's most dramatic footage—and some of the most dangerous to execute, requiring perfect timing and concentration to prevent accidents.

In addition to contributing their time and effort, every re-enactor brought his or her own carefully researched clothing and equipment to the set—a considerable investment, with a typical military "impression" costing $1,500. For those in the "Core Company" who portrayed both Union and Confederate soldiers, out-of-pocket expenses could reach $5,000. Some "Hollywood uniforms" were manufactured because of special costume requirements for early-war militia scenes and the Battle of First Manassas, but the re-enactors preferred their authentic personal gear.

Re-enactors come to any movie set with built-in motivations: the chance to practice their vocation in a marquee setting, and to share with audiences their passion for this remarkable historical period. With *Gods and Generals*, they also had the opportunity to help preserve physical history (*see sidebar*) and try to make the best Civil War movie ever. The re-enactors' presence brought "a large group of historians" to the set every day, explains Bob Tolar, who worked as a logistics coordinator. And besides their own

Above: *Director Ron Maxwell, center, films the doomed Union charge up Marye's Height at the Battle of Fredericksburg, as described in Jeff Shaara's foreword.* Opposite: *Filming the early-morning aftermath of the Battle of Fredericksburg. Re-enactors worked whenever the light and time of day were right for the historical event and the effect the director wanted.*

uniforms, weapons, and accoutrements, the re-enactors supplied their vast knowledge of nineteenth-century military tactics and skills. "We gave *Gods and Generals* a ready-to-field army," says Dana Heim. The re-enactors would "rather do something twenty times to get the correct maneuver than just once in incorrect formation." As Tolar concludes: "You can buy uniforms and props, but you cannot buy the desire and dedication that every individual re-enactor brought to the production."

Ron Maxwell agrees. "They bring the picture much, much more than mere extras could," he observes. "Not just because they have proper uniforms and weapons but because they know what the weapons mean; they know the protocol of the drill; they know how the weapons are used tactically in battle; and they know the structure of military units in the Civil War."

Stephen Lang, who portrays Stonewall Jackson, shares Maxwell's enthusiasm for the re-enactors' contributions. They're not extras," opines Lang. "They don't think or work like extras. They're a phenomenon. No matter how hard I worked, there's no way I can be Stonewall Jackson without—not only the support but the real belief—of the re-enactors around me."

Perhaps the most succinct acknowledgment of the re-enactors' role comes from Robert Duvall, who inspired them with his portrayal of Robert E. Lee: "You could not do this movie without the re-enactors."

DENNIS E. FRYE, Associate Producer for *Gods and Generals*, is the former Chief Historian at Harpers Ferry National Historical Park. He is also a founder and past president of the Association for the Preservation of Civil War Sites, Inc. (today's Civil War Preservation Trust) and the Save Historic Antietam Foundation, Inc.

"IT'S OUR WAR, TOO"

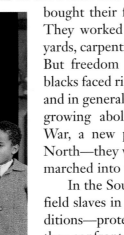

At the start of the war there were approximately 344,000 free blacks living in the Northern states and about 133,000 in the South. A much higher number—three million—were slaves in the South.

Free blacks in the North had either won their emancipation by law, bought their freedom, or were born of free parents. They worked in tobacco and textile factories, shipyards, carpentry shops and as servants in white homes. But freedom in the North did not mean equality: blacks faced rigid discrimination in most realms of life and in general were treated as inferiors, in spite of the growing abolitionist movement. During the Civil War, a new plight struck some free blacks in the North—they were seized by Confederate soldiers and marched into the South to be sold into slavery.

In the South, house slaves often fared better than field slaves in having better day-to-day working conditions—protected at least from the elements—but they confronted their own unique hardships. Martha, the Beale family's house slave depicted in *Gods and Generals*, is an actual historical figure; actress Donzaleigh Abernathy learned about her by reading Jane Beale's diaries as well as studying the lives of slaves in dozens of other books. Of the character she portrayed, Abernathy says:

> It was Martha's greatest desire to be free. She didn't stay behind during the Yankee occupation only to protect the house but also to secure her freedom. Her number-one priority was to experience freedom, to be able to govern herself, to dictate what time she got up, if she ate that day and if she worked that day. She showed courage in the midst of devastation. When they were in the cellar, Jane was frightened but Martha wasn't. That's when she found her strength, because she knew that freedom was coming. She loved Jane Beale, but she was loyal to herself, to her divine right.

Abernathy based her appearance and persona on a slave woman whose photograph she encountered during her research for the role. "The woman I finally based her on was the dress designer for Mary Todd Lincoln," she

Above: *Donzaleigh Abernathy as Martha, the Beale family's house slave, protecting the Beale house. Martha demanded that Jane Beale take her children to safety outside Fredericksburg, and Martha stayed behind in the home as the Yankees invaded and occupied the town.*

said, "who was a slave. This exquisitely beautiful woman, Elizabeth Keckley, was born a slave and she bought her freedom and rose to become Mrs. Lincoln's dress designer."

Some blacks in the South bought their freedom, and *Gods and Generals* highlights one free black man who, like Martha, is a real figure from history. Jim Lewis, a member of General Stonewall Jackson's staff, chose to work for Jackson. Director Ron Maxwell comments on why he brought this character into his screenplay:

> Jim Lewis joined Jackson's staff in the fall of 1861 as his personal cook and valet. Although inconclusive, the scant evidence about him suggests he was a free man of color, and that is how I have chosen to portray him. He stayed close to Jackson to the end. I hope to illuminate his relationship with the general, shedding light on Southern blacks who found themselves caught up with those who fought for the cause of secession.

As the Union army advanced south, their camps were inundated with blacks who fled plantations seeking freedom behind the Union lines. At first many were turned away, but later the Union chose to let them remain, arguing with the Confederacy that they were contraband and therefore appropriate to remain in the Army's possession.

The Union deliberated for years about whether or not blacks should be brought into the army and navy to fight beside white soldiers. But as casualties skyrocketed, the need for new enlistments overruled most qualms, and after the Emancipation Proclamation of September 1862 blacks were invited to enlist. The response was astounding. Eighty-five percent of those eligible for service joined up, with 180,000 blacks enlisting in the Union army and thousands more in the Navy.

Not surprisingly, black soldiers were not treated as equals in the Army. Within the 166 black regiments, the vast majority of officers were white. Black officers could not be promoted to a rank above captain. They did not receive the same clothing allowance as white soldiers, and therefore were more vulnerable to the elements and prone to get sick.

On September 27, 1862, the first black soldiers were officially sworn into the Union Army as the 1st Regiment of the Louisiana Native Guards. Black troops went on to participate in every major campaign of 1864–1865 except General Sherman's invasion of Georgia.

Above: *A black camp cook. Many black soldiers were given menial duties in the Union Army.* Below: *Seven runaway slaves who found safety and freedom in a Union Army camp. Union forces used the argument that because they were slaves, they were contraband of the Army and therefore did not have to be returned to their masters. By the end of the war, black soldiers made up 10 percent of the Union Army. Among them, approximately one-third lost their lives in battle or to disease.*

BIG NAMES
in Small Roles

S harp-eyed viewers will spot a number of distinguished non-actors playing cameo parts in *Gods and Generals*. The most recognizable is Ted Turner: the media mogul whose production company financed the film reprises the role he played in *Gettysburg*, Confederate Colonel Waller Tazewell Patton. Turner—who admits to saving his costume from the earlier film—worked a full day on location in Maryland, shooting a scene in which Confederate officers and enlisted men enjoy a USO-style camp show near Fredericksburg. Turner delivers a line of dialogue—"We owe your Texas boys a debt of gratitude for putting on these shows"—and joins in a rousing rendition of "The Bonnie Blue Flag." For his labors, Turner received a union-scale paycheck: $636.

Director Ron Maxwell also took a turn in front of the camera, playing a Union officer in Chamberlain's weary 20th Maine Regiment during the retreat to the north bank of the Rappahannock River. Maxwell—who liked the idea "doing a Hitchcock" and appearing briefly in his own films—had had a cameo in *Gettysburg* as well but says, "The beard covered me so well, no one could find me. I decided to try again."

While working to support the preservation and restoration of Civil War battlefields, Maxwell had met with national and local politicians, several of whom were offered roles in *Gods and Generals*. Senator Phil Gramm (R-Texas) appears in muttonchops and full costume as a member of the Richmond House of Delegates in the scene where Robert E. Lee accepts command of the Army of Virginia. Several local politicians, including Maryland state Senator Donald F. Munson, also appear in the scene.

Another cameo part went to veteran U.S. Senator Robert C. Byrd (D-West Virginia), who celebrated his 84th birthday on the set. Byrd spent a full day before the cameras in his role as Georgia Confederate General Paul Semmes in scenes

Above: *U.S. Senator George Allen of Virginia and his son as photographed by Rob Gibson.* Right: *U.S. Senator Robert C. Byrd of West Virginia portrayed a Confederate officer.*

depicting activity at Lee's command post at Fredericksburg. In a surprise birthday celebration, the film crew gave Byrd a cake in the shape of West Virginia, and Maxwell presented him with a miniature replica of a Civil War cannon.

On November 28, 2001, Sen. Byrd spoke before the Senate about his experience, saying, in part, "They [the actors] are not simply reciting words on a page; rather, they are bringing to life a period of American history that ended an inhuman practice and solidified our future as one nation."

Other politicians appearing in the Battle of Fredericksburg scenes were U.S. Senator George Allen (R-Virginia), Congressman Edward Markey (D-Massachusetts), and Dana Rohrabacher (R-California).

Several special appearances took place off camera. On one occasion, Robert E. Lee IV visited the set and met actor Robert Duvall, who portrays General Lee (and who is himself a direct descendant of the general). Another day brought the visit of Mrs. Cortlandt Creech, great-granddaughter of "Stonewall" Jackson. Introduced to Stephen Lang, who portrays General Jackson, Mrs. Creech exclaimed, "You look just like him!"

Former senator Phil Gramm of Texas played a member of the Virginia House of Delegates, here speaking with Gen. Robert E. Lee (Robert Duvall) in April 1861.

The Great Conflict

LIKE FIGHTING A WAR

"We are re-creating a time when the country confronted great challenges. People during the Civil War feared for their safety, just as we do now. And yet they rose to the occasion and assured freedom for us all."

—RON MAXWELL, AFTER
SEPTEMBER 11, 2001

The cast and crew of *Gods and Generals* came together in late August, 2001, to recreate three years of the costliest war in American history. They returned to the same rolling hills and beautiful valleys in Maryland, Virginia, and Pennsylvania where the conflict had originally been fought. The realism did not end there: In scope and complexity, making the film was not unlike fighting a war.

There was a "commanding general," director Ron Maxwell. There were logistical hurdles, budget constraints, and challenges of weather and terrain. There was tedious waiting…and unexpected terror. Throughout the filming, as in the war itself, there was a single objective: to complete the project.

"As Robert E. Lee says to General Longstreet in the middle of the battle of Fredericksburg, you must never ignore the unpredictable," says Ron Maxwell. "You must always have contingencies. As a producer and director, as with generals, that means making sure you have the very best people around you—people you can trust completely."

Principal photography began on August 28, 2001. On the very next day the filmmakers discovered the depth and range of the drama they had embarked on. In historic Lexington, filming took place at the Virginia Military Institute and in front of the adjoining Washington and Lee University, founded in 1749 (Robert E. Lee's name was added in 1871). Between August 28 and September 15, the company moved to several Virginia locations. Most shooting took place on two adjoining farming communities south of the historic city of Staunton. Here Maxwell recreated two of the war's most cataclysmic battles: Manassas I (Bull Run) and Antietam.

Gods and Generals was filming Antietam—called "the bloodiest day of the Civil War"—on September 11, when New York and Washington, D.C., were attacked by terrorists. The first to hear about the terrible events were teamster drivers listening to their car radios: the location of the shoot was out of cell phone range. The production came to a temporary halt, giving the cast and crew a chance to call home. A few hours later, Ron Maxwell addressed the solemn company surrounding him at the lower base camp. "We are making a film about another generation of Americans who were severely tested, who also didn't know what would happen the next day. Those who attacked America wanted to bring us to our knees," he said. "But the country must go forward." And so, he said, should *Gods and Generals*.

Although Maxwell offered the option of not returning to anyone who felt unable, every member of the company chose to continue filming. At sunset on September 12, a prayer vigil was held on the set. On the 13th, which had been designated a national day of memorial, cast and crew members attended local churches—whose congregants were startled by the sight of bloodied, bandaged re-enactors in full uniform for their battle scenes.

In mid-September, *Gods and Generals* returned to Maryland for filming on the Shenandoah River and in the historically preserved town of Harpers Ferry. The battle of Chancellorsville was staged near Keedysville on a 600-acre farm long owned by the Austin Flook family. Filming continued in October in several locations. The screen home of the Chamberlains was found in a Civil War–era mansion in Clear Springs, Maryland; the Christmas reception shared by Lee and Jackson was filmed at the Claymont Mansion near Charles Town, West Virginia. One of the most historically significant scenes is the swearing-in of Robert E. Lee as commander of the Confederate Army of Northern Virginia. Standing in for the Richmond House of Delegates is the Jefferson County Courthouse in Charles Town—the actual seat of justice where abolitionist John Brown was sentenced.

In late October, the company began a two-week hiatus to wait for winter weather. When cast and crew returned on November 13, it was to begin the battle of Fredericksburg, with Harpers Ferry doubling for the besieged town.

After weeks of filming horrific battles, the final day of shooting—December 12—was a relatively quiet and poignant one. Along the Potomac River, doubling for the Rappahannock, the company filmed a scene in which two soldiers, strangers fighting on opposite sides, exchange coffee and tobacco. The moment is a reminder of the fact that this catastrophic conflict was a civil war in more ways than one.

TIMELINE OF EVENTS PORTRAYED IN GODS AND GENERALS

MAY 11, 1861
The capital of the Confederacy moves from Montgomery, Alabama, to Richmond, Virginia.

APRIL 12, 1861
The Civil War begins with an attack on Fort Sumter in Charleston Harbor, South Carolina.

APRIL 23, 1861
Five days after being asked by President Lincoln to accept field command of the entire Union Army, Robert E. Lee accepts command of the Army of Virginia.

JULY 21, 1861
First battle of Manassas (Bull Run), where the "Rebel Yell" makes its debut.

JULY 22-23, 1861
President Lincoln signs two bills authorizing enlistments of a total of 3 million volunteers.

NOVEMBER 1861
Major General George B. McClellan replaces Winfield Scott as general in chief of U.S. armies.

APRIL 16, 1862
The Confederate Congress passes the first of three Confederate conscription acts—the first general military draft in American history.

MAY 8, 1862
Stonewall Jackson wins the first battle of his Shenandoah Valley campaign at McDowell, Virginia.

SEPTEMBER 16, 1862
Battle of Antietam (Sharpsburg). A total of 22,719 men are wounded, killed, or missing on the bloodiest single day of the war.

SEPTEMBER 22, 1862
President Lincoln issues the Preliminary Emancipation Proclamation.

DECEMBER 11-13, 1862
Battle of Fredericksburg, one of the worst Union defeats of the war

JANUARY 25, 1863
"Fighting Joe" Hooker replaces Ambrose Burnside as commander of the Army of the Potomac.

MAY 1863
Battle of Chancellorsville, Lee's biggest victory, against a much larger force led by Hooker.

MAY 6, 1863
General "Stonewall" Jackson is shot in the arm by one of his own troops during night maneuvers at Chancellorsville.

MAY 10, 1863
Jackson dies.

RAISING THE ARMIES

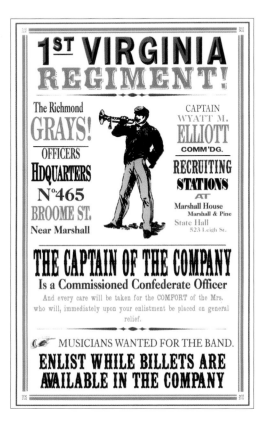

During the four years of the Civil War, approximately three million men served—and 620,000 died—in the Union and Confederate armies. But at the beginning of hostilities in April 1861, both sides had minuscule and poorly prepared forces. The United States Army, with just 16,367 officers and enlisted men, was actually smaller than the combined militias of the seven Confederate states. (The Confederacy would later comprise eleven states.) Drawn since Colonial times from state militias, these "armies" were largely untrained, ill-equipped, and inexperienced in the most fundamental aspects of military life.

During the first two years of the war, the Confederate leadership was clearly superior to the North's, with many distinguished West Point alumni—Robert E. Lee and C.S.A. President Jefferson Davis among them—casting their lot with the South. Also, as historian Brian Pohanka observes: "The South had an established military tradition that made the pursuit of an army career far more attractive than in the North" and responded to the imminent threat to its survival by recognizing and promoting its most talented leaders. The Federal army, on the other hand, "was saddled with the existing military structure, a hierarchy founded on seniority rather than ability."

When it became clear that the conflict would not end by Christmas 1861, as many on both sides had predicted, both the North and the South instituted general conscription for the first time in the nation's history. The draft was used largely as an incentive to volunteer: volunteers were paid, conscripts were not.

Above: *Recruiting poster for the 1st Virginia Brigade, created for the film.* Right: *Recruitment posters for (from left) the colorful Zouaves, 1861, the Anthon Battalion of Light Artillery, 1862, and Corcoran's Irish Legion, 1862.* Opposite: *Union troops at the Battle of First Manassas.*

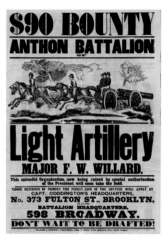

Down the Ranks

To accommodate the huge influx of men and the need for their rapid deployment, both sides had to adjust their staff structures. The Union and Confederate armies were virtually identical in their structure, setting the stage for U.S. military organization in the century and a half that followed.

Company Commanded by a captain; called a "battery" in artillery units. Theoretically 100 men; in reality between 30 and 50 due to attrition.

Regiment Commanded by a colonel. Raised by state governments, regiments comprised men from the same area and were the organizational unit that most men identified with. In the early years of the war, regimental officers were often elected by their men.

Brigade Commanded by a brigadier general. (Until 1864, the Union Army had only two "grades" of general—brigadier general and major general. The Confederacy had four grades; in ascending order, they were brigadier general, major general, lieutenant general, and general.) Brigades comprised between two and 15 regiments.

Division Commanded by a brigadier general or a major general. On both sides, a division could include 12,000 men organized in two to six brigades.

Corps On the Union side, commanded by a brigadier general or major general; in the Confederacy, commanded by a lieutenant general. The first corps in American history were organized by both sides during 1862; thereafter, they became standard wartime units of the United States Army.

Army The largest military field force, commanded by a major general (U.S.A.) or general (C.S.A.). Union armies were generally named after rivers, e.g., the Army of the Potomac; Confederate armies were usually named for the region where they were based, such the Army of Northern Virginia.

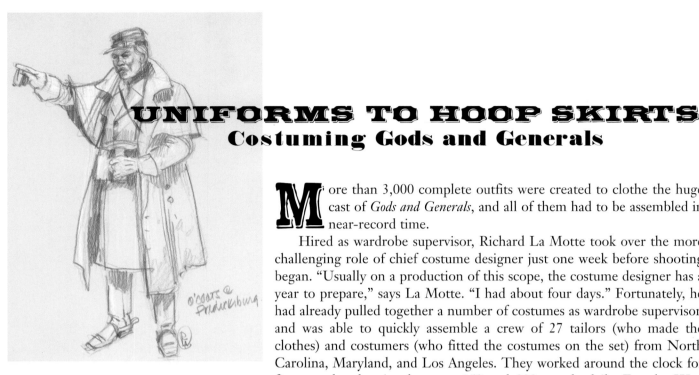

UNIFORMS TO HOOP SKIRTS
Costuming Gods and Generals

More than 3,000 complete outfits were created to clothe the huge cast of *Gods and Generals*, and all of them had to be assembled in near-record time.

Hired as wardrobe supervisor, Richard La Motte took over the more challenging role of chief costume designer just one week before shooting began. "Usually on a production of this scope, the costume designer has a year to prepare," says La Motte. "I had about four days." Fortunately, he had already pulled together a number of costumes as wardrobe supervisor, and was able to quickly assemble a crew of 27 tailors (who made the clothes) and costumers (who fitted the costumes on the set) from North Carolina, Maryland, and Los Angeles. They worked around the clock for five months, dressing between 150 and 800 people daily. For the West Virginia phase of shooting, a vacant department store near Harpers Ferry was transformed into a temporary wardrobe department.

"There was never an easy day," says La Motte. "On our first day of shooting, we had to costume 500 extras at Virginia Military Institute. The next day we costumed 200 soldiers for a scene in which they crossed a bridge." (Stunt doubles wore wetsuits under their uniforms.)

To speed the process, La Motte rented many costumes from sources in Hollywood and England. The rest—especially for the 20 principal actors—were created from scratch. Many costumes had to be made in multiples to account for damage, stunt doubles, and effects such as bloodying. For the scene in which "Stonewall" Jackson is shot, actor Stephen Lang had six uniform coats "just to get through the shooting," says La Motte.

Uniforms posed special challenges. The thousands of Civil War re-enactors who participated in the production brought their own carefully researched clothing and equipment to the set. In some cases, though, "Hollywood uniforms" had to be manufactured as well because of special requirements for early-war militia scenes and the Battle of First Manassas, and for scenes calling for blood, dirt, or damage to uniforms. To create these, La Motte relied on photographs from museums and a wealth of printed regulations that—thanks to the resurgence of interest in the Civil War—have been compiled over the last 20 years. He was assisted by a young historian, Jim Broomall, who consulted on uniform details.

Sometimes authenticity was sacrificed for expediency. Washable cotton flannel often substituted for wool; painted styrofoam balls doubled as pompons on Confederate shako hats.

The women's costumes presented an opportunity to underscore historical themes. "The North had more money, but it was colder and more mechanical," says La Motte. "The South was more romantic—but a little out of date." Thus Fanny Chamberlain wears an opulent gown to the theater in Baltimore (in the DVD version of the film only), while the costumes of Anna Jackson, Jane Beale, and other Southern women are more "pastoral—straw hats, shawls, and so forth. We also looked for gowns that were a bit antiquated—from the 1850s instead of the 1860s."

La Motte, who has worked in Hollywood for more than 25 years, can recall only one other production bigger than this one: *Hello, Dolly!* And *Gods and Generals* was more demanding, he says, because of its time span and scope. "We portrayed three years of fighting, four major battles, three seasons of the year. The cast included people from every walk of life: slaves, military officers, theater people." He credits his hardworking crew with the success of his mission. "Most of them had never worked together before, and some weren't familiar with the Civil War period. But they came through," he says. "They were fantastic."

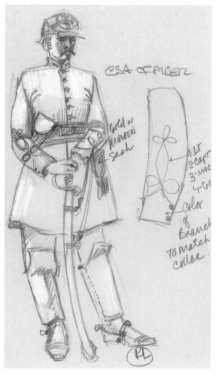

Above and opposite top: *Costume drawings by Richard La Motte.*
Opposite: *Royce Applegate (1939–2003) as Confederate General James Kemper.*

Military uniforms in the early years of the conflict were far from consistent; even the blue and gray of North and South had not been standardized. Some units wore clothes resembling civilian wear, while others—notably the flamboyant U.S. Zouave units, who modeled their uniforms after French Algerian troops'—were flashily attired. Union soldiers had just begun to wear colored corps symbols on their caps—the forerunners of contemporary unit patches—and Confederate soldiers were likely to wear the homespun cotton shirts and trousers they'd worn as farmhands or laborers. On both sides, materials were in short supply. Unscrupulous Union contractors sold uniforms made of "shoddy," an inferior fabric created by pressing together lint, sweepings, and fabric scraps and passing it off as wool. They looked acceptable when new, but disintegrated when dampened by rain or sweat. The term "shoddy" survives today as an adjective meaning substandard.

KILLING MACHINES
Weapons of the Civil War

Both sides fought the Civil War with a diverse array of weaponry, much of it antiquated and some of it terrifyingly innovative. (The writer Louis Menand has said the war "was fought with modern weapons and premodern tactics.") Because the war's scope quickly overwhelmed manufacturers' production capacity—especially in the South, which had few factories—both Union and Confederate governments bought many arms from European sources.

Three new weapons dramatically altered the character of the war. The first was the minié ball (or bullet), invented by Frenchman Claude Etienne Minié in 1848 and adapted over the next decade by the U.S. Army. The conical, .58-caliber minié ball became the standard infantry bullet on both sides; it was easier to load than previous bullets and had greater range and accuracy. It also caused terrible wounds: Instead of creating a neat hole, it shattered bone and lodged in the tissue, leading to infection. With no antibiotics available, field surgeons resorted to amputation.

The second innovation, the percussion rifle-musket, was also used by both sides. Unlike older muskets, it had a spiral-grooved ("rifled") bore, which doubled the weapon's range. The most popular models were Enfields, imported from Great Britain, and Springfields, made at the Federal arsenal in Springfield, Massachusetts, and by private contractors.

Finally, the Civil War saw the first use during wartime of repeating rifles, which held up to 16 rounds. Used almost exclusively by Union soldiers, these rifles—mostly Spencers and Henrys—were first tested in 1861 and became popular despite their weight and complexity. According to General George Armstrong Custer, the Union cavalry's success at Gettysburg was attributable to the Spencer rifle.

Above: *A Confederate battery at the Battle of Antietam (DVD version).* Right: *Twenty-pound Parrott rifled gun of the 1st New York Battery, near Richmond, Virginia, June 1862.* Opposite: *Jeff Shaara at VMI with the "Four Apostles" cannon he helped restore.*

More Civil War Weapons

Bayonet – Pointed metal weapon, socket or sword style, attached to the end of a rifle barrel and used in hand-to-hand fighting.

Flintlock – Muzzle-loading firearm dating back to the early nineteenth century or earlier.

Hand grenade – Used by both sides, mostly during siege or trench warfare.

Howitzer – Short cannon designed to fire explosive shells at medium velocity.

Lance – Used only by the Sixth Pennsylvania Cavalry ("Rush's Lancers"), lances consisted of long wooden poles with sharp metal tips.

Musket – Muzzle-loading, smooth-bore shoulder arm longer than 36 inches.

Musketoon – Shorter, muzzle-loading shoulder arm used by cavalry and artillery troops.

Napoleon – Smooth-bore cannon designed in France and named for Emperor Napoleon III. The Napoleon fired a 12.3-pound projectile.

Parrott gun – Cast-iron cannon in various sizes, including the 30-pound siege gun. Identified by the wrought-iron reinforcing band around the breech.

Single-shot rifle-musket – Loaded with a ramrod that pushed the bullet into the powder charge, it was capable of being fired three times a minute.

Sabers and swords – Used mostly ceremonially by officers; sabers had curving blades, swords had straight blades.

Whitworth sharpshooter – Imported by the Confederacy from Great Britain, this muzzle-loading rifle had outstanding accuracy at ranges of greater than 1,000 yards.

Matthew, Mark, Luke, and John

"The Four Apostles"—a battery of light cannon painted a distinctive red and black—got their name "because they spoke a powerful language." They had arrived at Virginia Military Institute in 1848; between 1851 and 1861, VMI artillery professor Major Thomas Jackson used them to instruct the cadets.

At the start of the war, the cannon were turned over to the Rockbridge Artillery, commanded by Rev. William Nelson Pendleton ("Old Penn"). They saw action at First Manassas (Bull Run); on May 14, 1863, they fired every half hour as a memorial to "Stonewall" Jackson, their old commander.

Captured after the fall of Richmond, the guns were returned to VMI in 1876; they were used in training drills until 1913 and again during World War I. In 2000, a generous gift from author Jeff Shaara enabled the restoration of the cannon to their original 1848 specifications. The guns now stand guard at the foot of the Jackson monument on the VMI campus.

MARCHING ON THEIR STOMACHS

W ar movies often portray soldiers standing in long lines with plates while company cooks ladle out food from tall, steaming pots. This type of organization came long after the Civil War, however. There were no mess halls during the Civil War and soldiers usually prepared their own meals. Some companies assigned mess duties to selected soldiers, but in most cases soldiers cooked for themselves over open fires or on camp stoves. Many officers, though, brought servants along who cooked their meals.

Basic rations included coffee, bacon, and salt pork—also called sowbelly—a fat cut of pork cured by salting. Given the choice, soldiers would rather march with salt pork than bacon because bacon fat melted in the heat and saturated everything in their haversacks with grease.

Union soldiers also were issued one-pound packages of hardtack, a square cracker made from flour, water, and salt. This thick, hard ration was loaded with salt so that it would keep for long periods and not entice mice or cockroaches. Weevils, however, didn't mind the salt and burrowed their way into the crackers, making it even less appetizing. Soldiers soaked hardtack in coffee and devised other ways to make it more appealing. "Hellfire stew," for example, was made by crushing hardtack into pieces, soaking it in water, and then frying it in bacon fat.

Above: *Noncommissioned officers mess of Company D, 93rd New York Infantry, Bealeton, Virginia, August 1863.* Below: *The film's Confederate winter camp near the Rappahannock River, January 1863.*

The Confederate bread staple was cornbread. Soldiers also ate hardtack captured from Union supplies, but cornbread was much more common in the South. Like hardtack, it attracted mice and insects and was difficult, if not impossible, to keep fresh.

Sutlers—people who followed armies to sell merchandise to the troops—provided other foodstuffs. Poor supplies of fruits and vegetables caused many health problems, and the Union army tried to offset this with dehydrated beans, beets, carrots, onions, and turnips pressed into small cakes. General Stonewall Jackson famously

"I was always a lover of coffee..."

The letters of soldiers offer rich details about how they ate in the field. The collected letters of Private Rufus Robbins of the Massachusetts Volunteers, for example, are filled with information about rations, cooking duties, recipes, and wish-lists that he penned to his parents. Making coffee, a staple that both sides tried to keep in good supply, was an important part of his day whether in camp or on the road:

"Coffee and sugar are dealt out to use twice a day, a large spoonful each night and morning. I mix mine in the little oil silk bag which mother made to keep my Bible in and have a supply on hand all the time as the rations are more than I want to use, except when on the march. If we halt for half an hour when on the march, coffee making is a lively business. Fires are made and the pots go on at short notice but sometimes are caught right in the middle of it. The order comes, fall in. Sling knapsacks. Take arms. Right face. Forward march. And away we go with the coffee half cooked turned upon the ground. You know, I was always a lover of coffee, but I prize it now more than ever."

sucked on lemons to prevent scurvy. Potatoes and onions were the most common vegetables available to troops on both sides, and officers encouraged soldiers to forage for onions as an important source of vitamins.

Gathering firewood and foraging for wild vegetables and game took up much of a soldier's time. "Every day I detail from a quarter to three quarters of my company to collect wood for cooking," wrote Union Captain John William De Forest from Ship Island in the Gulf of Mexico in the spring of 1862, "and this wood they must bring on their backs a distance of two, three, and four miles." Forced to store the company rations in his tent, De Forest lived among heaps of smelly rations:

We have no cook-tent, and no lumber wherewith to build cook-houses, so that I must store all the rations of my company in my own tent. Consequently I am encumbered with boxes of hardbread, and dispense a nutritious perfume of salt pork, salt beef, onions, potatoes, vinegar, sugar and coffee.

Rations were scarce toward the end of the war, especially for the Confederate troops whose supplies could not get through the Union blockades. Malnutrition and starvation followed these food shortages, and throughout the war those soldiers who were fortunate to receive packages from home fared better than those who did not.

Top: *Typical soldiers staples included hardtack, coffee issued individually in bags (the coffee can serving as a general mess tin) and "homespun" tobacco.*
Above: *Jim Lewis, right, played by Frankie Faison, with General Jackson. A free black man, Lewis worked as a cook on Jackson's staff.*

HARPER'S WEEKLY.

A JOURNAL OF CIVILIZATION.

Vol. VII.—No. 324.]   NEW YORK, SATURDAY, MARCH 14, 1863.   [SINGLE COPIES SIX CENTS.
$3,00 PER YEAR IN ADVANCE.

Entered according to Act of Congress, in the Year 1863, by Harper & Brothers, in the Clerk's Office of the District Court for the Southern District of New York.

TEACHING THE NEGRO RECRUITS THE USE OF THE MINIE RIFLE.—[See Page 174.]

WHAT THEY WERE READING

To keep up with the events of the war, readers turned to the many daily and weekly newspapers published in both the North and South. As supplies got short, some papers shrunk in size and at times publishers had to get creative about the printing process. Due to a shortage of newsprint in 1863, one edition of the *Opelousas Courier* came off the press on wallpaper.

The public demand for military news prompted journals such as *Harper's Weekly* and *Leslie's Illustrated Weekly* to send artists as well as reporters to the front. Once completed, battlefield illustrations were rushed to New York newspaper offices on horseback. *Harper's Weekly*, with its comprehensive reporting and dramatic illustrations, printed 250,000 copies a week at the war's peak.

When they weren't reading newspapers or letters from loved ones in uniform, many women at home were reading magazines such as *Godey's Lady's Book*. This popular and influential monthly journal ran fiction, poetry, sheet music (for the parlor piano), fashion illustrations, and articles on housekeeping, etiquette, and sundry topics to enlighten the female mind, providing a lively and beautifully illustrated distraction from the gloomy news of the day. During the war, Godey's editorial policy was to ignore the subject altogether and provide an "oasis" from the nation's troubles.

American books published during the war included Louisa May Alcott's *Hospital Sketches*, a widely read memoir of her volunteer work in a Georgetown military hospital. (Alcott's biggest seller, *Little Women*, would be published five years later.) Other books written by famed authors during the war were Henry Wadsworth Longfellow's *Tales of a Wayside Inn*, Henry David Thoreau's *The Maine Woods* and *Cape Cod*, and James Russell Lowell's *Fireside Travels*.

Soldiers' tastes in reading fell more to the inexpensive, action-packed dime novels—all the rage during the war. Priced at 10 cents vs. the 25-cent price of a regular novel, these 100-page books spun tales of pioneer life, Indian

Opposite: *Cover of* Harper's Weekly *from March 14, 1863.*
Right: *The* New York Herald*'s "headquarters" in Bealeton, Virginia, August 1863.*

A SAMPLING OF CIVIL WAR-ERA NEWSPAPERS

THE NORTH
Cincinnati Daily Gazette
Hartford Evening Press
National Police Gazette
Newark Daily Advertiser
New York Daily Tribune
New York Herald
New York Times
Philadelphia Enquirer
The Oregonian Statesman

THE SOUTH
Army & Navy Messenger
Charleston Daily Courier
Chattanooga Gazette
The Daily Press (Nashville)
Galveston Tri-Weekly News
Houston Daily Telegraph
Louisville Daily Journal
New Orleans Daily Delta
Opelousas Courier
Richmond Enquirer

fighting, and frontier adventure. One of the best-selling dime novels of the period was *Malaeska* by Ann S. Stephens, the story of an Indian maid who married a white hunter. Another was Edward S. Ellis's *Seth Jones*, the tale of a New England hunter described by the author as "a splendid specimen of nature's nobleman." Easy to afford and read, dime novels were exactly the kind of entertainment soldiers were looking for, and the Beadle & Adams publishing company sold more than 4 million copies by mid-1865.

A scene in the DVD version of the film dramatizes the high level of literary among Civil War fighting men. Around a campfire, Jackson aide and inveterate punster Sandie Pendleton regales his fellow officers with an endless stream of puns from his favorite source: *The Punster's Pocketbook, or The Art of Punning* by Bernard Blackmantle (London, 1826).

Right: *Cover of* Beadle's Dime Novels. Facing Page: Top: *Artist Alfred R. Waud of* Harper's Weekly, *sketching on the battlefield.* Bottom left: *"Young Soldier" by Winslow Homer, 1864.* Bottom right: *"Wounded Soldier Being Given a Drink From a Canteen" by Winslow Homer, 1864.*

Writing the War

Newspapers were big business by the time the war began, and competition to be the first to break the latest news was fierce. Some 500 war correspondents were hired to cover the action for northern, southern, and international newspapers. Young would-be reporters envisioned the war correspondent's job as a glamorous life of travel, adventure, and meeting famous people.

But both novice and veteran newspapermen soon learned that the job was anything but glitzy. Living the soldier's life, coming under fire, witnessing the bloody realities of war, and meeting deadlines made the war correspondent's job difficult and dangerous. Some died while observing combat; one reporter, standing six feet from General Grant, was decapitated by a cannonball. Others were victims of accidents such as drowning or being crushed by fallen horses. Approximately 50 were taken as prisoners of war for varying lengths of time. On top of the obvious hardships, correspondents were generally unwelcome within the armies they followed.

Most came from the prosperous Northern papers in big cities such as New York, Philadelphia, and Chicago. By far the most heavily invested paper was the *New York Herald*, which had 30 correspondents in the field by 1862 at a cost of $2,000 per week, and 63 by the end of the war. *Herald* correspondents received a circular stressing the importance of submitting stories before their rivals: "In no instance, and under no circumstances, must you be beaten."

Illustrations were extremely popular in the press at this time, and among the war correspondents were artists who delivered detailed pen sketches of locations, battles and personnel. Two young, prominent Civil War artists who went on to forge illustrious careers were Thomas Nast and Winslow Homer.

"When the times have such a gunpowder flavor, all literature loses its taste. Newspapers are the only reading. They are at once the record and the romance of the day."

—HENRY WADSWORTH LONGFELLOW, ONE WEEK AFTER THE ATTACK ON FORT SUMTER, 1861

IMAGES OF WAR

Photography was a new and developing art form at the outbreak of the Civil War. The daguerreotype—an image made on silver-plated copper—had been introduced in 1839, and daguerreotype portraits became so popular that by 1850 there were 77 photography studios in New York alone.

In the 1850s a revolutionary new process reduced exposure time and allowed multiple prints to be made from a glass-plate negative. Previously, only one daguerreotype could be made and that original could not be duplicated. The new collodion, or "wet-plate" process, was faster and less expensive and opened up new prospects for photography.

Civil War photographers traveled with cumbersome loads of chemicals and equipment to take pictures using the collodion process. Rough roads, fast processing speeds, delicate chemicals, and glass plates made it a tricky and high-pressured business. Their wagons were carefully covered to seal in darkness while they prepared and developed the glass photographic plates. Upon seeing these mysterious wagons, soldiers asked, "What is it?" so often that the wartime photographic cart came to be named just that—the "What Is It?"

Renowned Civil War photographers include Alexander Gardner, who made three-fourths of the pictures taken of the Army of the Potomac; Timothy O'Sullivan, creator of the famous Gettysburg photo entitled "Harvest of Death"; Captain A. J. Russell, the War Department's official cameraman; A.D. Lytle, a spy photographer for the Confederate Secret Service; and, the most famous of all, Mathew Brady.

Brady was already an institution by the time the war erupted. Anyone who was anyone had his or her portrait taken by Mathew Brady, including Abraham Lincoln. When the war began, Brady gained permission from federal government to accompany the troops and used his own money to fund a huge corps of photographers. "I had to go," Brady later said. "A spirit in my feet said 'Go,' and I went."

Brady spent much of his time managing this enterprise, supervising photographers sent into the field, overseeing supplies and handling the negatives. He published albums of the collected war photos under his name alone, however, which ignited animosity from photographers such as Gardner

Below: Timothy O'Sullivan's portrait of the Officers of Company D, 93rd New York Infantry in 1863.

and O'Sullivan, who were members of his corps for a time. Brady's own contributions came from trips to the field, where he saw plenty of action.

After the Battle of Antietam in 1862, Brady mounted a dramatic exhibit of battlefield photographs at one of his New York galleries. Those who filed in beneath the sign THE DEAD OF ANTIETAM were shocked by images of corpses and horrifying carnage. With this exhibit, Brady brought the realities of war to many people for the first time.

The War Department also utilized photography during the war, sending up manned hot air balloons to gather information about Confederate positions.

Above: *"Confederate Dead Along the Hagerstown Pike," 1862 by Alexander Gardener.* Below left: *Mathew Brady, 1861.*

Brady at Bull Run

The plucky photographer was forced along with the rest; and as night fell he lost his way in the thick woods which were not far from the little stream that gave the battle its name. He was clad in the linen duster which was a familiar sight to those who saw him taking his pictures during that campaign; and was by no means prepared for a night in the open. He was unarmed as well, and had nothing with which to defend himself from any of the victorious Confederates who might happen his way, until one of the… company of… Union forces gave him succor in the shape of a broadsword. This he strapped about his waist, and it was still there when he finally made his way to Washington three days later.

—Article in *Humphry's Journal* in 1861 describing Mathew Brady's experiences at the Battle of Bull Run (First Manassas)

LETTERS HOME
"We forage like the locusts...."

One of the most popular ways in which soldiers passed away the long, idle hours of the war was writing letters to their families back home. They wrote about the details of camp life, of their personal reflections on the war, of their loneliness and homesickness. "I mention all these little details," wrote Lieutenant William W. Gordon of Georgia to his wife, "to keep you posted as to the events which now make up the sum of our life."

Officers wrote to their wives to share their struggles, using their beloved partners back home as sounding boards for frustration and dismay. Soldiers wrote home to keep families informed of how they were getting along, offering personal notes more often than battle information because they knew that the newspapers reported the facts much more quickly than they could.

The vast amount of letter writing during the Civil War swelled the demand on the Federal postal service. At the outset of the war, mail in the eastern half of the nation traveled by rail, and with the increased volume came new efforts to streamline the system. In a major innovation in 1862, workers began sorting the mail on the train as it rushed from stop to stop. Another new efficiency measure was the creation of three categories of mail: first, second, and third class.

The South established its own postal department in early 1861, but service was hampered by interruptions in rail service, supply blockages, shortage of Confederate stamps, and invading Union armies.

Realizing that they were living through a momentous chapter in history, many in the field also kept private journals, recording experiences that they could read and reflect upon in years to come. Colonel Charles Wainwright of New York wrote of an exciting parcel of books that had just arrived. "By books, I do not mean to read, but books to write in. We are making history, not studying it." Several volumes later, Wainwright summed up his goals in keeping his diary: "I think I have accomplished my object in the journal, which is to fix the events of my soldiering in time and place, that I may easily recall them in years to come, should my life be spared. I do not expect that anyone else will see it."

Above: *In a scene from the film, General Jackson reads the news of the birth of his baby daughter.* Below: *Soldiers reading letters, papers, and playing cards, Petersburg, Virginia.*

Above: *Fanny Chamberlain (Mira Sorvino) reads a letter from her husband, Col. Joshua Chamberlain.*

Below: *Envelopes imprinted with political images were popular during the war, such as caricatures, flags, camp scenes, battleships, male and female designs, eagles, and many other designs. These envelopes and stationery are a fascinating glimpse into how the covering of a simple letter could represent both patriotism and biting criticism.*

In a letter to his wife, Union Captain John William De Forest described the chaos and hunger of the army as it marched through Louisiana in the autumn of 1863:

As I wrote you about a fortnight ago, the army crossed the Atchafalaya without opposition. It is a large column, counting two divisions. . . . but I cannot imagine what we are here for unless it is to make believe to carry on war, and so furnish an excuse to keep General Banks in charge of a department. We are slowly following a body of Confederate mounted infantry . . . who do nothing but burn bridges and then scamper away.

We forage like the locusts of Revelations. The Western men plunder worse than our fellows. It is pitiful to see how quickly a herd of noble cattle will be slaughtered. . . .

I was sent up [to Alligator Bayou] with my company to guard a bridge against a raid which was expected in our rear. We started in a hurry and with empty haversacks, expecting that rations would follow us. Then the commissary forgot us, or the transportation arrangement broke down, and we were left without food for two days. Luckily Sergeant Weber had served in the Seminole War and knew by experience that alligators' tails would make soup . . . so I sent a foraging party to look up one of the innocents of the bayou and borrow his tail . . . for twenty-four hours we rioted on alligator soup. We pronounced it delicious.

105

FIRST MANASSAS
Baptism in Battle
by James I. Robertson, Jr.

It was the first major engagement of the Civil War, but it was more a collision of two armed mobs than a battle between opposing sides. Today there is an unreal quality about First Manassas (or Bull Run, as Northerners call it), for most accounts describe it in terms of later struggles fought by experienced generals and trained soldiers. What happened at Manassas was not like that at all. Nothing went the way it had been planned.

Early summer, 1861: the Civil War was barely three months old. Yet North and South alike had instantly seen the value of a new form of transportation called the railroad. Because of it, any Union force starting southward from Washington, D.C., toward the Confederate seat of government at Richmond first had to gain control of an unimpressive village slightly off the main route. It was called Manassas Junction because the Orange & Alexandria and the Manassas Gap railroads came together there. Those lines were arteries into the Shenandoah Valley and the central (Piedmont) regions of Virginia.

Pressure for action came early and steadily from Northern authorities. A Union army must quickly form, go to Manassas Junction, crush the rebellion there, and march triumphantly to Richmond. Commanding the hastily assembled Union forces was Gen. Irvin McDowell, a former staff officer with no battle experience.

In mid-July, McDowell reluctantly started forward. He was leading 33,000 recruits—a host larger than the one Gen. Winfield Scott had commanded in Mexico. Yet disorganization reigned because of the newness of everything. When the head of his "army" began to move into Virginia, the tail of it was still being put together in Washington.

Thirty miles away, behind the southern bank of a sluggish stream called Bull Run, were 22,000 equally untutored Confederates. At their head

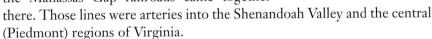

"First rank—lie down! Second rank—kneel!" Confederate troops prepare to fire at First Manassas.

107

was Gen. P. G. T. Beauregard, who had been one of McDowell's classmates at West Point. The eight-mile Southern defense line stood a mile north of the railroad junction. Most of a second Confederate force came in from the Shenandoah Valley to reinforce Beauregard's position. This put the contending sides at about equal strength.

Union scouts uncovered a crossing of Bull Run two miles north of the Confederate flank. On Sunday morning, July 21, McDowell made a feint against Beauregard's right flank to get the Southerners leaning in that direction. Meanwhile, the Union commander had sent 13,000 men northwestward to sweep around and behind the Confederate left.

The mistakes of inexperience continued. The Union attack was not only late; it came in short—that is, the Federal movement hit the left tip of the Southern line rather than curling around the flank. About 900 Confederates moved out to meet the threat. With the help of 1,000 hastily dispatched reinforcements—and aided by the disjointed Federal attacks—the little band of Southerners fought stubbornly and held back the Union turning column. Late in the morning, however, sheer Federal numbers overran the improvised Southern line.

McDowell then committed a major mistake by ordering a three-hour pause in the assaults while he reviewed the situation. This gave the Confederates time to rush troops from the right and center to the battered left. The most prominent height in the area was Henry House Hill, and posted out of sight on its reverse slope were 3,600 Virginians. This brigade formed the anchor of the reconstructed Southern position.

The brigadier general in charge of those troops was a former college professor, Thomas J. Jackson. Then thirty-seven, he was a shy, withdrawn man full of ferocious Presbyterianism. His reticence concealed determination and faith inside one who was born to fight.

Near 2:30 p.m., Federals surged forward toward Henry House Hill, driving back fragments of shattered Confederate units to the base of the eminence. Then came one of those dramatic moments that live in legend. Confederate Gen. Barnard E. Bee was trying to rally his broken ranks when he saw fresh soldiers advance to the hilltop. "Look, men!" Bee shouted as he pointed upward. "There stands Jackson like a stone wall! Rally behind the Virginians!" Bee fell mortally wounded a few moments later, but he had given American military history its most famous nickname.

The 1st Virginia Brigade in full charge.

Some 10,000 exuberant Federals swept up Henry House Hill in grand expectation. Jackson calmly watched their approach. He instructed his men: "Reserve your fire until they come within fifty yards! Then fire and give them the bayonet! And when you charge, yell like furies!"

His brigade did as told. Suddenly Jackson's five infantry regiments and 13 cannon unleashed a point-blank burst of gunfire. Confederates rose and dashed down the hill. Their screams above the battle noise marked the birth of what became known as the "Rebel Yell." This counterattack splintered the advancing Union lines. Federals recoiled in momentary confusion, then started forward again.

Union gunners rolled a battery of four cannon partway up the hill and opened an oblique fire. Jackson's artillery and infantry responded with a concentrated volley. A Union officer watching this action through field-glasses wrote: "It seemed as though every man and horse of that [Union] battery just laid right down and died right off."

An hour and a half passed as the two sides grappled back and forth on the hillside. "For one long mile the whole valley is a boiling crater of dust and smoke," a newspaperman observed. Then fresh Confederate reinforcements arrived by rail from the Shenandoah Valley. Their attack slammed into the exposed Federal flank.

McDowell saw that his great effort had failed. He ordered a retreat. The green Union recruits had fought well, but making an orderly withdrawal under fire from a losing field was too much. Brigades and regiments began to disintegrate. Next the soldiers encountered several hundred civilians who had come out from Washington to enjoy picnic lunches while they watched the Civil War end. They now decided it was time for them to go home. Within minutes, a major traffic jam formed on the main road to Washington. Anxiety became desperation that quickly changed to panic. A mob scene followed, with soldiers and civilians fleeing 30 miles back to the capital. An English observer sarcastically dubbed the spectacle the "Bull Run Races."

Opposite: Gen. Barnard Bee (Jim Choate) rallies his men defending Henry House Hill, pointing to Jackson's troops advancing in support: "There stands Jackson like a stone wall. Rally behind the Virginians!"

Fighting at Manassas had lasted seven hours. On both sides, it had been waged by poorly trained civilians who were trying to become soldiers. The wonder of it all is that the battle lasted as long as it did, and was marked with so much determination and courage. Casualties were 800 killed and 2,700 wounded. By the standards of later Civil War engagements, these losses were not excessive, yet they gave bloody evidence that this was not going to be a small, quick contest.

A few days afterward, a Confederate soldier informed his wife: "Sunday last … was the happiest day of my life, our wedding-day not excepted. I think the fight is over now." One of this man's compatriots saw the future more realistically. "I have no idea that they intend to give up the fight," he wrote of the Federals. "On the contrary, five men will rise up where one has been killed, and in my opinion, the war will have to be continued to the bloody end."

So each side went back to where it had started and prepared for another campaign. First Manassas was a traumatic beginning. Beneath the gaudy uniforms, gay flags, and lilting songs could now be felt a deep grimness and a new resolution. A long, terribly costly struggle lay ahead.

What the film *Gods and Generals* commendably underscores about First Manassas is the emergence to prominence of Gen. Thomas J. Jackson. After ten years as a dull, plodding college professor, he seemed a totally unlikely figure for stardom in the Civil War. The film shows us otherwise. Jackson's characteristics, demonstrated on the high ground overlooking Bull Run, made him the Confederacy's first enduring hero and—eventually—one of the living legends of American history.

JAMES I. ROBERTSON, JR., historian and great-grandson of a Confederate soldier, has taught Civil War history to thousands of college students and received every major award in his field. He is the author of *Stonewall Jackson: The Man, The Soldier, The Legend* and other acclaimed books, and appears regularly on the Arts & Entertainment network, the History Channel, and public television. He is an Alumni Distinguished Professor at Virginia Tech.

BLOODY ANTIETAM
"The most terrible clash of arms..."
by Dennis E. Frye

Stonewall Jackson knew Robert E. Lee was in trouble. The enemy had advanced unexpectedly. Lee's scattered Confederate army had just escaped disaster at South Mountain; renewed enemy attacks were expected at dawn. Outnumbered and without reserves, Lee's bedraggled Confederates could defend the mountain gaps no longer. The army must retire. The invasion into the North must end—immediately.

It was not supposed to end this way. Ten days earlier, on September 4, 1862, Lee had launched his first foray into Northern territory. Nearly 40,000 Confederates had splashed across the Potomac and entered Maryland during the second week of September, commencing an advance that Lee hoped would win the war for the Confederacy. "Should the results of the expedition justify it," Lee proclaimed boldly to President Jefferson Davis, "I propose to enter Pennsylvania."

Lee also hoped to recruit soldiers in Maryland and free that state from "the oppression to which she is now subject." Politically, he expected to embarrass Lincoln and his fellow Republicans, thus swaying votes to the Peace Democrats in the forthcoming Congressional elections. Just as significant, the presence of the Southern army in the North might persuade Europe to intervene in the war. At no time since the commencement of the war had Confederate independence looked so promising.

But General Lee's invasion ran into problems soon after it began. A Union garrison at Harpers Ferry remained in the Confederate rear, threatening Lee's avenue of supply and communication. To eliminate this threat, Lee divided his army into four segments, sending three columns under Stonewall Jackson to capture or destroy the Harpers Ferry nemesis. By September 13 "Old Jack" had surrounded the hapless Yankees.

Then disaster struck: Lee's instructions for the campaign fell into enemy hands. On September 13 Union commander George B. McClellan received a lost copy of Lee's orders at his Frederick headquarters, only 20 miles from the Ferry. An exuberant McClellan informed President Lincoln, "I have all the plans of the rebels and will catch them in their own trap."

The following day, McClellan attacked three gaps of South

Opposite: Gen. William Nelson Pendleton's battery at Antietam. Above: Associate producer Dennis Frye, in uniform, right, discusses battle strategy with line producer Ron Smith. Below: Burnside's bridge over Antietam Creek, photographed by Alexander Gardner in 1862. Federals captured the bridge after intense fighting.

Mountain in Maryland, where surprised but defiant Confederates saved Lee from extinction. With his invasion plan badly compromised, General Lee ordered a retreat—but then received promising news from Jackson and halted the retreat at Sharpsburg, hoping for Jackson's triumph. Before noon on the 15th word arrived. "Through God's blessing," Jackson's message began, "Harpers Ferry and its garrison are to be surrendered."

That settled Lee's decision to remain along the Antietam. But what if the enemy attacked before his army was reunited? Nearly 20 miles separated Lee from Harpers Ferry and Jackson, who had with him fully two-thirds of the Confederate army. Could Stonewall win the race to Sharpsburg before the Union army moved?

Jackson first had to deal with the fruits of his conquest: 73 pieces of artillery, 13,000 small arms, 200 wagons (and 1,200 mules), and 12,700 prisoners—the largest surrender of U.S. troops during the Civil War. Before moving to join Lee, Jackson arranged to have the equipment driven south into Confederate territory. Then he ordered Major General A. P. Hill to remain at the Ferry and to parole the Union prisoners.

At 1:00 a.m. on September 16, Jackson began marching his men toward Antietam Creek. With the Stonewall Division setting the pace, half of Lee's Harpers Ferry detachment reunited with their chieftain before dusk on the 16th. Still, even with his ranks thus bolstered, Lee still was outnumbered more than three to one. And McClellan was preparing to attack!

At dawn on September 17, 1862, the Battle of Antietam (called Sharpsburg in the South) commenced. The Union army launched assault after assault against the Confederate left—precisely where Lee had positioned Jackson. Fierce fighting raged incessantly for nearly four hours in the Cornfield, the East Woods, and the West Woods. About midway through the butchery, as Jackson's reserves were thinning, John Bell Hood rushed forward with his division, the Texas Brigade leading the charge. The fearless Texans halted the Union momentum but suffered heavy casualties—82 percent of the 1st Texas regiment alone. Even the veteran Hood was appalled at the human destruction, "the most terrible clash of arms," he wrote, "that ha[d] occurred during the war."

A shell, in fact, nearly killed Stonewall Jackson. During a conference near the West Woods with General Lafayette McLaws (whose division had just arrived from Harpers Ferry), a Yankee missile landed at the feet of the

Above: Ron Maxwell and the Confederate command filming the Battle of Antietam (DVD version). Opposite: Union troops under Gen. Ambrose Burnside prepare to advance.

114

two generals but did not explode—a very near miss for the Confederacy.

Four hours of tortured combat in Jackson's sector had littered the earth with nearly 8,000 dead and wounded Union and Confederate soldiers within a half-mile radius of a simple, white-washed brick church belonging to the Dunkers—a sect of pacifists. Jackson had thwarted attacks by six Union divisions that caused the Confederate left to buckle but not break. Fortunately for him, the battle then shifted south. But the situation for General Lee remained desperate.

Next came repeated attacks against Lee's center at Bloody Lane. The Confederate line broke here after three hours of valiant defense, but the Federals failed to exploit the breach. Pressure then mounted against Lee's right, where Major General Ambrose Burnside carried a stone bridge spanning the Antietam, then followed with an attack of 10,000 men—the largest assault of the day. Outnumbered on his right nearly five to one, Lee watched anxiously as Burnside's three divisions plodded forward.

Just as Burnside was about to smash Lee's right, more help arrived: A. P. Hill's division hurrying up from Harpers Ferry Hill's men swarmed onto the battlefield, stunning Burnside and driving him backward—thus securing Lee's line and ending the battle at dusk. It represented a remarkable effort by Hill, who had marched his men seventeen miles in seven hours and battled for another three, saving Lee's army from certain defeat.

But the invasion was over. Lee retreated from Maryland on the night of the 18th, and Antietam ended the political and diplomatic opportunities for the Confederacy in the fall of 1862. For both sides, the price was shockingly high: More than 23,000 men fell in twelve hours of brutal combat, forever engraving Antietam as the bloodiest single day in American history.

"Such a storm of balls I never conceived it possible for men to live through. Shot and shell shrieking and crashing, canister and bullets whistling and hissing most fiend-like. . . . In that mile's ride, I never expected to come back alive."

—SANDIE PENDLETON, WHOM JACKSON SENT FORWARD TO GET WORD FROM GEN. HOOD DURING THE HEIGHT OF THE UNION ASSAULT

BATTLING THE "THIRD ARMY"

Above: *Wounded soldiers being tended in the field after the battle of Chancellorsville, May 2, 1863.* Below: *Dr. Hunter McGuire (Sean Pratt) tends to the wounded General Jackson in a field hospital during the battle of Chancellorsville.*

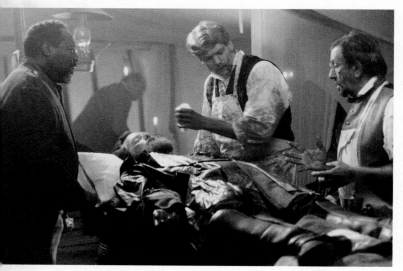

Grim scenes of bodies littering the fields after battle lead many to assume that most Civil War deaths occurred on the battlefield. But in fact, only a fraction did. Two-thirds of the approximately 660,000 deaths during the Civil War were caused by disease—the "Third Army" that struck equally against North and South. Physicians did not yet know that germs carried disease, even though important discoveries in that direction were underway in Europe. Had the war been fought just a few years later, methods to prevent infection would have been used in military hospitals and many fewer deaths would have occurred.

The risk of disease began in the training camps, where young men who had grown up in isolated country settings gathered in large groups for the first time. This ignited outbreaks of measles, mumps, and other "childhood" diseases that spread through the cramped and unsanitary camps. Once in the field, soldiers fell prey to typhoid, yellow fever, malaria, pneumonia, smallpox, and other diseases. Latrines were often nothing more than the nearest bush, which led to a contaminated water supply and rampant transmission of germs that caused diarrhea, cholera, and typhoid. Disease was also spread by the fleas, mites and lice that plagued every soldier, and the nutrient-poor military diet also advanced the Third Army's cause.

Even if a soldier survived the health hazards of camp life, he was still at risk of a life-threatening infection from battle wounds. Without sterile equipment, bandages, or conditions in which to work, the best efforts of field doctors were often futile. The first line of aid came just a few yards behind the battle scene, where surgeons and their assistants set up a dressing station. Armed with bandages, lint, opium pills, and morphine, medical personnel followed a rough protocol of emergency care. First, the wounded were given whiskey or brandy, which was believed to counteract shock. Then an assistant surgeon gave the soldier opium or rubbed morphine into the wound to buttress him for treatment. After examining the wound and trying to stop the bleeding, the doctor removed what-

ever bits of metal, clothing or other foreign bodies he could find; packed the wound with lint—unsterilized, of course—wrapped it in bandages; and attached a splint, if necessary.

After getting bandaged at a dressing station, soldiers who could walk made their way to the nearest division (field) hospital—generally at least three to five miles away—on foot. As the war progressed, hospitals were also set up in houses, schools, churches and other buildings after major battles to provide shelter for the wounded. Those who could not walk were loaded onto horse- or mule-drawn wagons for an agonizing journey over rough roads that jolted the fragile passengers into even worse condition by the time they arrived at a division hospital. Amputations were an all-too-common resort to save lives: due to the frightful wounds made by minié balls and the sheer numbers of wounded often arriving at once.

After being treated at the division hospital, surviving patients were either sent back to their regiment to continue fighting or transported to a general hospital for further treatment and recovery. By the end of the war there were 350 general hospitals in the North and 154 in the South.

Above: A filled-to-capacity military hospital, photographed by the Mathew Brady Studio between 1861 and 1865. Below: A field hospital, Savage Station, Virginia, June 30, 1862. Conditions at division hospitals grew worse and supplies thinner as the war drove on. Flimsy tents provided shelter for some, but many wounded were forced to lie on the ground in the open air where dirt and mud invaded their wounds.

Field doctors sometimes found themselves in the midst of battle when the fighting shifted toward the rear lines. In one of his letters, Union surgeon Daniel M. Holt described one unforgettable incident that took place while he was working just behind the lines: "One man was shot a second time while in my arms dressing his wound, and expired. For an hour bullets, shells and solid shot flew through our midst as thick as hail. I wonder why we were not killed."

FREDERICKSBURG
The Slopes of Death
by Frank A. O'Reilly

Abraham Lincoln had spent the better part of 1862 reassuring the North that the Civil War was going according to plan. Union reverses that summer, however, allowed Confederates to seize the initiative and move into Maryland and Kentucky. The bloody battles of Antietam (or Sharpsburg) and Perryville compelled them ultimately to fall back into Virginia and Tennessee, but Northern confidence had been badly shaken.

To restore voter confidence after a poor showing in fall 1862, Lincoln charged all of his armies to embark on a winter campaign (a treacherous undertaking normally criticized by military men) to gain total victory. When the armies responded unenthusiastically, Lincoln removed their commanders. Major General George B. McClellan, commanding the 135,000-man Army of the Potomac, halted around Warrenton, Virginia, and the president replaced him with Major General Ambrose E. Burnside. Anxious for immediate and decisive action, Lincoln demanded Burnside's plans at once. Burnside surveyed his maps and determined to move to Fredericksburg.

It was inevitable that the Civil War would come to Fredericksburg. Nestled on the Rappahannock River, fifty miles from Washington and Richmond, the quaint, Colonial city (population 5,060) stood midway between the two warring capitals and on the brink of a new era of military combat. The Richmond, Fredericksburg, and Potomac Railroad made an attractive supply route for the Union army.

Burnside's army would have to cross several significant rivers en route to Richmond, the first being the Rappahannock. He requested pontoon bridges (floating bridges constructed from boats) to meet him at Fredericksburg so he could cross there without slowing down. Lincoln approved the plan, and the Union army hurried to Fredericksburg. Robert

Above: *Union General Ambrose Burnside and his staff plan the attack on Fredericksburg.* Opposite: *The 20th Maine regiment under Col. Joshua Lawrence Chamberlain crosses the pontoon bridge across the Rappahannock River, December 13, 1862.*

"On we pushed, up slopes slippery with blood, miry with repeated, unavailing tread. We reached that final crest, before that all-commanding, counter-manding stone wall."

—GEN. JOSHUA LAWRENCE CHAMBERLAIN, FROM *BAYONET! FORWARD: MY CIVIL WAR REMINISCENCES*

E. Lee had divided his Southern army between Culpeper, Virginia, and the Shenandoah Valley. Fewer than 1,000 Confederates defended Fredericksburg when Burnside's army arrived on November 17. But Burnside could not capture the city because his pontoon bridges were late. They arrived ten days later, and by then Lee occupied a series of commanding ridges around Fredericksburg.

Burnside never intended to fight at Fredericksburg, hoping to use the city as a springboard for his drive on Richmond. Faced now with Lee's defenders entrenching along the Rappahannock and Lincoln's repeated demands for action, Burnside altered his plans. Discovering that the Confederates guarded almost thirty miles of river above and below Fredericksburg, and assuming Lee had spread his legions rather thin, Burnside determined to strike across the river at the city itself. A lightning thrust could cut the Rebel army in two, severing Lee's forces west of the city from those to the south.

Union engineers started constructing bridges in the early morning darkness of December 11. As their work neared the halfway mark, Mississippi sharpshooters, under Brigadier General William Barksdale, opened fire from the cover of the city's riverfront buildings. The engineers fled the terrible fire and work ground to a halt. Federal artillery tried to roust the Confederates from their strongholds, but without success, though it caused immense property damage and frightened civilians like Jane Howison Beale's family. Many abandoned their homes for safety behind Confederate lines.

Hours passed, and Burnside's plans, predicated on speed and surprise, collapsed. Brigadier General Henry J. Hunt, Burnside's chief of artillery, then suggested that the engineers should ferry infantry across the river and establish a bridgehead. Burnside agreed, and at a given signal, infantry volunteers jumped into the pontoons and paddled furiously across the Rappahannock. Attacking the nearest houses, Union troops drove the Confederates away from the river. Engineers could now erect their bridges in safety. Barksdale, though, saw an opportunity to further confound and delay the Yankee army. His troops contested the Union occupation, fighting from street to street and house to house until well after nightfall.

December 11 had been a momentous day in American military history.

Fredericksburg was the first city deliberately targeted for a bombardment. Union troops executed the first river crossing under fire and the first bridgehead established under fire. The city also witnessed the first urban combat in North America. Burnside had finally gained a toehold on the other side of the Rappahannock, but he was unable to exploit it.

Robert E. Lee had marshaled his Army of Northern Virginia on the ridges behind and downstream of Fredericksburg, along eight miles of front. As Burnside funneled troops across the river on December 12, Lee finalized his defenses. Lieutenant Colonel Edward Porter Alexander, one of his premier artillerists, rejoiced in the defensive scheme, boasting that "a chicken could not live on that field when we open on it."

Burnside struck on December 13, launching a two-pronged attack against Lee's right and left. His primary assault, against Lieutenant General Thomas J. "Stonewall" Jackson, met with initial success. Major General George Gordon Meade's division of Pennsylvania Reserves penetrated an undefended marsh in Jackson's front and breached the Confederate defenses. But Meade's men became disorganized and no one hurried to reinforce

Above and opposite: A 12-pound Parrott gun exploded near Generals Lee and Longstreet, knocking them off their feet. Lee commented: "It is not yet our time, gentlemen; it is not yet our time." Overleaf: Federal artillery on Stafford's Heights, opposite Fredericksburg. Inset: Georgia Irish Confederates of Cobb's Brigade at the stone wall.

Desperate Federal soldiers used their fallen companions as shields during the carnage on Marye's Heights, and later that night, as protection from the bitter cold.

them. This gave Jackson time to mount a punishing counterattack that drove Meade out of the gap and restored the Confederate line. Burnside's best attack of the day had failed. Losses were heavy. A Confederate wrote that "the scene which presented itself … in our front was sickening in the extreme." The Union army suffered 5,000 casualties, and Jackson's losses neared 4,000, which reflects how close either army had been to victory.

Meanwhile, Burnside had started a series of attacks on the other end of the line that would ultimately eclipse the battle between Jackson and Meade. In late morning, Federal troops issued out of the city and struck a particularly commanding hill. Burnside intended to pin down Lieutenant General James Longstreet's Confederates here on Marye's Heights so they could not send reinforcements to help Jackson. Bluecoat soldiers marched across a 900-yard open plain directly into the teeth of Longstreet's artillery and rifle fire. Southern cannon disrupted the neat formations as they paraded across the wide fields. As Union troops neared the foot of Marye's Heights, Rebel infantry under Brigadier General Thomas R.R. Cobb sprang up from a hidden sunken road and stone wall, firing into the confused mass of blue.

Amid the chaos and carnage, one glimmer of humanity rose above the tragedy. A young sergeant from South Carolina, Richard Rowland Kirkland, was touched by the tragic results of the battle. He heard the plaintive cries of the Northern wounded, trapped between the lines, begging for water. At the risk of his own life, Kirkland jumped the stone wall and brought water to his enemies. His selfless act of kindness gained him the nickname "the Angel of Marye's Heights," and provided a model of honor and respect that inspired leaders like Lee, Jackson, Hancock, and Chamberlain during the war and beyond.

The "Wild Geese" of the Irish Brigade

More than 170,000 Irish-born Americans—many of them recent refugees from the potato famine—fought on both sides of the Civil War. But the most famous contingent was the "Irish Brigade" created from the 69th and 88th New York regiments, the 63rd New York State Volunteers, and the 2nd New York Light Artillery Battalion. Although most of the brigade's soldiers were from New York City, some came from as far away as Buffalo, Boston, and Chicago. They came from all walks of life—bricklayers and attorneys, unskilled laborers and tenant farmers from the old country. Some spoke only Irish Gaelic. Many enlisted to escape desperate economic conditions.

To the men who served under its banners, the name "Irish Brigade" had resounding historical and patriotic echoes. In 1688, 5,000 Irishmen had gone to France to fight for James I, the English king in exile. Because it was illegal for the Irish—considered British subjects—to join foreign armies, the recruits were listed as "Wild Geese" on ships' manifests, and the nickname stuck.

The Union's Irish Brigade was formed by Brigadier General Thomas F. Meagher, himself an Irish immigrant with a colorful history: The son of a wealthy merchant, he studied law in Dublin, joined a radical Irish-independence movement, and was exiled to Tasmania. He escaped to America in 1852, where he became an attorney, lecturer, and political force among Irish immigrants. Meagher raised a company of Irishmen and armed them with "obsolete" .69-caliber smooth-bore muskets, which he preferred for their effectiveness at close range.

The Irish Brigade fought in every campaign of the Army of the Potomac, from First Manassas (where Meagher had his horse shot out from under him) up to the surrender at Appomattox. Among its most dramatic engagements was the tragic assault on Marye's Heights during the Battle of Fredericksburg. For the battle, the New York regiments joined with the 28th Massachusetts, the only regiment to carry a green flag (adorned with the harp of Ireland) that day. Instead of a flag, Meagher and his staff gave each of the New York troops a sprig of boxwood to wear in his hat.

The brigade went into battle with 1,200 men; only 263 survived. In one company, all but one man were slaughtered. Their courage was noted, surprisingly, in the generally anti-Irish *Times* of London, which reported, "Never at Fontenoy, Albuera, or at Waterloo, was more undaunted courage displayed by the sons of Erin."

> **"Boys! Look at that flag— remember Ireland and Fontenoy!"**
> —BRIG. GEN. THOMAS F. MEAGHER, JULY 21, 1861

Above: *Artist/historian Don Troiani's painting of the advancing Irish brigade,* Clear the Way, *1987.*

Above: *View of Fredericksburg, Virginia across the Rappahannock River, February, 1863.* Opposite: *The 20th Maine begins its ill-fated charge up Marye's Heights.*

FRANK A. O'REILLY is a former chief historian at the Fredericksburg & Spotsylvania National Military Park and permanent historian at the "Stonewall" Jackson Shrine. He has written numerous articles on the war in Virginia and is the author of *Stonewall Jackson at Fredericksburg* and *The Fredericksburg Campaign: Winter War on the Rappahannock.* He is currently researching a book on the Battle of Chancellorsville.

The Federal attack collapsed in turmoil. An entire division, some 4,000 men, had been decimated in thirty minutes. As Meade continued to need support in his battle with Jackson, Burnside launched wave after wave of attackers against the stone wall and Marye's Heights, including Brigadier General Winfield Scott Hancock's division. All met disaster, with Hancock losing in excess of 2,000 out of 5,500 men. To keep the Confederates from advancing and pushing his forces back into the Rappahannock, Burnside persisted in sending even more attackers into the field, among them the 20th Maine under Lieutenant Colonel Joshua Lawrence Chamberlain. Not one Union soldier reached the stone wall. Instead, thousands of wounded and dead bluecoats littered the plain. A 20th Maine soldier wrote, "The field was thickly covered with the fallen … mangled and bleeding, trodden under the feet of the charging column."

The losses were abysmally one-sided. Longstreet lost approximately 1,000 soldiers, while Burnside's right wing suffered 8,000 casualties. A Southern officer wrote that Burnside's actions had "led to two entirely separate battles fought three miles apart, between which there was no connection or interdependence." Under cover of night, Burnside abandoned Fredericksburg on December 15, and gave up the campaign.

The Battle of Fredericksburg was a milestone in the war—Robert E. Lee's most resounding victory and Abraham Lincoln's greatest embarrassment to date. Union morale collapsed in the aftermath of the futile assaults against Marye's Heights—what the men termed "sheer murder." Desertion became rampant as a result. On the other side, the battle convinced Lee's men that the war was about over and that one more victory might make Southern independence a reality

Union officers such as Hancock and Chamberlain would reflect on the battle for the rest of their lives. But in the immediate moment, both gathered a new resolve—steeling themselves for a harder road to restoring the Union. In the camps across the way, Confederates celebrated their easy victory, but Lee and Jackson felt troubled by the results. Both knew they had embarrassed Burnside's army but had not destroyed the Northern forces. Lee wrote after the battle, "I was holding back…and husbanding our strength and ammunition for the great struggle. Had I divined that it was to have been his only effort, he would have had more of it." Lee considered the battle only half won.

BURNISHING HISTORY
Digital and Special Effects

The authentic look of *Gods and Generals* owes a great deal to careful research and to the thousands of re-enactors who portray soldiers and civilians. But the verisimilitude was burnished by a team of expert technicians led by visual effects producer Thomas G. Smith.

Smith collaborated with production designer Michael Hanan, who shared his extensive library of Civil War images, and with history consultants Dennis Frye and Keith Gibson. And he worked closely with director Ron Maxwell. "Ron knew that visual effects would be needed to enhance the size of the armies and provide wide sweeping vistas of towns, true to their form during the Civil War," says Smith. "Because of budget constraints, our original plan called for a limited number of effects—fewer than 50 shots. But as the film progressed, nearly every day Ron called me to the set to show me something he wanted and ask if we could do it. In the end, we quadrupled our shot count." Virtually every effect was created for a single reason: to enhance the historical accuracy of the film.

"Accuracy" comprised two broad areas: scale and anachronism. The battles dramatized in the film often involved huge numbers of soldiers. "Even the thousands of dedicated re-enactors performing in the film were not enough," Smith explains. "We often needed to show tens of thousands. At Antietam, on one day alone, there were 20,000 casualties." Through digital cloning, Smith and his crew were able to enhance the panoramic battlefield scenes—many of which had been shot with no intention of using visual or digital effects. Only later were Smith and his crew called in and asked to add an effect.

Above: *A street in Frederick, Maryland, stands in for a residential neighborhood of Washington, D.C., in 1861.* Below: *Visual FX add the unfinished dome of the Capitol.*

Sometimes, visual effects were employed for more subtle purposes. Early in the film there is a scene showing Harpers Ferry in 1861. Still untouched by the war, a large armory sat on the banks of the Potomac and Shenandoah rivers, with the town set back from the water. Steam trains and horse-drawn wagons rolled past the factory. Today, 80 percent of the town has changed from the way it looked before the Civil War; only the rivers and a few old buildings remain. The crew filmed the town as it is now. Afterward, using still photos taken around 1861, digital matte artist Bob Scifo was able to recreate a detailed view of Harpers Ferry as it would have looked before it was altered by the 20th century.

Washington, D.C., has also changed dramatically since 1861. At that time, the Capitol dome was still under construction. In the movie, a street in Frederick, Maryland, substitutes for Washington, with horses and carriages in the foreground and a digitally created Capitol—with unfinished dome—in the background. "The movie becomes an artifact to help Civil War buffs see how it would have really looked if we'd had 35mm anamorphic color movies in 1861," says Smith.

Above: Harpers Ferry as it looks today; the two photos below show a 3D rendering and the final visual effect seen in the film of Fredericksburg in 1862.

Digital effects also were used to "erase" anachronistic elements—such as barbed wire, cars, and trucks in the distance—anything that would have betrayed the film's 21st-century origins.

Two of the most impressive effects were created by Toy Box, one of the visual-effects contractors used in the production. In one scene, as Robert E. Lee and Stonewall Jackson return to Fredericksburg after the battle, the camera pans up to reveal damaged and smoldering buildings. "In fact, there were no damaged buildings," says Smith. "It was all a digital effect." In the other scene, soldiers stare in awe as the aurora borealis streams across the night

sky above the battlefield at Marye's Heights. As stunning as it appears, this was one of the simplest effects in the movie, says Smith, who credits "the skilled artists at Toy Box."

The goal of visual effects is to be invisible, says Smith. "We hope people don't say, 'That was a good effect.' We want them to keep thinking of the story, not about the technical tricks it took to make it. The less the audience sees our work, the more we have succeeded."

CHANCELLORSVILLE
High-water Mark for the South
by James I. Robertson, Jr.

The May 1863 campaign at Chancellorsville was the grandest victory that Generals Robert E. Lee and Thomas J. Jackson gained together. On paper, it was a battle Lee could not win. Yet win it he did, brilliantly but at great personal loss to the Confederacy. That engagement in north-central Virginia was unquestionably a turning point in the fortunes of the South's major force, the Army of Northern Virginia.

Six months earlier, Lee had gained a lopsided victory over General Ambrose Burnside's Army of the Potomac at Fredericksburg. The dispirited Union host spent the winter of 1862–63 licking its wounds, regaining strength, and rekindling morale under a new commander, Gen. Joseph Hooker. Handsome, battle-proven, ambitious, and boastful, Hooker gave new life to what became a force of 134,000 thoroughly outfitted soldiers. Meanwhile, Lee and his 60,000 ill-equipped men stood defiant on the heights behind Fredericksburg.

Hooker had no intention of repeating Burnside's mistake by launching unimaginative head-on assaults against Lee. The 1863 strategy devised by Hooker was well conceived. Revitalized Union cavalry would gallop behind the Confederate army and create havoc all the way to Richmond. Part of the massive Union army would threaten Lee's front at Fredericksburg. Meanwhile, Hooker with some 73,000 Federals would advance 20 miles up the Rappahannock River and swing around Lee's left flank.

If the movements worked, Lee would be forced either to fall back into the open—where his smaller force would surely be destroyed—or to remain where he was and be squeezed in a huge vise formed by the two segments of the Union army. "My plans are perfect," Hooker chortled, "and when I start to carry them out, may God have mercy on General Lee, for I will have none."

Federals began moving upriver on April 27; initially, all went well.

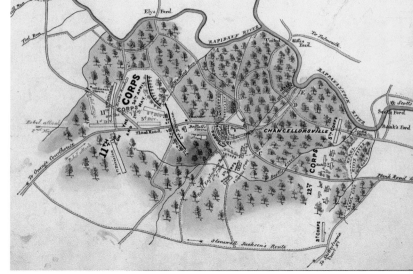

Above: *An 1863 map of the battlefield of Chancellorsville, Virginia, showing troop positions and movements, roads, railroad route, and vegetation.*
Opposite: *Confederates overrun the Union camp in Jackson's surprise attack on May 2, 1863.*

Hooker's men forded the Rappahannock and marched rapidly along country roads threading a 72-square-mile area known as the Wilderness. It was a confusing, almost roadless jungle of stunted pines, hardwood trees, vines, and undergrowth. Visibility was no more than 20 yards in any direction. The Wilderness was no place for an army—yet once Hooker got through, he would not only be in open country but behind Lee's forces as well.

The Union drive faltered at the critical moment, owing to several factors. First, Hooker fatally assumed that Lee would do what Hooker thought he would do. Lee did not, however, take the bait of Federal horsemen in his rear. He saw the Union raid for what it was: a diversion. His own cavalry, under dashing and aggressive "Jeb" Stuart, roamed the countryside and soon discovered Hooker's turning movement.

Lee was heavily outnumbered and about to be pinned down in the middle of a huge Federal army. Yet because the odds against him were so great, he could take enormous risks. Lee sent his most trusted lieutenant, "Stonewall" Jackson, westward with his corps to blunt the Union advance while Lee remained at Fredericksburg to watch the Federal forces there.

On May 1, Jackson's men slammed unexpectedly into the van of Hooker's army as it was emerging from the Wilderness. This counterattack was the turning point of the whole campaign. The surprise and strength of Jackson's assault so rattled Hooker that he ordered his forces back into the gloom of the Wilderness. A near-victorious Army of the Potomac went into a defensive posture where two country roads intersected. The clearing had a tavern and the name Chancellorsville.

"The surprise was complete. A bolt from the sky would not have startled [the enemy] half as much as the musket shots in the thickets… and then a solid wall of gray… bearing down upon them like an irresistible avalanche. There was no stemming such a tide."

— A Confederate officer
at Chancellorsville

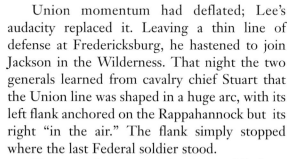

Union momentum had deflated; Lee's audacity replaced it. Leaving a thin line of defense at Fredericksburg, he hastened to join Jackson in the Wilderness. That night the two generals learned from cavalry chief Stuart that the Union line was shaped in a huge arc, with its left flank anchored on the Rappahannock but its right "in the air." The flank simply stopped where the last Federal soldier stood.

Here was the opportunity Lee and Jackson had sought. Near midnight on May 1–2, the two designed what has been called "one of the most audacious tactical moves in the history of modern warfare." Lee was going to divide his little army again. Jackson would take 28,000 soldiers, take a circuitous route to the exposed Union

flank, and then attack down the enemy line. Meanwhile, Lee with 14,000 Confederates would confront five times that number of Federals.

The daring plan caught the Union army totally off guard. Throughout Saturday, May 2, Lee gave a masterful imitation of a field commander about to launch an attack. That held Federal attention. Meanwhile, Jackson's veterans tramped twelve miles along forgotten wagon trails, through woods, over open fields, and into battle position. Near 5:15 p.m., Jackson gave the signal. His attack line, three miles long, moved forward through the dense foliage, gaining speed as his men approached the Union encampments.

Most Federals were cooking supper over campfires or lounging in camp when Jackson's troops struck. A Confederate officer declared: "The surprise was complete. A bolt from the sky would not have startled [the enemy] half as much as the musket shots in the thickets ... and then a solid wall of gray, forcing their way through the timber and bearing down upon them like an irresistible avalanche. There was no stemming such a tide."

For three miles Jackson's men drove the shattered Union lines. Nightfall, the blind tangle of the Wilderness, and exhaustion caused the Confederate advance to waver. Unsatisfied, Jackson sought with furious

Above: Confederates storm through the Union encampment, shattering the Union line and capturing precious artillery pieces. Opposite: General Jackson with his aide, Lt. Joseph Morrison, at Chancellorsville. Overleaf: Jackson and his staff ride through the Union camp. Mounted, left to right: Capt. James Powers Smith, Jackson, Henry Kyd Douglas, Sandie Pendleton, and Lt. Joseph Morrison.

133

Costs of War

Casualty figures of the Civil War vary, but a large consensus agrees that the human toll was approximately 620,000. This is the largest death toll of in any war the United States has fought, from the Revolutionary War to Vietnam.

The Union (2.5 to 2.7 million troops)

Battle deaths	110,070
Disease, etc.	250,152
Total	360,222

The Confederacy (750,000 to 1.25 million troops)

Battle deaths	94,000
Disease, etc.	164,000
Total	258,000

Other Reported Union Casualties:

Deaths in prison	24,866
Drowning	4,944
Accidental deaths	4,144
Murdered	520
Suicides	391
Sunstroke	313
Military executions	267
Killed after capture	104
Executed by enemy	64
Unclassified	14,155

Types of Conflict

Full-scale battles	76
Engagements	310
Skirmishes	6,337

Dollars and Cents

Cost of the war per day (in 1863): $2.5 million

Total cost (1879 official estimate): $6.2 billion

Additional cost for former Union soldiers' pensions and other benefits: $3.3 billion (The amount spent on benefits eventually well exceeded the war's original cost)

Approximate total cost for both sides: $15 billion ($350 billion in 1990 dollars)

Major Regiment Losses in Battle

REGIMENT	BATTLE	STRENGTH	PERCENT
1st Texas, CSA	Antietam	226	82.3
1st Minnesota, US	Gettysburg	262	82
21st Georgia, CSA	Manassas	242	76
141st Pennsylvania, US	Gettysburg	198	75.7
101st New York, US	Manassas	168	73.8
6th Mississippi, CSA	Shiloh	425	70.5
25th Massachusetts, US	Cold Harbor	310	70
36th Wisconsin, US	Bethesda Church	240	69
20th Massachusetts, US	Fredericksburg	238	68.4
8th Tennessee, CSA	Stone's River	444	68.7
10th Tennessee, CSA	Chickamauga	328	68
8th Vermont, US	Cedar Creek	156	67.9
Palmetto Sharpshooters, CSA	Frayser's Farm	215	67.7
81st Pennsylvania, US	Fredericksburg	261	67.4

single-mindedness to keep the battle going to a decisive conclusion. A night attack in force would bring complete triumph, he was convinced.

Oblivious to personal danger, the general took some of his aides and rode forward to determine the enemy's new position. He was returning to his own lines when some of his infantry mistook the riders for Union cavalry and opened fire. Jackson was hit; the worst of the three bullet wounds shattered the bone and tendons in his upper left arm. Soldiers struggled to get him to the rear on a litter. In the underbrush and confusion, they twice dropped the stretcher. Some five hours after Jackson was shot, his surgeon amputated the irreparable limb.

Fighting at Chancellorsville raged on for the next three days. Lee ordered Jackson removed to safety, which necessitated an all-day, 27-mile wagon ride over bumpy roads to the railhead at Guiney Station. Within two days, the first signs of pneumonia were visible. No positive treatment then existed for the illness, and the general's condition worsened. Jackson had always wished that he might die on the Lord's Day. In mid-afternoon on Sunday, May 10, Jackson emerged from a coma long enough to say: "Let us cross over the river and rest under the shade of the trees." With those words, he completed his earthly pilgrimage.

Chancellorsville was Lee's greatest victory. Thanks to Jackson's daring and aggressiveness, the Union army's 1863 effort to take Richmond and end the war failed. It was a costly failure: the Federals suffered 17,000 casualties in a campaign that accomplished nothing strategically. The victory was hollow for the South, too. It came at a loss of 13,000 soldiers, including Jackson. "I know not how to replace him," a crestfallen Lee declared.

It is appropriate that the film *Gods and Generals* ends with Chancellorsville. More than one historian regards that battle as the beginning of the end for the Confederacy in Virginia. With Jackson's passing went much of the mobility and audacity that were his trademark. Lee never again attempted a great flanking movement such as Jackson had executed so masterfully. Starting in mid-1863, the Civil War in Virginia became a standup, slugging fight between two mismatched hosts. Lee would win a round here or there, but over the long haul Union might would be the decisive factor. The road to Appomattox, then, probably began at Chancellorsville on a dark and confusing night in May 1863.

"He has lost his left arm; but I have lost my right."

— ROBERT E. LEE ON HEARING THE NEWS THAT GENERAL JACKSON'S ARM WAS AMPUTATED

General Jackson is severely wounded by friendly fire while returning from a late-night reconnaissance on May 2.

137

SOUNDTRACK TO WAR

Above: *Sheet music for "The Bonnie Blue Flag," a Confederate favorite second only to "Dixie" in popularity, and the North's response, "The Bonnie Flag with the Stripes and Stars," written by a Union colonel while being held prisoner of war.*

The music for *Gods and Generals* is operatic in scope—not surprising, given that director Ron Maxwell is an ardent opera enthusiast with a strong interest in music of all kinds. Lyrical orchestral themes blend with authentic period songs and military music; bracketing the film are two original songs, one by a talented newcomer, Mary Fahl, the other by the legendary Bob Dylan.

To weave together these diverse musical strands, Maxwell called on music producer David Franco, who had been the music supervisor on *Gettysburg*. Franco immersed himself in research, unearthing 1860s sheet music ("we followed the arrangements as closely as possible") and finding or re-creating period instruments. He was aided in the research by musicologist Pat Gibson of Lexington, Virginia, who scoured the Library of Congress for long-lost songs of the antebellum era.

Fortunately, the interest in Civil War re-enactment has spawned many musical groups as scrupulous about authenticity as are Maxwell and Franco. From their ranks, Franco selected outstanding brass bands, military bands, fife-and-drum corps, and minstrel groups. All the music was pre-recorded in a studio and filmed to play back on the set.

"One of the challenges of making a film that depicts mid-nineteenth-century America is to re-create its musical ethos," says Ron Maxwell. "Folks at home were buying sheet music of old and new songs to sing around the piano. Soldiers already burdened with the essential accoutrements of warfare also carried harmonicas, guitars, tins whistles, and banjos. Military brass bands and fife-and-drum corps paraded in city streets and played during actual battles. Congregations filled churches with hymns, while round many a Yankee or Rebel campfire, balladeers sang of home and loved ones left behind. *Gods and Generals* had to capture a mosaic of this musical expression."

In his research for the screenplay, Maxwell discovered the songwriter-performer Harry McCarthy, who wrote the lyrics for the Southern anthem "The Bonnie Blue Flag," set to an earlier Irish melody. He and his companion Lottie Estelle toured the South during the war years, performing for both civilian and military audiences. In the movie they perform an authentic period arrangement of the song for troops at the Confederate winter encampment at Moss Neck.

The "underscore"—or off-camera music—was created by veteran

movie composers Randy Edelman and John Frizzell. Edelman, who had composed the score for *Gettysburg*, wrote some themes after seeing early footage of *Gods and Generals*. "John and Randy have succeeded in creating an emotional soundscape that perfectly surrounds and embodies the film's protagonists, their passions, hopes, and loss," says Maxwell.

Frizzell conceived of the score as an audible expression of the characters' thoughts and feelings. "Some themes, like Jackson's, depict a single character," says Frizzell. "Others depict a sentiment or ideal, and were used for characters on both sides of the conflict." The last theme he wrote was for the Irish Brigade. "I watched the scene over and over and contemplated the tragic lives of these men," says Frizzell. "As soon as I thought I understood their pain I sat down and the melody came out very quickly."

The Irish Brigade theme, along with other "Irish" incidental music, is played on the Uilleann pipes by Dublin native Paddy Moloney, one of the foremost interpreters of Irish traditional music alive today. A founding member of the Chieftains, Moloney is also featured on the Irish tin whistle.

The other distinctive instrumental sound on the score is the fiddle. "I knew early on that Mark O'Connor—a great fiddle artist who has recorded with classical cellist Yo-Yo Ma—would be playing on the score," says

Top: *Composer John Frizzell (far left) supervises a recording session for his score at Air Lyndhurst Studios in Hampstead, London. The conductor is Nick Ingram.* Above: *Dana Stackpole as Lottie Estelle and Damon Kirsche as Harry McCarthy perform "The Bonnie Blue Flag" at a show for Confederate troops.*

Frizzell. "I kept looking for varied and expressive moments to showcase Mark's fiddle playing." One of his favorites is the scene when Kilrain and Chamberlain awaken on the battlefield to see crows circling overhead; the fiddle theme is both haunting and soaring.

The balance of the off-camera music is solidly within the European orchestral tradition; it's given voice by a 94-piece orchestra and 40 singers recorded at Air Lyndhurst, a state-of-the-art London studio.

The songs that accompany the opening and closing credits are new, original compositions written by the singers. Mary Fahl, formerly lead vocalist for the 1990s cult band October Project, wrote and recorded "Going Home" as a demo tape. "Mary's song sounds as if it must have been written in antebellum America, yet feels fresh as a sunrise," says Ron Maxwell. "The lyrics speak to the heart of the characters— their attachment to place, to a community, to a home worth defending." The song is heard over the opening credits.

As for Bob Dylan's seven-minute "'Cross the Green Mountain," which plays over the closing credits, Maxwell says it's "a moving ballad, reminiscent of Dylan's earliest work but with the added insights of a lifetime. It's at once specific to our characters and story and universal in its statement on the tragedy of war and the poignancy of the lives swept up in it. The poetry of the lyrics, the driving rhythms, the melodic line—it's classic Dylan."

Above: John Frizzell, *right, goes over the score with orchestrator Andrew Kinney.* Right: Civil War-era sheet *music.*

Civil War Playlist

The Bonnie Blue Flag Set to the tune of "The Irish Jaunting Car," this marching song describes how each state in turn joined the Confederacy. The flag of the title dated back to the West Florida revolt of 1810; it came to represent Southern secession in general.

Dixie Written in 1859 for a New York minstrel show, the song became the South's "Marseillaise" when it was played at Jefferson Davis's inauguration in 1861.

Maryland, My Maryland Baltimore native James Ryder Randall wrote the lyrics in 1861; it was later set to music familiar as "O Tannenbaum (O Christmas Tree)." In 1939 it was adopted as Maryland's state song.

Kathleen Mavourneen Frederick Nicholls Crouch wrote the tune. As war broke out, he was in Maine visiting his former music student, Fanny Chamberlain; he later became a bugler in the Confederate army. (DVD)

The Southern Soldier Boy Words by G. W. Alexander; music adapted from "Boy With the Auburn Hair." A sentimental favorite, it was played most often on fiddles and banjos, as in the film.

Steal Away to Jesus This Negro spiritual, sung by blacks in the Confederate night camp, acquires a double meaning, the coded message referring to escape to the North or eventual emancipation. (DVD)

GODS AND GENERALS

The Screenplay

PREFACE TO THE SCREENPLAY

This screenplay for *Gods and Generals*, though faithful to the structure of Jeff Shaara's novel and its main characters, has taken on a life of its own. The distinctions are in characterization, dialogue, and cinematic storytelling. I felt compelled to include the stories of Afro-Virginians and Virginia women who figured in the historical events covered in the film and who could illuminate the story in unique ways, revealing other facets of the "generals" as well as creating a richer tapestry of the times.

In doing my research for the screenplay, for example, I came across the journal of Jane Howison Beale, who lived in Fredericksburg through the war years and was present, with her children, during the siege and battle of Fredericksburg. Neither Anna Jackson nor Fanny Chamberlain endured a rival experience, and I deemed it important to see the war from the aspect of a civilian, a woman, who found herself momentarily at its epicenter.

As is always the case when delving into the facts, wonderful coincidences emerged. The Reverend Beverly Tucker Lacy was both Jane's pastor and Jackson's wartime chaplain. The Beale family also provided me with the opportunity to introduce Roberta Corbin of Moss Neck manor, where the Confederate army wintered in the early months of 1863. There, Jackson would meet Mrs. Corbin's enchanting five-year-old daughter Jane, and Sandie Pendleton, Jackson's youthful aide, would encounter his future wife, Catherine Corbin.

One story opened up into another and characters miraculously crossed paths; some would escape harrowing circumstances, some would die suddenly from a fever. Altogether, the women gave the story a dimension that put battles and combat in relief, and that made the soldiers more human, more vulnerable. The Civil War is as much a saga of the home front as the front lines, and with this film I wanted to make that connection better known.

Jeff Shaara's book is great reading. To be sure there is lots of warfare, but in some measure the book succeeds because he also takes you through long passages of characters' thoughts or describes their inner lives. In film, much of this needs to be externalized. Silent passages or musical interludes can be effective, as are "voiceovers" of thoughts. But at the end of the day, character is largely revealed through dialogue and action, especially if the characters are inherently loquacious and sometimes eloquent. As was the case on *Gettysburg*, a linguistic dialect coach worked with the cast to discover actual speaking "solutions"— which became organic, invisible touches of character, in contrast to the seeming heavy-handedness of the written word on the page.

Poetic license is the art of what might have been. Not a snapshot, it is more like a retrieved memory, a window opened to reality. When we read Hugo or Tolstoy, we know we are reading fiction, not history, but we are convinced of its authenticity, its honesty, its rigorous conception of what might have been, what could have been. Poetic license is not an excuse for sloppiness and slipshod research; it does not confer authorization to make it all up. Filmmakers, playwrights, and novelists, like historians, are fiercely preoccupied with the truth—poetic, dramatic, and historical. When truth is rendered with artistry, it yields *War and Peace*, *Les Misérables*, *The Gods Will Have Blood*. Through these novels we know European history as well as or better than we know it from historical works.

The Civil War was a brutal episode in our history. More than half million were killed, more than a million wounded. Tens of thousands were made refugees. The suffering was beyond our reckoning. Individual heroism and courage, duty and honor, make sense only in the context of these trials and tribulations. I have not shied away from either in the screenplay for *Gods and Generals*. The last thing the world needs is a mindless, glossy entertainment on the Civil War. So it is important to accept the seriousness of this challenge: to keep our eyes wide open, to be relentlessly honest, to refrain from perpetuating myth and folklore—to get to the truth of the matter. Nothing will be more dramatic and nothing will be more worthwhile.

—*Ronald F. Maxwell*
St. Michaels, Maryland, September 2000

EXT. ARLINGTON HOUSE – DAY

A handsome carriage is drawn up to the front door. A man descends the steps, entering the carriage.

INT. CARRIAGE – DAY

ROBERT E. LEE sits inside, preoccupied.

EXT. BLAIR TOWNHOUSE, WASHINGTON – DAY

SUPER TITLE: Washington City, April 18, 1861

The carriage draws up to the imposing townhouse. In the distance can be seen the Capitol dome, still in construction.

INT. BLAIR HOME, WASHINGTON – DAY

Lee is met at the door by a BLACK HOUSE SERVANT, who leads him to the study, where he meets...

INT. BLAIR STUDY, WASHINGTON – DAY

...FRANCIS PRESTON BLAIR JR., Postmaster General, and Lincoln's personal friend.

> BLAIR
> Welcome, Colonel Lee, welcome to my home. I apologize for the short notice and thank you for your promptness.

> LEE
> No apologies required, Mr. Blair, I am most happy to see you.

> BLAIR
> Colonel, please be seated. Allow me to get to the point. I've been authorized by President Lincoln himself, with the full blessings of the War Department, to offer you the position of Major General in command of the army, the army being formed to put down the rebellion and preserve the Union.

> LEE
> I'm assuming, Mr. Blair, this army is to be used to invade those areas — to eliminate the rebellion by force.

> BLAIR
> Of course, Colonel. The Federal government has been challenged by rebels who've been most effective in turning the sentiments of several state legislatures against their central government, against the Constitution. The attack on Fort Sumter could not be ignored.

> LEE
> General, my home's right there, across the Potomac. Why, you can see Arlington House from your front door. My family's spread all over this part of Virginia. If you invade the South, your enemy territory will be there — right across that river.

> BLAIR
> Colonel, there's no great cry for secession in Virginia. It's not a foregone conclusion that Virginia, or Tennessee, or Arkansas, or Kentucky will join in the rebellion.

> LEE
> My friend, may I humbly submit that you are mistaken about Virginia. As you know, the legislature is convening in Richmond this very day to discuss the very issue of secession. Perhaps you know their mind better than they themselves. I regret to say the President's hasty calling up of seventy-five thousand volunteers to suppress the rebellion in the Cotton States has done nothing to ameliorate the crisis. It has only deepened it.

> BLAIR
> I hope you are not being hasty yourself, Colonel. This could be a great opportunity for you to serve your country.

> LEE
> My country, Mr. Blair? I never thought I would live to see the day that a president of the United States would raise an army to invade his own country. No, Mr. Blair. I cannot lead it. I will not lead it.

> BLAIR
> I am sorry to hear you say so. I fear you are making a terrible mistake.

Lee stands.

> LEE
> Sir, would you please convey my deepest sense of honor and gratitude to the President, but I must decline his offer. Please tell him, please be clear, I have never taken my duties lightly, but I have no greater duty than to my home, to Virginia.

The two men shake hands and Lee takes his leave.

EXT. VIRGINIA MILITARY INSTITUTE – DAY

SUPER TITLE: Virginia Military Institute, Lexington, Virginia

The building has an imposing facade. CAMERA TRACKS IN to a window. We hear Jackson in voice-over.

> JACKSON (V.O.)
> Gentlemen, if you are going to succeed at this institution, you have one common goal — to learn your lessons. If you are placing your energies elsewhere, you will not succeed, either with me or with your careers as military officers.

INT. CLASSROOM OF THE VIRGINIA MILITARY INSTITUTE – DAY

THOMAS JONATHAN JACKSON stands stiffly, facing seated rows of cadets.

> JACKSON
> Gentlemen, I had hoped you would see that with a proper grasp of the artillery principles I have laid before you today, you would eventually learn to apply these principles with great effectiveness in your own field experiences. But since you seem unable to grasp them, I am forced to conclude

---

The screenplay published here represents the complete shooting script for Gods and Generals, *which was filmed in its entirety. It contains some scenes that do not appear in the theatrical release but are included in the DVD version.*

that I must repeat this lesson tomorrow, word for word. Word for word. And if you, if all of you, will pay a bit closer attention, perhaps it will be understood.

A commotion outside distracts the class. Jackson steps over to the open window. He can hear the distinct cry...

VOICE-OVER
Secession!

EXT. WASHINGTON COLLEGE CAMPUS – DAY
SUPER TITLE: Washington College

Jostling crowds. Cheering students surround a flagpole, as the United States flag is lowered, the new Confederate flag, the stars and bars, is hoisted.

JACKSON, in VMI uniform, pushes his way through the crowd. Some of the students cheer him. He sees Dr. JUNKIN, the president of the university, who is being jeered by students.

STUDENTS
Lincoln Junkin! Lincoln Junkin!

JUNKIN (trying to make himself heard)
This is the essence of immorality.

No one takes any notice of him. Jackson pushes toward him. Junkin is nearly in tears. The following conversation is continually interrupted by the jostling students, and by shouts directed against Junkin.

JUNKIN (Cont'd)
Major! Listen to them — the leaders of our intellectual future, screaming for the destruction of our nation.

STUDENTS
Abolitionist! Abolitionist!

JACKSON
Sir, President Lincoln is raising troops.

JUNKIN
I will not stay in a place where my students dishonor their country's flag. Major, I'm leaving for Pennsylvania tomorrow.

JACKSON
War is the sum of all evils. But if I know myself, all I am and all I have is at the service of my country.

Junkin is not angry with Jackson, only with the students.

JUNKIN
Your country, Thomas? Your country, my country — it's all one.

Junkin tries to make his way through the jostling students. Jackson gestures to them, and they allow the old man through.

JUNKIN (Cont'd)
All one, Thomas. All one.

INT. VIRGINIA HOUSE OF DELEGATES, RICHMOND – DAY
SUPER TITLE: House of Delegates, Richmond, Virginia

The assembly is in session. At the center of the imposing chamber stands a statue of George Washington. On the walls hang portraits of Jefferson, Madison, Monroe and Patrick Henry. Lee sits near the podium, where JOHN JANNEY, president of the convention, is concluding his remarks.

JANNEY
... that amid the searching of souls and the gnashing of teeth, the delegates of this convention, harried by the rash actions of a belligerent usurper and the radicals of his party, have stumbled into secession. God knows I and many in this room have resisted it. But how could there be union with a section that would impose its will through coercion? Now that Virginia confronts the armed might of the United States, we Virginians are determined that no spot of her sacred soil be polluted by the foot of an invader. In the memory of the great Virginian George Washington, who was first in the hearts of his countrymen, and summoning also on the memory of his own gallant father, Lighthorse Harry Lee, the Convention calls upon Robert Edward Lee to take command of the armed forces of the citizen army of Virginia.

To general applause Lee ascends to the podium.

LEE
Mr. President and Gentlemen of the Convention: Profoundly impressed with the solemnity of the occasion, for which I must say I was not prepared, I accept the position assigned me by your partiality. I would have much preferred had your choice fallen on an abler man. Trusting in almighty God, an approving conscience, and the aid of my fellow citizens, I devote myself to the service of my native state, in whose behalf alone will I ever again draw my sword.

EXT. MARSHALL THEATER, RICHMOND – DAY
JOHN WILKES BOOTH steps out the stage door of the Marshall Theater, where THREE FEMALE ADMIRERS await him. Out on the street civilians muster into two lines of city militia, the RICHMOND BLUES and the RICHMOND GRAYS.

BELLE #1
Mr. Wilkes, sir. Would you be kind enough to autograph my play bill?

BELLE #2
I was never much interested in Shakespeare till I saw you play Richard the Third. "A horse, a horse, my kingdom for a horse."

BOOTH
"Was ever woman in this humour woo'd? Was ever woman in this humour won?"

The threesome swoon at this gem of thespian genius, as Booth completes his autographs and glides past them into the street. He strolls past the line of smartly uniformed militiamen, notices the many sweethearts kissing and cheering them on. A nearby band strikes up "I'm Goin' Back to Dixie." Meanwhile the stage-door admirers have caught up.

GRAY #1
Say, haven't I seen you someplace?

BELLE #3
Why, of course you have. This here is Mister Wilkes Booth, the finest actor in all of Richmond!

Booth is mildly rankled at the parochial intimation, but only smiles.

BOOTH
All the world's a stage and we but its poor players! What better role than a soldier's, in the defense of his home, his honor, and his beloved.

INT. JACKSON'S HOUSE, LEXINGTON – MORNING
Jackson and his wife, ANNA MORRISON JACKSON are standing together. The doorbell rings. A black house servant, HATTIE, opens the door to a cadet, CHARLIE NORRIS, who stands at attention, salutes.

CHARLIE NORRIS
Good morning, Major. This just arrived for you.

Jackson takes the envelope, breaks the wax seal, reads.

JACKSON
Cadet, return to the institute. Give Colonel Smith my compliments, and inform him I will be at his office within the half hour.

The Cadet salutes.

CHARLIE NORRIS
Sir!

The Cadet goes. Anna takes the letter and reads.

ANNA JACKSON
You are ordered to report immediately with the Corps of Cadets to Camp Instruction, to begin the formal training and organization of the Provisional Army, for the defense of the Commonwealth of Virginia.

JACKSON
My esposita! Come, before I leave, we must sit, read together... a verse...

Jackson finds his Bible on the center table.

JACKSON (Cont'd)
Yes, yes, here. Corinthians, Second Corinthians, chapter five, I have been thinking about this verse.

Anna puts her hand on his, and they read it together.

JACKSON & ANNA JACKSON
"For we know that if our earthly house of this tabernacle were dissolved, we have a building of God, a house not made with hands, eternal in the heavens."

They kneel together. His arm is around her.

JACKSON
O Almighty God, grant that, if it be Thy will, Thou wilt still avert the threatening danger, and grant us peace. Keep her whom I love, oh Lord, in Thy protecting care, and bring us all at last to the joy of Thy eternal kingdom.

EXT. PARADE GROUNDS, VMI, LEXINGTON – DAY
The cadets march in formation in time to a single fife and drum, Jackson at their head. Riding with him are professors Rodes and Colston. Immediately behind them is a three-man color guard, bearing the white VMI flag with the blue and grey Virginia seal in the middle. We notice some of the students from his class, faces we will come to recognize. The youngest among them is seventeen-year-old Charlie Norris.

Anna Jackson stands with Hattie in the crowd of onlookers.

ANNA JACKSON
God, how could You make this day so beautiful?

EXT. SHENANDOAH VALLEY (MONTAGE) – DAY
The following montage is underscored by the music of a solitary bagpipe, playing "Scots Wha Hae."

Farmers lift their heads to the sound of the pipes and drop their plows; students put down their books and leave their classrooms; laborers leave their chores and walk away; bank tellers close their windows; shop keepers shutter their doors; an Episcopal rector (Old Penn) steps down from his pulpit. Singly, in pairs, in small groups, in clans they march to the sound of the pipes. Droves of men, a motley assemblage of individuals, whose sartorial diversity speaks of their age — a time before mass production and the tyranny of fashion. They carry flintlocks and shotguns and swords, pistols and knives. They assemble at the town of Harper's Ferry, at the northern end of the Shenandoah Valley.

EXT. HARPER'S FERRY – DAY
SUPER TITLE: Harper's Ferry, Virginia

EXT. BOLIVAR HEIGHTS, HARPER'S FERRY – DAY
The men are standing in formation, a ragged band of brothers, the "cousin-wealth" of the Shenandoah Valley. Jackson is mounted. Nearby, also mounted, his aides de camp, SANDIE PENDLETON and JAMES POWER SMITH.

JACKSON
Men of the Valley! Citizen soldiers! I am here at the order of General Robert E. Lee, commanding all Virginia forces. On April fifteenth of this year of our Lord, 1861, Simon Cameron, the Secretary of War of the United States, sent a

telegram to our governor John Letcher, directing him to raise three regiments of infantry to be sent to assist in suppressing the Southern Confederacy. Governor Letcher's answer is well known to you, but perhaps not his words. His wire to Washington stated, "You have chosen to inaugurate civil war, and having done so we will meet you in a spirit as determined as the Lincoln administration has exhibited towards the South." Two days later, the Virginia legislature voted for secession. Just as we would not send any of our soldiers to march in other states and tyrannize other people, so will we never allow the armies of others to march into our state and tyrannize our people. Like many of you, indeed most of you, I have always been a Union man. It is not with joy or with a light heart that many of us have welcomed secession. Had our neighbors to the north practiced a less bellicose form of persuasion, perhaps this day might not have come. But that day has been thrust upon us, like it was thrust upon our ancestors. The Lincoln administration required us to raise three regiments. Tell them we have done so.

Jackson rides his horse down the ragged line of volunteers.

JACKSON (Cont'd)
Dismissed!

EXT. VIEW OF FREDERICKSBURG – DAY
SUPER TITLE: Fredericksburg, Virginia

The bucolic setting of a small town, church steeples, neat rows of town- and detached houses, and graceful bridges over the Rappahannock River. Drifting over all the graceful notes of a piano melody by Beethoven.

INT. BEALE HOUSE, FREDERICKSBURG – DAY
LUCY COOKE BEALE, age twenty-three, is seated at the forte-piano, providing a splendid and melancholy performance for her widowed mother JANE HOWISON BEALE, the black house servant MARTHA and Lucy's four brothers, JOHN BEALE and CHARLES BEALE, both wearing new uniforms of the First Regiment of Virginia Volunteers, and the two youngest, SAM and JULIAN. Also with them are their friends ROBERTA CORBIN, in her early thirties, her daughter JANE CORBIN, a toddler of four, and CATHERINE CARTER CORBIN, age twenty-one and Pastor BEVERLY TUCKER LACY. The women are sewing the finishing touches onto a home-made battle flag. As the last chord hangs in the air, Jane rises to embrace her daughter.

ROBERTA CORBIN
Why, Lucy Cooke Beale, that is the most sublime playing I have ever heard. You must have practiced your fingers to the bone.

Jane Beale steps closer to her sons.

JANE BEALE
We must not fear the final result of this war, but many a loved one will fall and many a heart throb with anguish before we can breathe the exhilarating atmosphere of freedom or feel the sweet assurance of safety and peace once more. There is nothing in this life more dear to me than my children, except perhaps the memory of your wonderful father. When you leave for Richmond, and wherever this war takes you, you must not worry for us. We will be with you wherever you go. "Surely goodness and mercy have followed me all the days of my life."

One by one John and Charles embrace their mother and sister. Jane Beale hands the folded flag to her sons.

JANE BEALE (Cont'd)
Now. Be on your way. And God bless you.

MARTHA (stepping up to embrace them)
Y'all be comin' back, ya hear.

JOHN BEALE
We'll be back, Martha, and we'll be thinkin' of you all every day we're gone.

The boys pick up their sacks and leave.

LUCY BEALE
I know there are a thousand brothers leaving a thousand homes, and I know we're not the only ones, Mother. But I've never felt sadder in my life.

EXT. HANCOCK'S HOUSE, LOS ANGELES – NIGHT
We see the semi-desert landscape of California in the moonlight — so different from the landscape of Maine or Virginia. Horses are tied to the railings. Soldiers stand on guard. We hear the sounds of a party from inside the house.

INT. HANCOCK'S HOUSE, CALIFORNIA – NIGHT
A party has been in progress for some hours. WINFIELD SCOTT HANCOCK is there, as host. There are about a dozen OFFICERS as guests, some with their WIVES. The hostess is HANCOCK's wife MIRA. Also present is the Hancocks' Virginian friend LEWIS ARMISTEAD. All the men are wearing their blue United States Army uniforms.

ARMISTEAD
A toast to our hostess. Till next we meet.

Glasses are raised. Mira smiles her thanks at them.

MIRA (taking Hancock's arm)
Pennsylvania. (taking Armistead's arm) Virginia. So close. How could this have happened? My two heroes in blue. Why couldn't time stand still? Why must either of you go?

Mira looks from one to the other, wistfully. She goes to the piano, leafs through some music, then, as if by chance, chooses a song, starts to play, and then to sing — "Kathleen Mavourneen."

All the officers and wives gather round the piano.

ARMISTEAD
If I ever raise my hand against you, Win, may God strike me dead.

MIRA (singing)
Kathleen Mavourneen, the gray dawn is breaking,
The horn of the hunter is heard on the hill,
The lark from her light wing the bright dew is shaking,
Kathleen Mavourneen, what? Slumb'ring still?
Kathleen Mavourneen, what? Slumb'ring still?
Oh, hast thou forgotten how soon we must sever?
Oh, hast thou forgotten this day we must part...

INT. CHAMBERLAIN PARLOR, BRUNSWICK, MAINE – NIGHT
JOSHUA LAWRENCE CHAMBERLAIN and his wife FANNY sing at their piano. FREDERICK CROUCH is seated nearby.

CHAMBERLAIN, FANNY, & CROUCH (singing)
It may be for years, and it may be forever;
Then why art thou silent, thou voice of my heart?
It may be for years and it may be forever;
Then why art thou silent, Kathleen Mavourneen...

FREDERICK CROUCH
I can hear you still keep up your singing, Fanny. It gives me pleasure to know you've not forgotten what I taught you.

FANNY
Professor, it is our pleasure to have the composer of such a famous song with us in our own home.

CHAMBERLAIN
Are we wrong to enjoy music and literature while men — and boys — are volunteering to fight, and perhaps die for the preservation of our country?

FREDERICK CROUCH
How could time spent on music — or the teaching of rhetoric — be wrongly spent?

FANNY
Well, Professor, our country's quarrels are not yours. I wish you could stay here with us in peaceful Maine. I'm sorry to hear you are to return to Virginia, for I fear there may be fighting there, now that Virginia has seceded.

FREDERICK CROUCH
My dear Fanny, I am a mere musician. I do not think that training a choir in Virginia is likely to drag me onto the battlefield.

EXT. BOLIVAR HEIGHTS – DAY
Columns of troops are marching, four abreast, shoulder arms, back and forth across the open fields. Four drummers stand in the middle of the field, among them the youngest and oldest members of the brigade, aged 16 and 57. Two privates, McCLINTOCK and POGUE, converse in the ranks of marching men.

McCLINTOCK (commenting on the sartorial dis-uniformity)
Blue, green, red, gray uniforms. How we supposed to know who the enemy is?

POGUE
You dang fool. Just shoot at the fella that's shootin' at you.

McCLINTOCK
I thought we were going to be trained. I could have done all this much walking on my own back in Staunton.

POGUE
I never seen you walk in your whole life when you didn't have to. Nor me neither. What man in his right senses would cross his street when he could be jes' sittin' on his porch?

McCLINTOCK
God knows I've walked more in the last week than my whole life and my daddy's whole life put together. Who'll give us fresh shoes when there's nothing left of these but tatters and bits of laces?

EXT. BOLIVAR HEIGHTS, ANOTHER PART OF THE FIELD – DAY
The Rockbridge Artillery, Rev. WILLIAM NELSON PENDLETON (OLD PENN) commanding, trains in limbering and unlimbering its cannon. JOHN McCAUSLAND, ROBERT E. LEE JR. (ROBB LEE), D. GARDINER TYLER, and the four CARPENTER brothers, among others, work the guns and caissons.

EXT. BOLIVAR HEIGHTS, FIELD – DAY
Captained by JOHN AVIS and GEORGE W. KURTZ, members of the Continental Morgan Guards (attired in blue Colonial uniforms) practice loading and firing.

EXT. STREET, HARPER'S FERRY – DAY
Jackson and Sandie Pendleton inspect a wagon laden with personal items belonging to a newly arrived band of volunteers.

JACKSON
Do you think the Yankees will be impressed with your toiletries and comforts? Where we're going you'll need no more than a gum cloth, a blanket, a toothbrush, a musket and forty rounds of cartridges. That and the gospels is all that's required of a gentleman soldier. As for the rest of this baggage, clear it out of my camp.

Jackson and his aide leave the stunned newcomers.

EXT. BOLIVAR HEIGHTS, CAMP – NIGHT
The encampment is dark except for the moonlight. McClintock

and Pogue sleep side by side tucked in their blankets, under the stars.

POGUE
No fires, No tents. Just like I always dreamed it would be.

McCLINTOCK
Did you suppose the Virginia legislature was goin' to buy you your own personal tent?

POGUE
That's fine for now, but you'll be hummin' a different tune when its a rainin' or you're all covered with frost, or when you need me to dig you out of a snow drift. So damned dark the bats are runnin' into each other.

McCLINTOCK
Old Hickory jes wants us fit fer the fightin'.

POGUE
Old Hickory, Old Jack, Old Blue Light. How many names you got for the old man anyway?

McCLINTOCK
Them VMI boys gives him a choice one. They calls him Tom Fool when he's lookin' the other way.

POGUE
I'll be a fool if I keep on listenin' to you all the livelong night.

McCLINTOCK
Yeah. Old Tom Fool. That name ought to stick to him like a tick on a mule.

EXT. BOLIVAR HEIGHTS, ENCAMPMENT - DAY
On the drill ground are the "Liberty Hall Volunteers," mostly former students from Washington College, commanded by Captain JAMES J. WHITE. They sing in cadence as they march.

LIBERTY HALL MEN
Oh great Lord at what a wonder
Colonel Jackson — Hell and Thunder!

EXT. BOLIVAR HEIGHTS, ENCAMPMENT – EVENING
Campfire of the "Emerald Guards," Company E, 33rd Regiment. Their regimental flag is posted near the fire. MULLIGAN is seen at a distance, carrying two buckets of slops. McCARTHY calls out to him.

McCARTHY
Hey Mulligan, boyo! You're a fine sight carryin' those buckets of slops!

The other men laugh at Mulligan's expense.

MULLIGAN
Slops is it? This is not slops, McCarthy, it's patriotism!

Mulligan continues on his way, to the cheers of his former hecklers. Captain MARION SIBERT approaches the fire.

SIBERT
Mulligan has shamed us all.

CONNER
Sir, will you share in our meager dinner?

SIBERT
I will! But it's the nourishment of song I'd hoped to find by the fire.

McCARTHY
C'mon then, Fitzgerald, let's have a verse.

The men prepare a tin plate of grub for their captain, as FITZGERALD clears his throat for his tune, "The Irish Green."

FITZGERALD (*in a fine Irish tenor*)
The Irish Green shall again be seen
As our Irish fathers bore it,
A burning wind from the south behind,
And the Yankee rout before it!

Unnoticed, Jackson, Pendleton and Colonel ARTHUR CUMMINGS have strolled nearby, and stop to listen.

FITZGERALD (*Cont'd*)
O'Neill's red hand shall purge the land —
Rain fire on men and cattle,
Till the Lincoln snakes in their cold lakes
Plunge from the blaze of battle!

EXT. RAILROAD DEPOT, HARPER'S FERRY – DAY
An east-bound freight train is detained at the depot. Rolling stock is filled with horses. The horses are being led down ramps out of the cars. Quartermaster Major JOHN A. HARMAN walks with Jackson and Pendleton.

HARMAN
This train was on its way to Washington. Its livestock have been requisitioned by the Confederate government. There's enough beef here to keep us fed for quite a while, and as many steeds to supply our current needs. With your permission, sir, we've made a selection of some of the more promising horses.

Harman leads Jackson to a makeshift corral, containing half a dozen of the larger horses. After a quick inspection, Jackson settles on a powerful-looking gelding.

JACKSON
March, countermarch and march. This animal looks fit for the duty.

HARMAN
Then he's yours, sir.

Jackson motions to a smaller horse in another corral.

JACKSON
That small horse over there. Has he been assigned?

HARMAN
A well rounded sorrel, but too small for you, sir. You'll have your feet draggin' in the dust.

JACKSON (*looking over the little sorrel*)
I was thinking of my wife, Anna. He would make a fine gift for her.

HARMAN
That it would, sir. Shall I arrange for the purchase?

JACKSON
Leave the bill of the sale at my headquarters. I will buy them both.

HARMAN
The Confederate treasury is honored, sir. And may you both sit well in the saddle.

EXT. BOLIVAR HEIGHTS, PARADE GROUND – DAY
Jackson rides across the fields on the "little sorrel," approaching the Rockbridge artillery's battery of four guns. Commanding the artillerists is Old Penn, who wears his frock-coat and starched Episcopal collar.

OLD PENN
Good morning, sir!

JACKSON
Reverend Pendleton, how goes it today with the artillery?

OLD PENN
You are just in time for a christening, sir. The men have decided to name our howitzers. Matthew, Mark, Luke and John.

JACKSON
Reverend, I'm sure your men will do their utmost to spread the gospel wherever they encounter the enemy.

Jackson salutes the men, who return a stiff salute as he rides off.

EXT. BOLIVAR HEIGHTS, PARADE GROUND – DAY
Not far off he arrives at the company of Liberty Hall Volunteers, drilling with Captain White.

JACKSON
Captain White, how fare the scholars of Washington College? Are they making the transition from books to bullets?

WHITE
A few more days of drill, and my boys will surpass the cadets of VMI.

JACKSON
Drill, drill, drill, Professor White. Remember Alexander in Anatolia, Caesar in Gaul, Napoleon in Iberia.

WHITE
We march by day and read Xenophon by night. We will be your Greek phalanx!

JACKSON
Then you must begin with the bayonet. The bayonet must be for the Virginian what the sarissa was for the Macedonian. If the Yankees once dare to set foot in Virginia, we must show them the bayonet. Train with the bayonet, Captain White, and we shall keep our freedom.

Jackson salutes them and rides off...

EXT. BOLIVAR HEIGHTS, PARADE GROUND - DAY
...just as he is joined by Pendleton. They ride together.

PENDLETON
Sir, Harmon has a detachment ready to take your little sorrel to Mrs. Jackson in Lexington. The horse you chose for yourself is waiting for you at headquarters.

JACKSON
Mister Pendleton, I've decided to keep this little sorrel for myself. I prefer his gait to the larger horse. And unlike the other one, he has an even temper. He will need it where we are going. Yes, I will keep him.

PENDLETON
And Mrs. Jackson sir? What shall we send her?

JACKSON
Instruct Mr. Harmon to make another selection. I have complete trust in his judgement.

PENDLETON
Yes sir, at once, sir.

Pendleton rides off, leaving a very contented Jackson, who puts his little sorrel into an easy canter across the fields of Bolivar Heights.

INT. JACKSON'S HDQS, HARPER'S FERRY – DAY
The Reverend DAVID S. JENKINS is seated alongside his son, GEORGE JENKINS, wearing the uniform of the 4th Virginia. Jackson listens intently.

D.S. JENKINS
Secession is inexcusable. Southerners and Northerners can still work together. Slavery will eventually die of natural causes. The breakup of the Union will inaugurate wars of a hundred generations in America, only to repeat the bloody history of Europe.

JACKSON
Reverend Jenkins. You have my deepest sympathy and understanding. Aside from my wife Anna, there is no one I hold more dear to my heart than my beloved sister Laura. She sits in Beverly, an outspoken Unionist. We who once wrote letters to one another when I was away at West Point or with the army in Mexico, now hardly write at all. I fear I will not see her until this war is over. I regret my sister's Union sentiments, as I regret yours. But I will always respect

her, and can say no less of you. *(he turns to George)*
Your son George has volunteered to fight with the fourth
Virginia regiment, with his neighbors, with his friends.
I know he respects you, as all sons should respect their
fathers. But he is his own man now, and can make his
own decisions.
(turning back to Jenkins)
As a Christian man, my first allegiance is to God, and then
to my state, the State of Virginia; and every other state has
a primal claim to the fealty of her citizens, and they may
justly control their allegiance. If Virginia adheres to the
United States, I adhere. Her determination must control
mine. This is my understanding of patriotism, and though I
love the Union, I love Virginia more.
(turning back to George)
Private Jenkins, because of the high regard with which I
hold your father, you are free to do as you please. You may
return with him to his new home in Pennsylvania. It is your
decision. But if you decide to stay with us, you may never
again leave. If you do, you will be treated as a deserter.

GEORGE JENKINS
Colonel Jackson, sir. Father. I am a soldier in the Fourth
Virginia. And in the Fourth Virginia I will stay, and if needs
be, die.

Reverend Jenkins' eyes fill with tears, but not without admiration
for his son. He stands.

D.S. JENKINS
Then I will take my leave.

JACKSON
No sir, it is I will leave the two of you to have some time
together, on your own. You may have this room for as long
as you require it.

Jenkins takes Jackson's hand.

D.S. JENKINS
Farewell, Colonel. May we meet again in happier times.
If not in this troubled world, may we meet in...
(his voice breaks)

JACKSON
...in heaven.

EXT. BOLIVAR HEIGHTS, FIELDS – DAY
The Liberty Hall Volunteers train with the bayonet. So do all the
regiments of the brigade. Pogue and McClintock drive their bayonets into straw dummies.

McCLINTOCK
As if you'd ever get close enough to stick a man with this.

POGUE
You can give your bayonet to me if you have no use for it.

McCLINTOCK
What'd you do with two of 'em?

POGUE
You never heard of spare parts?

McCLINTOCK
Pogue. Your only hope is some Yankee puts you out of
your misery.

EXT. FIELD HDQS – HARPER'S FERRY – MAY 10, 1861
JAMES EWELL BROWN STUART rides up with a flourish.

STUART
Lieutenant Colonel Stuart reporting for duty, sir.

JACKSON
Sit down, Colonel. I see from your record that you are West
Point, class of '54, and that you have served since in the
cavalry. Fort Clark, Texas, operations against Apache and
Comanche. Most impressive, you are a native of Virginia.

STUART
Fought with Longstreet and Ewell, sir. A nasty business.
A pitiless climate. Glad to be home, sir. The Apache were
defending their homes, as we will be defending ours, sir. If
we fight as well as the Apache I pity the Yankee invader.

JACKSON
Colonel Stuart, if I had my way we would show no quarter
to the enemy. No more than the redskin showed your troop-
ers. The black flag, sir. If the North triumphs, it is not alone
the destruction of our property, it is the prelude to anarchy,
infidelity and the ultimate loss of free and responsible government on this continent. It is the triumph of commerce,
banks and the factory. We should meet the Federal invaders
on the outer verge of just and right defence, and raise at
once the black flag. No quarter to the violators of our homes
and firesides. Our political leadership in Richmond is too
timid to face the reality of the coming war. They should look
to the Bible. It is full of such wars. Only the black flag will
bring the North quickly to its senses and rapidly end the war.

STUART
One way or the other, we will give them a warm reception.

JACKSON
You will be in charge of the cavalry in the Harper's Ferry
district. Your experience and your zeal will be invaluable.

EXT. HARPER'S FERRY TELEGRAPH OFFICE – DAY – MAY 27
Troops mill around. The Reverend Pendleton exits the office
holding a note, from which he reads to a waiting crowd of soldiers
and civilians.

OLD PENN
The ratification vote for secession is in. Reporting from all
the counties of Virginia, the vote is four to one in favor!

The crowd cheers, some throwing their hats in the air.

OLD PENN *(Cont'd)*
And I am proud to report that the vote in the Shenandoah Valley is 3,130 in favor, ten against.

Another cheer.

OLD PENN *(Cont'd)*
And in my own Rockbridge County, only one person voted against leaving the Union.

General laughter.

A VOICE (o.s.)
Pro'bly the village idiot!

More laughter.

EXT. BOLIVAR HEIGHTS—PRE-DAWN
Reveille is sounded, followed by shouted orders.

VOICE-OVER
On your feet, men! Take your gear! We're moving out!

The Emerald Guards crawl out of their bed-rolls.

FITZGERALD
Sometin's up.

MULLIGAN
Marching. Marching. Always marching. Where are we marching to?

CONNER
We don't know. Nobody knows. But Old Jack knows.

McCARTHY
Yeah. Old Jack knows. He don't tell no one. But he knows.

EXT. SHENANDOAH RIVER FORD – DAY
SUPER TITLE: Shenandoah River

The entire brigade is assembled, preparing to ford the river. Sandie Pendleton rides up, reading aloud from a written order.

PENDLETON
Soldiers! Commanding General Johnston's orders! General Beauregard is being attacked at Manassas Junction by overwhelming forces. We have been ordered to cross the Blue Ridge to his assistance! Every moment is now precious, and the General hopes that his soldiers will step out and keep closed ranks, for this march is a forced march to save our country!

The troops cheer with shouts of joy! The bugles blare and the orders are shouted to move out. The army plunges into the Shenandoah ford with eagerness and determination.

EXT. ASHBY'S GAP, BLUE RIDGE MTS., VA – DUSK
The exhausted troops rest for the night, many falling asleep where they drop. It is a beautiful night. Far below, the snaking Shenandoah glistens in the moonlight. The sound of crickets fills the air. Jackson is propped against a fence as Dr. HUNTER McGUIRE joins him.

McGUIRE
You must sleep, sir.

JACKSON
I'll sleep better when Captain Pendleton and the artillery make it up this mountain.

McGUIRE
They'll make better time tomorrow, sir. It'll be all downhill. If you will trust me to wait for the guns, sir?

JACKSON
You are an excellent practitioner, Doctor McGuire. I will take your prescription.

Jackson settles down into the tall grass along the fence.

EXT. PIEDMONT RAILHEAD – DAY – JULY 19
SUPER TITLE: Piedmont Railhead

The army boards rail cars. Locals bring food items and drink to the troops, cheering them on. ISAAC R. TRIMBLE directs the loading of the men onto the train.

TRIMBLE
That's it, step lively. Two at a time, quick as you can. No dilly. No dally. One foot forward, then the other. Nothing pretty, nothing fancy. Into the train. Do it lovely, do it ugly, all the same to me.

Trimble takes notice that he is being watched by Jackson, whom he now salutes.

JACKSON
Understand you're a train man, Colonel Trimble.

TRIMBLE
Baltimore & Ohio. Spent most of my life building those lines up in Maryland and the past six months tearing them up. No use leaving them in such fine fettle for the meddling Yankee. If you'll excuse me, sir. Got to move these men where they can do the most damage to the enemy.

He salutes and returns to loudly herding the troops. Jackson comments to Smith and Pendleton on Trimble's fine black army hat with its gold cord and sweeping feathers.

JACKSON
That's the finest dressed man in the whole Confederate army.

TRIMBLE *(to the troops)*
In you go. Up and over. Through the brush and in the clover. Crowd on in. Move it over!

EXT. MANASSAS JUNCTION – DAY
SUPER TITLE: Manassas Junction

Smoke bellows from a locomotive. Jackson's troops have already disembarked from the boxcars and are marching to the sound of the guns.

EXT. NEAR BULL RUN, MANASSAS – NIGHT
A driving rain soaks the exhausted troops as they approach Blackburn's Ford along Bull Run. As they march they pass a row of fresh dug graves with crude wooden markers. A couple of horse carcasses and wrecked caissons litter the field. Trees are lopped and mangled. "Halt" is shouted down the ranks. Followed by "Fall out." The men break ranks to find what shelter they can in the downpour.

EXT. JACKSON'S CAMP, MANASSAS -PRE-DAWN
Jackson is alone in prayer, which he speaks softly.

> **JACKSON**
> Dear Lord. This is your day, and you have admonished us to keep it holy. If it is your will that we fight this day, then your will be done. Dear Lord, this is also my darling Anna's birthday, and if it is your will that we fight this day, your will be done. I ask your protection over Anna, your faithful servant and my loving wife. I ask you to shine your face down upon her, Lord, on her thirtieth birthday, and to fill her heart with the conviction of how much she is loved and missed by her husband. Dear Lord, you have called me to this place in this hour, far from my home and my loved ones, but I know it is your will that leads me here. If it is your will that we fight today, I am ready, Lord, thy will be done. It is your sword I will wield into battle, your banner I will raise against those who would desecrate our land. I am your humble and obedient servant, Lord. If it is your will that we fight on the sabbath, then the fight will be all the more righteous, all the more holy. And if it is my time to be with you, Lord, then I come to you with all the joy in my heart. Amen.

Cannon fire in the distance.

EXT. BLACKBURN'S FORD, MANASSAS – DAWN
The men are formed into ranks and quickly double-timed through woods and across fields, pulled up behind the crest of Henry House Hill.

EXT. HENRY HOUSE HILL, MANASSAS – DAY
Jackson rides up to the crest of the hill. The battle is already raging.

EXT. JACKSON'S POV, MANASSAS – DAY
Jackson can see masses of blue troops heading his way.

EXT. HENRY HOUSE HILL, MANASSAS – DAY
Jackson looks to his Courier.

> **JACKSON**
> Kindly inform General Bee that the First Virginians are on the field. Ask him, can he hold long enough for me to deploy my men?

> **JACKSON'S COURIER**
> Yes sir, I'll ask him how long he can hold.

The Courier gallops off.

> **JACKSON**
> They may not hold, gentlemen, and we must assume they cannot. Instruct captains Imboden and Stanard to position their batteries in the center of the crest. I want the Fourth and Twenty-seventh regiments stationed as support. I want the Fifth Regiment posted to their right, and the Second and Thirty-third to the left. Understood, gentlemen?

The assembled officers nod, salute and move off. Shells start to explode overhead and on all sides.

> **JACKSON** (*Cont'd*)
> Instruct the men to stay down. Hug the ground. There's no use in standing until we must.

A stream of wounded starts to trickle through their ranks, some limping, some crawling, unnerving two of the fresh troops.

EXT. MANASSAS, ANOTHER PART OF THE BATTLE – DAY
Demoralized Confederate troops are seen falling back through their positions. The din of battle grows louder, the crack of musketry closer.

EXT. MANASSAS, WITH BEE – DAY
General BARNARD E. BEE, spattered with dirt, his sword in hand, rides up to Jackson's position.

> **BEE**
> General! Our line on Matthew's Hill has broken! They are beating us back!

Jackson looks calmly at...

EXT. MANASSAS, JACKSON'S POV – DAY
... the tidal wave of Federals rolling down the opposite hillside towards his position.

EXT. MANASSAS, JACKSON'S POSITION – DAY

> **JACKSON**
> Then, sir, we will give them the bayonet!
> (*to his officers*)
> First Brigade, move up to a position just below the crest of the hill. And stay low!

The order is quickly relayed, and the brigade scurries up the crest.

EXT. MANASSAS, WITH BEE – DAY
As the fragments of the retreating brigades continue to move through Jackson's positions, Bee spurs his horse to gallop

among them. He rises in his stirrups, pointing his sword back to the crest.

> **BEE**
> Look! There is Jackson standing like a stone wall! Let us determine to die here, and we will conquer! Rally behind the Virginians!

EXT. MANASSAS, JACKSON'S POSITION – DAY

The sight of Jackson calmly astride his horse, with his brigades crouched in readiness at the ridge...

EXT. MANASSAS, WITH BEE – DAY

... has the effect of inspiriting the scattered troops. They begin to assemble around their officers, regroup into formations and march back towards the battle, taking up positions in reserve of Jackson's men.

EXT. MANASSAS, PENN'S ARTILLERY – DAY

Old Penn's red-wheeled four-gun battery, pulled by teams of lathered horses, bounces up the hill, unlimbering to take its positions at the top of the ridge.

EXT. MANASSAS, JACKSON'S POSITION – DAY

Amid the deafening roar of shot and shell can now be heard the cheers of the advancing Federals. A yellow haze of smoke and dust floats up and over the ridge, enveloping the Confederates. Jackson, always mounted, moves like a ghost through the murkiness, along the front line of his troops.

> **JACKSON**
> Steady, men. Steady.

At that moment Jackson is struck in the left hand. Noticing a broken finger, he wraps the hand in a handkerchief.

EXT. MANASSAS, FEDERAL BATTERIES – DAY

Two Federal batteries begin a direct fire into the left of Jackson's lines as the Federal infantry closes on the center...

EXT. MANASSAS, 33RD VIRGINIA POSITIONS – DAY

...where Colonel Cummings is in command of the 33rd Virginia regiment.

> **CUMMINGS**
> They are coming, boys. Now wait until they get close before you shoot.

> **MULLIGAN**
> They're close enough for me!

> **CUMMINGS**
> Stay in ranks. We will see them soon enough.

EXT. MANASSAS, FEDERAL ATTACK – DAY

The first thing to be seen by the prone troops are the tops of the regimental flags, then mounted officers. A Yankee officer, a surprised look on his face, sees the mass of Confederates crouched behind the ridge.

EXT. MANASSAS, 33RD VIRGINIA POSITIONS – DAY

Without rising, a number of the Confederates fire at the officer and the advancing troops.

EXT. MANASSAS, FEDERAL ATTACK – DAY

> **A VOICE** (o.s.)
> Fire!

The Federals stop and fire a fearful volley...

EXT. MANASSAS, 33RD VIRGINIA POSITIONS – DAY

...but as most of the Confederates are still lying on the ground, almost none are hit.

> **CUMMINGS**
> Give 'em hell, boys!

The 33rd Virginians rise as if one man and deliver a withering volley into the ranks of the Federals...

EXT. MANASSAS, FEDERAL ATTACK – DAY

...staggering their advance.

EXT. MANASSAS, 33RD VIRGINIA POSITIONS – DAY

The Virginians rush forward, firing as they go. CHARLIE NORRIS, in full dress VMI uniform, leads a company.

> **CHARLIE NORRIS**
> Come on, boys! Quick and we can whip 'em!

EXT. MANASSAS, FEDERAL ATTACK – DAY

The stunned Federals break and back away, back towards the opposite hill.

EXT. MANASSAS, 33RD VIRGINIA POSITIONS – DAY

> **CUMMINGS**
> Easy, men. We have no orders to advance.

But the blood is up, and there's no holding them back. In groups they charge after the fleeing Federals.

> **CUMMINGS** (Cont'd)
> Damn it! Charge!

Now the whole center of the line moves forward, racing to capture the Federal guns under Ricketts and Griffin.

EXT. MANASSAS, JACKSON'S POSITION – DAY

> **PENDLETON**
> That's Cummings' boys. What're they doing?

> **JACKSON**
> Easy now, easy. It's good to have your dander up, but it's discipline that wins the day.

> **PENDLETON**
> Should we send them support?

> **JACKSON**
> We'd only be hacked up by their artillery. It's we will do the hacking today.

EXT. MANASSAS, RICKETT'S BATTERIES – DAY
With a sweeping fire that fells many of the Yankee gun crews, the 33rd Regiment overwhelms Rickett's batteries, momentarily unsupported by their infantry.

EXT. MANASSAS, RICKETT'S BATTERIES – DAY
The withdrawing Federals manage to drag off three guns, but the rest are captured.

EXT. MANASSAS, FEDERAL COUNTERATTACK – DAY
At that moment the New York Zouaves and the First Michigan launch a ferocious counterattack.

EXT. MANASSAS, RICKETT'S BATTERIES – DAY
The Emerald Guards are caught in the thick of it. Sibert is felled by a shot through both his legs. Conner and Fitzgerald drag him to the rear as the 33rd Virginians are driven away from their newly won trophies and back up the hill in a hail of bullets.

MANASSAS, BEE'S POSITION
Nearby, Bee is toppled from his horse by a fatal bullet.

EXT. MANASSAS, CREST OF THE HILL – DAY
The returning men of the 33rd collide with the 2nd Virginia regiment, still at the crest of the hill. An OFFICER OF THE 33RD approaches Jackson, who still holds his wounded hand aloft.

> **AN OFFICER OF THE 33RD**
> General, the day is going against us!

> **JACKSON** (privately, to the officer)
> If you think so, sir, you had better not say anything about it.

EXT. MANASSAS, FEDERAL COUNTERATTACK – DAY
The Federals press the momentary advantage to resume their attack up the hill, covered by a blanketing fire from batteries at their rear.

EXT. MANASSAS, CREST OF THE HILL – DAY
Jackson turns to the officers of the Fourth and Twenty-seventh regiments, standing beside him.

> **JACKSON**
> Order the men to stand up. We'll charge them now and drive them to Washington.

Jackson rides out in front of the troops, shouting so that all may hear him above the roar of artillery and muskets.

> **JACKSON** (Cont'd)
> Reserve your fire until they come within fifty yards, then fire and give them the bayonet! And when you charge, yell like furies!

EXT. MANASSAS, CREST OF THE HILL – DAY
Orders are barked down the line, as all the regiments rise to their feet, delivering a tremendous fire into the approaching Federals. Like wild men, shrieking the rebel yell, the Virginians charge...

EXT. MANASSAS, HILLSIDE – DAY
...into the dazed and broken ranks of the Yankees, breaking through the center.

EXT. MANASSAS, RICKETT'S BATTERIES – DAY
Lt. FRANK PAXTON of the 4th Regiment reaches the abandoned guns, planting his colors at the battery. This invites Federal fire, which riddles the flag, leaving Paxton miraculously untouched. Cummings finds the wounded Captain RICKETTS lying next to one of his guns.

> **CUMMINGS**
> Captain Ricketts, can you hear me, sir?

Ricketts sees Cummings, but can only moan.

> **CUMMINGS** (Cont'd)
> I'll have you moved to the rear.
> (to a soldier)
> Bring a stretcher at once. This man is a hero of the War with Mexico and a gentleman.

EXT. BATTLEFIELD, MANASSAS – DAY
Elsewhere, with the lines fully enmeshed, vicious hand to hand fighting continues. The tide of battle already turned by the explosive Confederate assault, the Yankees gradually if begrudgingly give ground. When fresh troops under E. KIRBY SMITH arrive on the battlefield, it is the final demoralizing blow for the Yankees, whose retreat turns into a rout.

EXT. BATTLEFIELD, CAVALRY, MANASSAS – DAY
Jeb Stuart's cavalry pursues the fleeing Federals. The Confederate infantry cheer them on.

EXT. BATTLEFIELD, MANASSAS – DUSK
Jackson is walking through the debris of the battlefield — corpses, dead horses, broken guns. His hand is bandaged, and his arm in a sling. Three VMI cadets, dressed in their double buttoned coatees, lie together in a heap. Not far away is another, lying slumped over a Yankee cannon, sword still clenched in death. It is Charlie Norris, shot through the heart. Captain Smith comes up alongside.

> **SMITH**
> General, how is it that you can keep so cool, and appear so utterly insensible to danger in such a storm of shells and bullets as rained about your head when your hand was hit?

> **JACKSON**
> Captain, my religious belief teaches me to feel as safe in battle as in bed. God has fixed the time for my death. I do not concern myself about that, but to be always ready, no matter when it may overtake me.

He pauses, looks out over the battlefield.

JACKSON (*Cont'd*)
Captain, that is the way all men should live, and then all would be equally brave.

EXT. CONFEDERATE CAMP, MANASSAS – DUSK

PENDLETON
The preliminary reports for the brigade, sir. One hundred and eleven dead, 373 wounded and missing. If I may ask, sir, how is your hand?

JACKSON
It was just a spent bullet. Only a bruised finger. Mr. Pendleton, I am more than satisfied with the part performed by the brigade during the action. Through the blessing of God it met the thus far victorious enemy and turned the fortunes of the day. Good night, sir. Tomorrow is a new day.

PENDLETON
Good night, General.

JACKSON
And Mr. Pendleton. Thank you for the report. I will never forget those men. We must never forget them.

PENDLETON
Yes sir.

He salutes and is off, leaving Jackson alone in the moonlight.

INT. BACKSTAGE HOLLIDAY STREET THEATER, BALTIMORE – NIGHT
SUPER TITLE: Holiday Street Theater, Baltimore, Maryland

Booth applies his makeup for Richard III. Another actor, JAMES HARRISON, enters.

HARRISON
Which is it tonight, John — Hamlet, Richard Three or the Scottish play?

BOOTH
The schedule is posted. Relieved to see you've prepared for your role.

HARRISON
I'll admit my concentration has been impaired by the distractions of this war.

He holds up two different wigs.

BOOTH
Then think "winter of our discontent," and what "a glorious summer" it will be when the South is free of the meddling Yankee.

Harrison has his answer and keeps the wig for Richard III, settling down to his make-up mirror.

BOOTH (*Cont'd*)
Sometimes, when I'm up on that stage, brandishing the

prop sword, threatening with the mock word, I wonder if it's more farce than tragedy, more posturing than art. Harrison, as we recite and declaim others march and die.

HARRISON
Down in Mississippi when all the other boys went out hunting or fishing, I was the one reading books, learning Shakespeare's sonnets by heart. My daddy said that art was the hardest thing in the world — that everything else seems more important at the time, but that we needed it, more than air, more than food even. So now it's politics instead of hunting. Same old thing. Got to stay concentrated on what really matters. Shakespeare matters. Acting matters.

Booth, who has been listening intently, resumes the application of his make-up.

EXT. JACKSON'S TENT, CENTREVILLE, VA – DAY
Jackson is surrounded by his aides and officers.

JACKSON
Gentlemen, we have received new orders from the War Department. The Confederate Army has been re-organized into three districts. That of the Potomac will remain under the command of General Beauregard and the Aquia under General Holmes. I have been promoted to the rank of major-general and assigned to the command of the forces in the Shenandoah Valley. The entire army together will now be known as the Army of Northern Virginia. Although I am being transferred to Winchester, the brigade must remain here at Centreville.

There is a murmur of surprise and indignation.

SMITH
Begging your pardon, sir, but the men will much prefer remaining under your command.

PENDLETON
That's right, sir, couldn't the entire brigade be transferred with you to the Valley?

JACKSON (*holding up a hand*)
Gentlemen. Such a degree of public confidence and respect as puts it in one's power to serve his country should be accepted and prized. But, apart from that, promotion among men is only a temptation and a trouble. Had this communication not come to me as an order, I should instantly have declined it and continued in command of my brave old brigade.

McGUIRE
May we hope, sir, that a formal entreaty to the authorities in Richmond may effect a transfer of the entire brigade to the Valley army?

The assembled officers echo "Hear, hear."

JACKSON
I will not stop you from making such a request, but for now we must prepare ourselves. My trust is in God for the defence of our country. We shall all have our labors to perform, but through the blessing of an ever-kind heavenly Father, I trust that He will enable us to accomplish them. You are dismissed.

The officers and aides salute.

EXT. JACKSON'S CAMP, CENTREVILLE, VIRGINIA, AUTUMN – DAY
November 1861. Some fall leaves are still on the trees, but many have been blown off.

Jackson's brigade is drawn up on parade. Jackson rides up, followed by Paxton, Pendleton and aides.

The men present arms. Jackson returns the salute.

JACKSON
I'm not here to make a speech, but simply to say farewell, and leave you in the care of your new commander, Colonel James Preston. Throughout the broad extent of country through which you have marched, by your respect for the rights and property of citizens, you have always shown that you are soldiers not only to defend, but able and willing both to defend and protect. You've already won a brilliant reputation throughout the army of the whole Confederacy; and I trust, in the future, by your deeds in the field, and by the assistance of the same kind Providence who has hitherto favored our cause, you will win more victories and add lustre to the reputation you now enjoy. You have already gained a proud position in the future history of this our second War of Independence. I shall look with anxiety to your future movements, and I trust whenever I shall hear of the First Brigade on the field of battle, it will be of still nobler deeds achieved, and higher reputation won!

Jackson starts to leave, but turns back. He stands in his stirrups, draws his sword, and raises it high.

JACKSON (Cont'd)
In the Army of the Shenandoah, you were the First Brigade! In the Army of the Potomac you were the First Brigade! In the Second Corps of the Army you are the First Brigade! You are the First Brigade in the affections of your general, and I hope by your future deeds and bearing you will be handed down to posterity as the First Brigade in this our second War of Independence. Farewell!

The men cheer — wild enthusiasm. The cheer echoes across the hills. Jackson salutes them, turns his horse, and leaves.

EXT. BOWDOIN COLLEGE, AUTUMN – DAY
SUPER TITLE: Bowdoin College, Brunswick, Maine

INT. CLASSROOM, BOWDOIN COLLEGE, MAINE – DAY
The students are listening intently to JOSHUA LAWRENCE CHAMBERLAIN, who stands at the podium.

CHAMBERLAIN
... and yes, I know. Some of you — perhaps all of you — regard yourselves as unsuitable students of rhetoric. Have no fear. I, standing here as your professor of rhetoric, also regard myself as unsuitable for this study.

Rhetoric requires a man of rules, of easy exactness, of commonplace infallibility. Whereas I am a person of little respect for arbitrary rules, and of a slight vein of originality ... in my style at any rate.

He smiles at the students; some of them smile back.

CHAMBERLAIN (Cont'd)
But the easy exactness, for which we are striving in our study of rhetoric, can only come through respect for these rules which may at first seem arbitrary, alien. The Universe itself is subject to rules, to law. The super-abounding life lavished on this world of ours is proof that the play of infinite freedom is here to work out the will of infinite law. The nature of the Universe demonstrates that freedom can only exist as a part of law.

A STUDENT
Begging your pardon, Professor, but how does the study of philosophy intersect with real life? If freedom can only exist as part of law, how can we continue to tolerate slavery protected by law?

INT. CHAMBERLAIN'S HOUSE, AUTUMN – NIGHT
Fanny watches Chamberlain as he descends the staircase of their home.

FANNY (whispering)
Lawrence, I know.

CHAMBERLAIN
How?

FANNY
I've noticed the way you've been looking into the children's room each night.

Chamberlain steps into the parlor, wanting to avoid the conversation he knows he must have.

INT. THE CHAMBERLAIN'S PARLOR, AUTUMN – CONTINUOUS

FANNY
Blue. Why blue uniforms? It should be like the English — red — the color of blood.

CHAMBERLAIN
Are you angry with me?

FANNY
Lawrence, my darling Lawrence. Do you remember when you were thinking of being a missionary? You wrote me saying you wished your "little wife" was willing for you to take the course you thought best, and was ready to help you in it with all her heart.

CHAMBERLAIN
"Little wife"! How could I ever have called you that? Your spirit is vaster than oceans. Then you wrote back — and I've never forgotten what you said — "Well dear, she is willing, and she feels that you know better about the matter than she does."
(smiling)
But now I never think I know better than you.

FANNY
I couldn't bear to have you feel you must forever remain at a stand because you're married. I always want to help you on in your... excelsior striving.

"Excelsior striving" is a kind of code phrase between them, referring to Lawrence's utter determination to pursue the best.

FANNY *(Cont'd)*
I dreamt about you, Lawrence. Last night, while you were away, offering your services to the Governor... I saw you in my dream... boys in blue, marching past... some of the boys we know...and there you were, riding at the head of them, on a great white horse.

CHAMBERLAIN
Fanny, my love... I felt I had to go. I offered the Governor my services, wherever he wanted to place me. I thought he'd probably order me to an office... speeches, administration.

FANNY
No, Lawrence, I know. If you do a thing, you do it *à l'outrance*. He gave you a commission, didn't he?

CHAMBERLAIN
They need serving officers. Five new regiments are being formed now. Maine has already sent fifteen. How could I refuse?

FANNY
And Lawrence — damn you — you'll be good at it. Good at soldiering, like you're good at everything else. Go, do your duty for your country's flag, get your medals for bravery, get yourself killed...

Suddenly, her control leaves her, and she quietly weeps.

Then Fanny lifts her head, with one of her dazzling smiles that can transform her face into sudden sunshine.

FANNY *(Cont'd)*
That poem of Lovelace. That beautiful... horrible...

damnable... sad... lovely... poem. I think you recited it in my dream.

CHAMBERLAIN
Lovelace — off to the English Civil War? I would not dare presume to quote it now.

FANNY *(quoting by heart)*
Tell me not, sweet, I am unkind
That from the nunnery
Of thy chaste breast and quiet mind
To warlike arms I fly.
True, a new mistress now I serve,
The first foe in the field,
And with a sterner faith embrace
A sword, a horse, a shield.
Yet this inconstancy is such
As thou too shalt adore.
I could not love thee, dear, so much,
Loved I not honour more.

They both love the poem. But this is the first time in their lives that they have had to face its meaning.

FANNY *(Cont'd)*
You will be wounded. You will be changed by the horrors of it... But you will come home. I do believe that, my love. You will come home.

She takes him in her arms and they embrace.

EXT. ALTA VISTA, JACKSON'S HQ, WINCHESTER – DAY
SUPER TITLE: Winchester, Virginia, November 1861

INT. JACKSON'S HDQS, WINCHESTER, AUTUMN – DAY
JIM LEWIS, a black man in his fifties, enters Jackson's office. Jackson greets him, offering his hand.

JACKSON
Come in, come in. You must be Mister Lewis.

JIM LEWIS
They's some that calls me Uncle Jim, and some that calls me Big Jim. Some folks jes calls me Jim, but I ain't heard no white man yet calls me Mistuh Lewis.

JACKSON
I don't suppose you've heard any of the names I get called.

JIM LEWIS
I heard "Stonewall" more'n once.

JACKSON
Well, that name properly belongs to the First Virginia Brigade, not to me. They were the ones who earned it.

JIM LEWIS
Some folks say otherwise. Folks say men cain't fight wiffout no one up front to lead them on.

JACKSON (*changing the subject*)
I'm told you're a first rate cook.

JIM LEWIS
Yes sir. They wasn't lyin' told you that. Whatever it is you likes to eat, I can cooks it. Pan fry, griddle, boil, bake or roast it!

JACKSON
And I understand you're from Lexington. You come highly recommended to me, Jim.

JIM LEWIS
Lexington is my home, General, same as you'n. If I c'n do my share in defendin' my home, I'll be doin' same as you. I heard it was Napoleon hisself that says an army can't march but on its stomach.

JACKSON
If you love your country, fear the Lord and have no trouble getting up at five o'clock in the morning, you've got the job.

JIM LEWIS
You's got you'self a deal, General, sir.

An aide enters.

WINCHESTER AIDE
General, sir, you have some visitors.

Jackson walks to the ante-room, to discover his former staff.

SMITH
We've been re-assigned, sir. Back to your command. And the entire brigade as well.

Jackson cannot hide the slightest smile.

EXT. TAYLOR'S HOTEL, WINCHESTER, DECEMBER – DUSK
A stage coach draws up before the hotel, discharging a small group of passengers, among them Anna Jackson. Out of the shadows, muffled up in his military overcoat and low cap, appears Jackson. He takes Anna in his arms...

JACKSON
My esposita!

...and they embrace.

INT. ALTA VISTA, WINCHESTER – MORNING
Jackson and Anna lie in each other's arms.

ANNA JACKSON
I was thinking, Thomas, that it may have been a blessing that the battle at Manassas was fought on my birthday.

JACKSON
And why is that?

ANNA JACKSON
In our old age you will never forget it.

JACKSON
I will forget my own before I ever forget yours.

He kisses her gently on the forehead, then tenderly on her lips.

JACKSON (*Cont'd*)
Everything in this life seems so fragile, so temporary. When we are separated I fear I may never see you again. I fear we may never have a child. I fear I may lose you if we dare to have a child. I know I should trust in the Lord. But then I see the face of my dear mother, of my first wife dead and cold with our dead daughter, dead in birth before she could take her first breath in this world. And I am afraid, Anna, afraid to feel happiness, afraid to hope for it again. Afraid of God's judgment.

She holds him tight in her arms.

ANNA JACKSON
We serve a loving God, Thomas. We are in each other's arms. We are together and we are happy together. And is our love not proof of his? We must not fear, Thomas. We will survive this war and we will have a child. So help us God.

EXT. CAMP MASON, MAINE – DAY
SUPER TITLE: Camp Mason, Maine, Spring 1862

The volunteers for the 20th Maine regiment are drawn up as if on parade. No one has any uniform, and they are not exactly standing in line. They wear every variety of clothing. One officer wears a brown cutaway, striped trousers, and a silk hat, carrying a ramrod instead of a sword. Many of the men do, however, have guns — a variety of ancient hunting weapons.

Standing to one side is Chamberlain. He wears a civilian suit, but stands erect in a military fashion.

In sharp contrast. Colonel ADELBERT AMES, rides up with Major GILMORE. Both are in uniform. Both are obviously experienced soldiers, though they are both little more than twenty.

AMES (*to Gilmore*)
This is a hell of a regiment.

As Ames and Gilmore approach the men, there is a deafening noise, and a group of men playing fifes and drums walk in front of the parade. They do not walk in step, the drums are beating several incompatible rhythms, and the fifes play several different tunes, "Yankee Doodle," "Columbia," and "Camptown Races." The group forms up roughly between the regiment and Ames, and continues its noisy cacophony.

AMES (*Cont'd*) (*shouting over the noise*)
Major Gilmore, stop that damned drumming. Stop that damned drumming.

GILMORE (*shouting*)
Quiet! Quiet!

163

One by one, with no sense of coordination, the "musicians" peter out.

GILMORE (*Cont'd*)
Men of the Twentieth Maine Regiment of Volunteers, this is your commanding officer, Colonel Adelbert Ames.

The men give a cheer.

GILMORE (*Cont'd*)
Quiet. You do not cheer an officer. You salute him... when you have learnt to salute.

Gilmore gives Ames a smart salute.

GILMORE (*Cont'd*)
Twentieth Maine ready for inspection, sir.

AMES (*to Gilmore*)
Not much to inspect as yet, is there, Major?
(*to the regiment*)
Twentieth Maine, I commend the enthusiasm which has made you volunteer for service in President Lincoln's army. I can see that many of you are strong and fit. We Maine men know that life in the woods of Maine toughens the muscles, and stretches the sinews. I have no doubt that many of you have become good shots by hunting deer. But tough muscles and skillful shooting are not enough to make a soldier. That requires discipline.

Major Gilmore tells me you are in the habit of holding discussions with your officers. This will cease from now. An officer's orders are to be obeyed instantly, and without question. This regiment must learn to move as one man. Otherwise we will all be killed.

Major Gilmore, see if you can teach them to march.

Gilmore turns to the volunteers.

GILMORE
When I say "Twentieth Maine, Attention," bring your feet together

Ames goes to Chamberlain.

AMES
Come with me, Colonel Chamberlain.

Ames and Chamberlain walk off together, while Gilmore gives the regiment the beginnings of drill.

EXT. CAMP MASON, ANOTHER PART OF THE CAMP – MOMENTS LATER
Ames and Chamberlain are walking.

AMES
Governor Washburn and Adjutant General Hodson have sent me an impressive report about you. They say you will master any assignment you are given.

CHAMBERLAIN
I shall certainly try, sir. I understand you were in the battle of Bull Run.

AMES
Wounded, too. It taught me the need for discipline and proper procedure. Take the act of shooting, for example. When we're hunting in the Maine woods, there's no great difficulty about loading a rifle. But in the panic of war, men act foolishly. During Bull Run I saw a soldier forget to remove his ramrod from the barrel. When he fired, out it flew with a dismal twang. He lost the means of firing again, and was killed soon after by a rebel bullet.

As they walk on, they pass one of the recruits, JOE, leaning against a wall, with his legs crossed.

JOE
How d'ye do, Colonel.

AMES
For God's sake, man, draw up your bowels.

Ames and Chamberlain walk on.

AMES (*Cont'd*)
This is a hell of a regiment.

EXT. CAMP MASON, ANOTHER PART OF THE CAMP – DAY
Chamberlain comes out of his tent, still in his civilian suit. TOM CHAMBERLAIN comes up.

TOM (*smiling*)
Sergeant Chamberlain, reporting for duty, sir.

CHAMBERLAIN
Tom! What on earth? What are you doing here?

TOM
Lawrence, I joined up. I'm in this regiment. I'm coming with you.

CHAMBERLAIN
How did — did Father approve this? How will he run the farm?

TOM
Lawrence, once he heard you was gonna be a colonel, he couldn't say no. You know him, he'll be all right, they both will. I'm giving him one less thing to cuss at. And Mama said so many prayers for both of us — we got nothin' to worry about.

CHAMBERLAIN
Well, I guess I have one more responsibility — I have to look after you.

TOM
Me? Lawrence, Mama told me to look after you.

INT./EXT. CAMP MASON, A SHED – DAY

A line of men are being issued uniforms. One lad of sixteen is over six feet tall, but very skinny. He is trying on uniform pants. The only ones long enough for him are vastly too big in the waist. We see him wearing the pants, but pulling them out in front of him, as if he was preparing to fit someone else inside. Meanwhile the more ordinarily shaped men file by, receiving folded uniforms.

They move on to another part of the shed, where each man is issued with a woolen blanket, a rubber blanket, a haversack, a canteen, a tin plate, a tin dipper, a knife, fork, spoon, and a towel. GLAZIER ESTABROOK oversees the disbursements.

> **ESTABROOK**
> Just remember, lads, even a tin cup is a great weight after twenty miles. Your precarious pegs won't last if you turn yourselves into pack mules. And only one leg to a pants if you please. You'll soon be at the worn end of it, where formal attire will be your shirt collar and boots.

EXT. CAMP MASON, ANOTHER PART OF THE CAMP – DAY

Ames and Chamberlain are walking round the camp.

> **AMES**
> We have what is called "The School of the Soldier" in which the soldier is trained in By the Numbers Drill. Loading the musket, for example, is done in nine movements, performed over and over again until they become automatic — as we call it, "Loading in Nine Times."

They come across a small group of soldiers who have just been issued with muskets, and are examining them cautiously.

> **AMES** *(Cont'd)*
> Ah! Loading in Nine Times. Let's see Sergeant Chamberlain demonstrate this.

As Ames describes them, Tom performs the actions, but very slowly, without confidence.

> **AMES** *(Cont'd)*
> Assume the musket has just been fired. One — reach into cartridge box and withdraw cartridge. Two — place one end of cartridge between teeth and tear paper open. Three — empty powder into barrel. Four — insert ball with pointed end uppermost. Five — withdraw ramrod from pipes beneath barrel. Six — ram the ball home. Seven — return the ramrod. Eight — half-cock the hammer, and remove old cap. Nine — reach into cap pouch, get a new cap, and press it down on the nipple.
>
> All right, Sergeant, you have the idea. But this must be done without thinking, and much, much faster.

Ames takes the musket from Tom, and performs the nine actions at speed, calling each number as he does so.

> **AMES** *(Cont'd)*
> One. Two. Three. Four. Five. Six. Seven. Eight. Nine.

He hands the musket back to Tom.

> **AMES** *(Cont'd)* *(to the group)*
> Practice until you can do it as fast as that. It may save your lives.

INT. CAMP MASON, AMES'S TENT – DAY

Chamberlain and Ames are sitting at a table. Ames has a piece of paper and a pencil, with which he draws diagrams of the formations he is describing.

> **AMES**
> Line of battle consists of two lines of men, one behind the other, so that while one line fires, the other reloads. Behind them is the line of file closers — lieutenants and sergeants.
>
> But two lines makes a regiment unwieldy on the move. So we form column of fours. We need to be able to change from column of fours to line of battle, and back again, quickly.

EXT. CAMP MASON, ANOTHER PART OF THE CAMP – DAY

A company is drawn up. Gilmore stands in front of them. Chamberlain and Ames walk up and watch. Captain ELLIS SPEAR of Company G, puffing on his pipe, stands with Gilmore.

> **GILMORE**
> When I say "Form line of battle," you form up in two ranks, facing the front. Now count off your numbers — one, two, one, two.

The soldiers count off, shouting alternately "One" "Two" down the line.

> **GILMORE** *(Cont'd)*
> Right. Now we are going to form a column of fours. On the command "Company — Right Face," turn to the right, and the even numbers — those who shouted "Two" — take one pace smartly to their right. On the command "Double" the even numbers — those who shouted "Two" — take one pace smartly forward, so that they are standing next to their odd numbers — those who shouted "One." From there, the command will be given "By the flank, forward — march." Captain Spear, will you give the commands.

> **SPEAR**
> Company! Form line of battle.

The soldiers, with difficulty, form up in two lines.

> **SPEAR** *(Cont'd)*
> Company! Number off!

The soldiers shout "One," "Two," somewhat raggedly, down the lines.

> **SPEAR** *(Cont'd)*
> Company! Right face!

The right turn is performed reasonably. The stepping up is a shambles. Spear looks on helplessly. Ames steps forward.

AMES
Men — I can't call you soldiers yet — let me make this clear. Unless you learn these drills, you will be slaughtered.

Ames walks on with Chamberlain.

AMES *(Cont'd)*
To move from line of battle into column of fours is not difficult. It is harder to move from column of fours into line of battle. And if we are called to make that move, it will be when we are under fire. I'm sure you can understand, Colonel, how important it is that these movements are learnt so thoroughly that the men can perform them in their sleep.

EXT. CAMP MASON – DAY
The regiment is marching past in column of fours, watched by Ames.

CHAMBERLAIN
Battalion! Halt!

The company halts, more or less together.

CHAMBERLAIN *(Cont'd)*
Battalion! Front!

It is not a perfect drill movement by any means. But at least the regiment manages to turn to the front and form two lines instead of four.

The sergeants and lieutenants form the file-closer rank, behind the other two ranks.

CHAMBERLAIN *(Cont'd)*
Battalion! Prepare to fire!

The regiment brings rifles up ready for firing.

AMES *(to Chamberlain)*
Well done, Colonel. That's a beginning. But that movement needs to be practiced and practiced and practiced. Another month, and we'll be ready. But we leave for Washington tomorrow.

Tom is standing next to BUSTER KILRAIN, among the other sergeants.

TOM *(quietly to Kilrain)*
It's good being a sergeant, isn't it? If you shoot a sergeant, you have to fire through two men first.

KILRAIN
A sergeant never fires his gun until the men in front are killed, and then not unless you want to show off.

EXT. LEE'S HDQS, NORTHERN VIRGINIA – DAY
It is hot, late summer. Lee, Longstreet, and Jackson lean over a map table, in conference with their staffs.

LEE
Gentlemen, it is only September. Too soon for winter camp. We have the momentum. I propose we advance our army north, into Maryland. The farms there are plentiful and nearly untouched. With the fall harvest, we can feed our troops well. There's one other consideration. Maryland is being held in the Union by force. Our arrival may be viewed as a liberation. We might receive some hospitality, and we might even receive a number of volunteers for service in the army.

LONGSTREET
General, might this not be considered an invasion?

LEE
I don't believe so, General. The Federal invasion of Virginia, of the entire Confederacy, proved to all who is the aggressor here. We did not bring this war, and we fight now only to free the South of Federal occupation. If Washington will end their side of the fighting, and recall their armies, this war will be over. But we must show the enemy that they cannot win. By moving into Maryland, we'll be in a position to push into Pennsylvania. So far, gentlemen, the bloody fields are Southern fields. If we threaten the Northern cities — if we threaten to bring the fight into the North, there will be great pressure on Mr. Lincoln to end this war. Our presence, just the threat, could be sufficient.

LONGSTREET
General, we'd be cutting ourselves off from our base of supply, from communications. We'd be vulnerable from the rear.

LEE
General Longstreet, you marched with General Scott, into Mexico, did you not?

LONGSTREET
Yes, sir.

LEE
And did not General Scott cut himself off from his supplies, from all communication, and by doing so, did he not bring a rapid end to that war? And did he not accomplish all of that in a foreign land? Well, this is not a foreign land. The citizens will see we're not coming to vandalize, as the Yankees did to us. We come to end the war, quickly, and without any need to conquer or subdue anyone. We've proven our superiority on the battlefield. The threat of that superiority may be all we need.

JACKSON
General Lee, I'm pleased to hear we're finally taking the war to the enemy. Let them feel the scourge of this war that they began.

166

EXT. POTOMAC RIVER FORD – DAY
SUPER TITLE: Potomac River, September 1862

Watched by a group of EXCITED BOYS on the banks, the Army of Northern Virginia is crossing the river into Maryland. In chest-deep water, holding their weapons above their heads, regimental flags flapping in the breeze, hundreds of men sing "Maryland, My Maryland."

EXT. TWENTIETH MAINE CAMP, MARYLAND – DAWN
A sea of tents and men and wagons, the men getting to work.

Sergeant Kilrain holds out a tin cup, steaming hot.

> **KILRAIN**
> A good mornin' to ye, sir. Colonel Ames sent me to get you. Says you might be needin' a drop o' this.

> **CHAMBERLAIN**
> Thank you...uh...

> **KILRAIN**
> Kilrain, sir. Sergeant Kilrain. Glad to be of service, sir. The boys, we been a' watchin' you, that we have. You've learnt fast, sir. Becomin' a pleasure to serve under you.

Chamberlain takes the hot cup, drinks a painful gulp.

> **CHAMBERLAIN**
> You a veteran, Sergeant?

> **KILRAIN**
> Aye, Colonel, I suppose you could say that. Did me duty in the regular army for a while. Made the great long walk with General Scott, south of the Rio Grande.

> **CHAMBERLAIN**
> Some of the men you fought with in Mexico are on the other side. Almost all of their generals.

> **KILRAIN**
> Ah, but it gets worse than that, Colonel. Some of the boys I left Ireland with are on the other side as well. Imagine that. We left together to escape a tyranny, only to end up shootin' at one another in the land of the free.

> **CHAMBERLAIN**
> I too have friends on the other side, Sergeant... And enemies.

> **KILRAIN**
> Yes, sir. No shortage of enemies, and that's for sure.

Kilrain salutes and goes. A distant rumble of guns.

EXT. TWENTIETH MAINE CAMP, MARYLAND – DAWN
Chamberlain sees Ames talking to the company commanders, and joins him.

> **CHAMBERLAIN**
> Thank you for the coffee, sir.

> **AMES**
> Good morning, Colonel. We've been ordered to remain in place. The army's spreading out in front of us, a couple miles up. The enemy's dug in behind a small creek, Antietam Creek, just this side of Sharpsburg. We may be put into the attack at any time. For now, get the men to step it up, finish their breakfasts, then wait for the orders to move. Got that?

> **CHAMBERLAIN**
> Certainly, Colonel. Colonel, whose guns are those? Is the attack begun?

> **AMES**
> Likely it's the first feeling out, probing, testing the strength. It's a game to the artillery boys, letting you know they can hit you when the time comes.

Ames moves away, and Chamberlain follows, toward the wagons and the plates of food — biscuits and bacon, a steaming pot of thick coffee. They stuff bacon into their mouths. Ames puts hardtack in his pocket. Chamberlain follows suit. The bugle sounds, and the men fall in.

Tom comes out of the mess tent, with hardtack in his hands, which he is trying to chew. He meets Chamberlain.

> **TOM** (*holding up the biscuits*)
> Look at this, Lawrence. This is what we eat every day. But d'you know what? I've gained weight. Strange to think of gaining weight on a diet of worms.

EXT. CONFEDERATE POSITIONS, ANTIETAM – DAY
The Confederate batteries are firing away near the Dunker church. Lee and staff ride up near the Rockbridge artillery.

> **OLD PENN** (*saluting Lee*)
> Good morning, sir. The Yankees are coming thick and fast in the woods before us, sir. We're making it hot for them.

> **LEE**
> We must hold this ridge. Pour it into them, Reverend.

A begrimed gunner calmly walks up to General Lee and salutes. Lee unconsciously returns the salute, then prepares to ride off.

> **ROB LEE**
> Sir, it's me, Rob!

Lee turns back to realize that the man is his son.

> **LEE**
> My dear son. I'm sorry. I could not tell it was you. How are you, boy?

> **ROB LEE**
> I am well, sir.

LEE
I congratulate you for being in the fight and unhurt. May God keep you so. We must all do what we can to drive these people back.

ROB LEE
Yes sir. We'll do our best, sir.

Rob Lee salutes. Lee salutes his son, turns, and rides off.

EXT. ANTIETAM BATTLEFIELD, JACKSON'S POSITION – DAY
A heavy cloud of battle smoke obscures the field. Artillery fire is intense. Jackson is mounted with his aides, including Captain JOSEPH G. MORRISON.

JACKSON
Mister Pendleton, ride to General Hood. Ask him, can he maintain his position?

PENDLETON
Yes sir, can he maintain his position.

He salutes and is off into the smoke.

EXT. ANTIETAM BATTLEFIELD, FEDERAL BATTERIES – DAY
A line of guns on a rise: they start to fire.

EXT. ANTIETAM BATTLEFIELD, 20TH MAINE POSITIONS – DAY
Chamberlain is on his horse, by the column of his regiment. Ames canters back to him.

AMES (*pointing*)
Colonel, move the men into this field. Wait for further orders. We're part of the reserve.

Ames rides past him, to the bugler, who sounds a call. With the signal, the men move quickly off the road.

EXT. ANTIETAM BATTLEFIELD, FEDERAL BATTERIES – DAY
The guns begin to fire again, a loud and thunderous volley, and the hill becomes a great, thick fog bank.

EXT. ANTIETAM BATTLEFIELD, DUNKER CHURCH – DAY
The fighting is fierce, a living hell. Hood's Texans are nearly enmeshed with and firing at close range with elements of Doubleday's division. Pendleton miraculously rides through shot and shell to reach General JOHN BELL HOOD.

PENDLETON
Compliments from General Jackson, sir. He wants to know, can you maintain your position?

HOOD
Tell General Jackson, unless I get reinforcements, I must be forced back. But I am going on while I can.

PENDLETON
Reinforcements. Yes sir.

Pendleton salutes and is off, back the way he came, seemingly immune to the hailstorm of lead.

EXT. ANTIETAM BATTLEFIELD, HANCOCK'S DIVISION – DAY
Hancock's brigade is in formation, ready for battle.

General GEORGE BRINTON McCLELLAN, the army commander, rides up, his aides in tow.

McCLELLAN
General Hancock, have you heard? General Richardson has been wounded.

HANCOCK
I heard he'd been wounded, sir.

McCLELLAN
I'm sorry to tell you he died a few minutes ago. You will assume his command.

HANCOCK
Yes, sir. Of course, sir. I am honoured to accept the command.

McCLELLAN
Thank you, General. I'm sure you'll perform this duty with the skill and courage you've shown already. We are on the move now. We'll push the rebels into the river before the sun sets. Hold this position against any assault by the enemy.

McClellan wheels his horse and rides off.

EXT. ANTIETAM BATTLEFIELD, JACKSON'S POSITION – DAY
Pendleton returns at a gallop. General McLAWS is with Jackson and Morrison.

PENDLETON
Reply from General Hood, sir. Tell General Jackson unless I get reinforcements I must be forced back. But he will hold while he can.

JACKSON
Good, good. General McLaws, advance your division.

At that moment a shrieking Federal shell lands at the feet of their horses. Inexplicably, it does not explode. They exchange glances.

JACKSON (*Cont'd*)
Captain Morrison, it may be advisable to keep your distance from me when we are in the fight. It would not do for Anna to lose both her husband and her brother on the same day.

EXT. ANTIETAM BATTLEFIELD, 20TH MAINE POSITIONS – DAY

CHAMBERLAIN (*to Spear*)
The battle may be moving our way. Keep them ready!

Shot and shell falls everywhere. A Maine soldier is suddenly hit by a cannon ball which takes off his head. Tom is splattered with blood.

SPEAR
Get down! Everyone, on the ground!

Joe is hit in the hand. He drops his musket, and screams in pain.

KILRAIN
Blast your soul, you old woman. Stop cryin'. You're makin' more noise t'an the man t'at lost his head.

EXT. ANTIETAM BATTLEFIELD, NEAR DUNKER CHURCH – DAY

The Confederates have held the high ground around the church, the fighting now more desultory. Wounded men are being carried toward the rear. Hunter McGuire, his shirt sleeves bloody, walks up to Jackson. He reaches into his pockets, extracting a couple of fresh peaches. He offers one to Jackson.

McGUIRE
Courtesy of a lady admirer in Sharpsburg.

Jackson devours the peach.

JACKSON
God has been very kind to us today, but this is the first food I've eaten. I thank you, sir, and the kind lady.

McGUIRE
Can we hold against another attack?

JACKSON
I think they have done their worst. There is little danger now of our line being broken.

McGUIRE
Your disposition for the wounded, sir. Where should we bring them?

JACKSON
No need to move them further back. They'll be safe behind this line.

EXT. ANTIETAM BATTLEFIELD, 20TH MAINE LINES – EVENING

It is late in the day. Long shadows. Ames rides up.

AMES
We won't be needed today, Colonel.

Other officers gather, and Ames addresses them.

AMES (Cont'd)
The Fifth Corps was not needed today, gentlemen, not in the judgment of the commanding general. The battle has been extremely costly. The enemy's been checked, at great loss to both sides. From what we can observe so far, we've gained little. It's possible the fight will resume tomorrow.

Ames walks away. Chamberlain watches him, but does not follow. Instead he walks up the hill and looks over the crest, where all that can be seen are rows of corpses in blue and gray, dead horses, broken muskets, pieces of torn clothing and abandoned equipment.

BOOTH (V.O.)
How all occasions do inform against me/And spur my dull revenge! What is a man/If his chief good and market of his time/Be but to sleep and feed? A beast, no more.

INT. McVICKER'S THEATER, CHICAGO – EVENING
SUPER TITLE: McVicker's Theater, Chicago

A performance is in progress.

BOOTH (As Hamlet)
Now, whether it be Bestial oblivion, or some craven scruple Of thinking too precisely on th'event — A thought which, quartered, hath not but one part wisdom/And ever three parts coward — I do not know/Why yet I live to say, This thing's to do," Sith I have cause, and will, and strength, and means/To do't. Examples gross as nature exhort me. Witness this army of such mass and charge/Led by a delicate and tender prince/Whose spirit, with divine ambition puffed/Makes mouths at the insatiable event, Exposing what is mortal and unsure To all that fortune, death, and danger dare/Even for an eggshell. Rightly to be great/Is not to stir without great argument/But greatly to find quarrel in a straw/When honor's at the stake. How stand I then/That have a father killed, a mother stained/Excitements of my reason and my blood, And let all sleep, while to my shame I see/The imminent death of twenty thousand men/That for a fantasy and trick of fame/Go to their graves like beds, fight for a plot/Whereon the numbers cannot try the cause, Which is not tomb enough and continent/To hide the slain? O, from this time forth/My thoughts be bloody, or be nothing worth!

INT. TAVERN, CHICAGO – NIGHT
Booth is seated with a female companion. Both have drinks. He has an open newspaper on the table.

BOOTH
He's actually going to go through with this? Have you seen this? He's mad! It's nothing less than a call for a slave uprising.

COMPANION
Darling, I hardly ever get to see you. Can't we put away the paper this one evening? It'll put you in the foulest mood. It always does.

BOOTH
Well here, read it for yourself. Lincoln plans a general emancipation on New Year's day for all slaves from states

still in rebellion. Yet another page from the Constitution torn to shreds.

She looks over the article.

COMPANION
But this is harmless, John. See, it says right here, an emancipation of all slaves from the states still in rebellion. But can't you see? Those are the very states where the President has no authority and no power.

BOOTH
Why yes, you're quite right. I hadn't considered it in that light.

COMPANION
Now, can we fold up the paper into a nice little square so that I can cut it up into a hundred little pieces and throw it into the street?

Booth melts in the face of such charm and good humor. He turns to the BARTENDER.

BOOTH
Boyo, another round if you please.

EXT. JACKSON'S CAMP, BUNKER HILL, VIRGINIA, AUTUMN – NIGHT

Jackson, Pendleton, McGuire, Smith, Morrison, young BOSWELL and other officers are sitting around a large campfire. Two fiddlers, a guitarist and banjoist play "The Southern Soldier Boy."

PENDLETON
It says here, in Blackmantle's "Art of Punning," that punning is an art of harmonious jingling upon words, which, passing in at the ears, and falling upon the diaphragm, excites a titillary motion in those parts; and this being conveyed by the animal spirits into the muscles of the face, raises the cockles of the heart. Alright then, everyone ready? Counties of England! Which has the most dogs?

SMITH
Bark-shire!

PENDLETON
Where did the first hermaphrodites come from?

McGUIRE
Middle-sex.

PENDLETON
From whence the first circus tumblers?

A pause. All are stumped.

PENDLETON *(Cont'd)*
From Somer-set.

All howl with feigned derision.

PENDLETON *(Cont'd)*
I see you have all learned Rule number six, never to speak well of another punster and never to laugh at his puns.

EXT. THE FIELD KITCHEN, BUNKER HILL, AUTUMN – NIGHT

Jim Lewis is preparing a hot meal with WASHINGTON, another black cook.

WASHINGTON
De Rebel sharpshooters was in de house. Dat's what made dem Yankees shell it so.

JIM LEWIS
Whey was d'is?

WASHINGTON
Outside Winchester. You know dem Yankees been t'ru d'at town mo' times dan dey is flies on a mule.

JIM LEWIS
Where is your massa now?

WASHINGTON
I ha'nt got no massa no mo'. Now he my boss. I was sold at auction in Fredericksburg oncet, and he bought me fo' twelve hundred dolla's. But when da wo' come, it didn't sit right wi'd him, so he gave me my freedom papers and now he pays me wages.

JIM LEWIS
No sir!

WASHINGTON
Thirty dollas a month!

JIM LEWIS
What he pay you fo'?

WASHINGTON
I kin do whatever I turns my hand to. Den dem Yankees come and burn down his house and next thing I know de man who's payin' my wages is in the Confederate army and so am I.

Jim and Washington have a good laugh.

EXT. JACKSON'S CAMP, BUNKER HILL, AUTUMN – NIGHT

JOHANN HEROS VON BORCKE, of Stuart's staff, rides up.

VON BORCKE
Greetings! General, goot evening.

JACKSON
How is our fine Prussian officer this evening? I would have thought that general Stuart would have you at least twenty miles beyond the enemy lines creating havoc and bewilderment in Washington.

Jackson's aides voice their approval.

VON BORCKE
I vood zertainly prefer zuch a mission, but tonight I come bringing you a present! General Chackson, I am grreatly pleased to bring you this present from General Shtuart. The general has gone to grrreat lengths to secure for you — zis!

Von Borcke holds out a package wrapped in brown paper, and Jackson stares at it, does not move. Pendleton reaches out, takes the package.

PENDLETON
Would you like me to open it, sir?

Jackson nods. Pendleton tears at the paper and holds up the neatly folded gray of a new uniform.

PENDLETON (Cont'd)
General, this is some fine material. Look here, there's gold braid.

Jackson stares at the gift.

JACKSON
Major, you may tell General Stuart I deeply appreciate his present. Please assure him I'll treat it with the greatest of care, and see no harm comes to it. Captain Pendleton, will you kindly place the uniform in my tent, and keep it neatly folded.

VON BORCKE
No General, no, you do not understand. General Shtuart vas most insistent. He says now zat you are Lieutenant General, corps commander, you deserve new uniform. He vas most insistent you try it on. He vill certainly ask how vas the fit. Please, General. Try it on.

Jackson looks at Pendleton, who smiles broadly, holding the uniform out to him. Jackson reaches out slowly, feels the material, then takes it, cradling it with both hands, and changes into the new jacket. It fits him perfectly.

Just at that moment Jim Lewis approaches the fire with a large coffee kettle. He has to look twice at what he sees. Then tries, unsuccessfully, to suppress a big grin.

JIM LEWIS
Gen'ral, d'ats some mighty fine coat!

Everyone has a good, hearted laugh at Jackson's expense.

As the laugh subsides an eerie sound can be discerned, almost floating in the wind. Gradually, it grows in strength, sobering the mood around the campfire. It is the rebel yell, moving like a wave across the vast Confederate encampment. Jackson steps away from the campfire, to a fence rail not far off.

EXT. JACKSON'S CAMP, JACKSON'S POV – NIGHT
From there he can see across the valley, the thousands of tents, the hundreds of campfires. Finally, as mysteriously as it began, the yell dies off in scattered voices far away.

EXT. JACKSON'S CAMP, BUNKER HILL – NIGHT

JACKSON
That was the sweetest music I ever heard.

EXT. FEDERAL HQ, CHATHAM – DAY
SUPER TITLE: Falmouth, Virginia, December 1862

It is winter. A stately home overlooking the Rappahannock River. Couch and Hancock ride up.

Guards salute as they dismount. Hancock and Couch glance around the yard, see vast gardens, vine-covered walkways, brown stems peeking out through the snow.

INT. FEDERAL HQ, CHATHAM – DAY
The main living room. A pallor of cigar smoke. Standing in the middle of the room, amid a cluster of buff facings and gilt buttons, is General AMBROSE EVERETT BURNSIDE.

COUCH
Excuse us, General Burnside, General Hancock has some information you may find useful.

BURNSIDE
Yes, General Hancock, a pleasure.

General EDWIN VOSE SUMNER enters from an adjoining room.

BURNSIDE (Cont'd)
General Sumner? We have visitors.

COUCH
Sir, General Hancock reports the river can be forded a short way upstream. There'd be no difficulty crossing. With your permission, we could move right away.

BURNSIDE
General Hancock, I certainly appreciate your efforts at reconnaissance, but that possibility has been considered and rejected. The pontoons will be here any time now, and then we'll be able to cross, not only the men, but the wagons and supplies as well. It'd be foolhardy to send the men without the wagons, without the big guns.

HANCOCK
Excuse me, General, but am I correct in my observation that there's little force opposing us across the river?

BURNSIDE
Yes, General, you are correct. For once we seem to have caught old Bobby Lee by surprise.

HANCOCK
Well, then, sir, if I may suggest — isn't it possible General Lee's moving this way? Certainly he's aware of our intentions. If we could occupy the town with infantry it'd make our job much easier when the bridges do arrive, sir.

BURNSIDE
General, that's risky, I'm afraid. Those men could be cut off.

This weather — it snows one day, melts the next. The river could rise unexpectedly. It will be best, I assure you, if we wait until the entire army can cross together.

HANCOCK
General Burnside, if we don't cross the river very soon, I'm confident General Lee will make every effort to stop us. He's not going to let us move toward Richmond unopposed. Where are General Jackson's forces now? We don't know. Shouldn't we make some attempt to occupy Fredericksburg, and possibly the heights beyond, now, while we have it for the taking?

Couch can see that Burnside is impervious to the arguments.

COUCH
Please allow me, sir, to send at least General Hancock's division across the river. Surely, they can carry enough supplies with them, and the artillery from this side can protect them from any advance by Lee.

BURNSIDE
Gentlemen, we'll cross the river when the bridges arrive, and not before. You must understand, I do not have the luxury of deviating from the larger plan. The President has approved my strategy, and I'll stick to it. Once this army's across the river, we'll advance on Richmond. In force. We must not allow him the luxury of attacking us as divided and separated units, as he has done in the past. I will not make the mistake of my predecessors. No, General Hancock. You will hold your division on this side of the river until the pontoons are in place and the entire army crosses together, an irresistible, impregnable force.

EXT. WILDERNESS, CHANCELLOR HOUSE – EVENING
A light snowfall. Jackson and his aides approach a large brick tavern in the midst of the tangled forest.

JACKSON
What place is this?

SMITH
Chancellor's crossing. We're another four hours or so from Fredericksburg.

JACKSON
We'll rest here for a moment.

SMITH
I'll see what the good folks can provide.

Smith dismounts and enters the house. Jim Lewis approaches Jackson, who remains mounted.

JIM LEWIS
Will the gen'rl be fixin' to eat somethin' warm?

JACKSON
No, Jim. We've got to keep riding through to General Lee. Don't want to get all warmed up just to feel the cold all over

again. You never seem to mind the cold much.

JIM LEWIS
Oh, I minds it. I jes don't shows it.

Lewis reaches into a saddlebag, pulls out a cornstalk, offers it to Little Sorrel, who hesitates.

JIM LEWIS (*Cont'd*)
Now, Little Sorrel, I know dis co'n look poo'ly, but it sure does beat no co'n at all.

Little Sorrell snatches it up.

JACKSON
Heard from your family lately?

JIM LEWIS
Ain't heard much for some time. Yankee mail used to run quicker than Secesh mail.

Lewis chuckles, Jackson smiles.

JACKSON (*praying softly aloud*)
Lord, From where you sit you can see the great distance that separates our Southern men from their wives and children. We pray that you watch over our families. Lord, I ask you to watch over Jim's family, over his friends, over his loved ones, wherever they may be.

JIM LEWIS (*picking up with the prayer*)
Lo'd, I know you sees into da heart of all men jes like you sees into da heart of ol' Jim Lewis. An Lo'd, I knows deres no lyin' or deceitfulness can hide from you. You find out de truth in de bottom of de deepest pit a darkness. Dey be no hidin from your truth an' your ever watchful eye.

JACKSON
Amen.

JIM LEWIS
How is it, Lo'd, can you 'splain sumpin' to dis ol' Virginy man? How is it a good Christian man like some folks I know can tolerate dey black brothers in bondage? How is it, Lo'd, dat dey don't jes break dem chains! How is it, Lo'd, my heart is open and achin' and I wants to know!

Jackson opens an eye, stealing a quizzical glance over to Jim, then shutting it as quickly.

JACKSON
I want to know too, Lord. Speak to your children, Lord. Speak to Jim Lewis and Thomas Jackson, your humble and obedient servants. Speak to all of us. Our hearts are open. Show us the way and we will go.

JIM LEWIS
Amen.

JACKSON
Amen.

An awkward moment. Lewis starts to leave.

JACKSON *(Cont'd)*
Jim.

JIM LEWIS
Yes, Gen'rl.

JACKSON
What's the status of your family, Jim?

JIM LEWIS
'Bout half is free, half slave. Dat's countin' all de cousins an' such.

JACKSON
You must know, Jim, that some officers in this army are of the opinion that we should be enlisting Negroes as a condition of freedom. General Lee is among them, as is Jefferson Davis.

JIM LEWIS
Dat's what dey says 'round de camp.

JACKSON
Your people will be free one way or the other, Jim. The only question is whether the Southern government will have the good sense to do it first, and soon. And in so doing to seal a bond of enduring friendship among us.

JIM LEWIS
Dat's what dey say, Genr'l.

JACKSON
All in God's time. His plan is a great mystery that will be revealed to us.

Lewis offers another corn stalk to Little Sorrel.

JIM LEWIS
Dat's all de fodder you git dis night. We goin' into a country whar d'eres nothin mo' fo' an animal to eat than thar is in the palm of my hand.

EXT. RAPPAHANNOCK RIVER, FREDERICKSBURG – DAY
Across the Rappahannock River is the town of Fredericksburg. On the hills beyond are lines of gray-uniformed soldiers. They are digging in. Lee's army has arrived.

EXT. HILLS ABOVE FREDERICKSBURG – DAY
Lee sits on his horse, observing the lay of the land. Taylor is near him, also on horseback.

TAYLOR
Did you know, General, that George Washington spent his boyhood not far from here, and that it's across that river down there that he's supposed to have thrown that silver dollar and cut down that cherry tree?

LEE
That may be so, Mister Taylor. But it has an even

greater significance for me. It's where I met my wife... It's something these Yankees do not understand, will never understand. Rivers, hills, valleys, fields, even towns: to those people they're just markings on a map from the war office in Washington. To us, they're birthplaces and burial grounds, they're battlefields where our ancestors fought. They're places where we learned to walk, to talk, to pray. They're places where we made friendships and fell in love... They're the incarnation of all our memories and all that we are.

EXT. LEE'S POV, FREDERICKSBURG – DAY
The town, the Rappahannock River, to the Federal encampments on Stafford Heights.

EXT. HILLS ABOVE FREDERICKSBURG – DAY
Lee rides along his vantage point. Lt. Colonel EDWARD PORTER ALEXANDER is positioning his guns.

ALEXANDER
General Lee, a fine day, sir. We have batteries all along the hill, covering our front to the river. By tomorrow we'll have batteries in those trees to the south. We'll be able to cover the entire open ground — all of it.

Lee and Alexander are looking down a steep slope...

EXT. LEE'S POV, FROM MARYE'S HEIGHTS – DAY
...at the bottom of which is a stone wall. Below the wall, the ground continues to slope down, though less steeply, toward the town, and the river.

EXT. HILLS ABOVE FREDERICKSBURG – DAY
It is a commanding position for these guns.

ALEXANDER
General Lee, d'you think they'll come at us here?

LEE
Colonel Alexander, the Federal Army's massed together across that river watching us prepare for them. If I were General Burnside — no, I would not attack here. I would move back upstream, come across above us.

LEE *(Cont'd)*
But General Burnside is not a man with the luxury of flexibility. He's being pushed from behind, by loud voices in Washington, by newspapers who demand quick action. We're here, and so he will attack us here.

ALEXANDER
General, we have guns covering every inch of the open ground. If they try to cross that canal, it'll slow them down, and we'll hit them from every angle. Sir, a chicken could not live on that field.

A lone horseman rides toward them, through the lines of laboring soldiers. It is Captain Smith. He salutes.

SMITH
General Lee, sir. General Jackson sends his respects, and advises his corps will begin deploying to the south of this position by tomorrow, as you instructed, sir.

LEE
What are his men made of! He was a hundred and fifty miles away.

SMITH
Begging your pardon, sir, but to General Jackson, dawn is one minute after midnight.

INT. JACKSON'S TENT, FREDERICKSBURG – NIGHT
Jackson sits on a small stool, staring at an oil lamp. His chief of staff, Captain PENDLETON, stands outside the flap.

PENDLETON (O.S.)
Sir? Forgive me, General ...

JACKSON
You may enter, Captain.

Pendleton lifts the flaps. It is snowing. He leans into the warmth of the dull light.

PENDLETON
There's a letter for you, General. The courier was slow today. I thought you'd want to see it, sir.

Jackson reaches out, takes the letter from Pendleton's out-stretched hand and glances at the envelope.

PENDLETON (Cont'd)
Good night, sir.

Pendleton backs out, dropping down the tent flaps.

Jackson stares now at the letter. He is nervous. He takes a deep breath, tears open the envelope. His hand shakes slightly as he holds the paper out, catching the lamp light.

JACKSON (V.O.)
My own dear father, as my mother's letter has been cut short by my arrival, I think it but justice that I should continue it. I know that you are rejoiced to hear of my coming, and I hope that God has sent me to radiate your pathway through life. I am a very tiny little thing. I weigh only eight and a half pounds, and Aunt Harriet says I am the express image of my darling papa... My mother is very comfortable this morning.

Jackson puts the letter down.

JACKSON (Cont'd) (whispering)
Thank you, Lord, thank you, thank you, thank you.

INT. FEDERAL HDQS, STAFFORD HEIGHTS NIGHT
Hancock and Couch are leaning over a map table lit by an oil lamp.

HANCOCK
They've occupied all the buildings along the river front. Our boys will be lining up those pontoon bridges through a hail of lead. Once across, the rebs will make us pay for every block. Beyond the town is the canal which cuts across this open field — a field we'll have to cross to reach their entrenchments on Marye's Heights... another difficult obstacle in the face of artillery fire.

COUCH
Down to the left, we could push through, turn Jackson's lines, push him back, trap Longstreet on top of the hill, surround him. It's ...possible.

HANCOCK
Turn Jackson's lines? No, General, we'll meet them head on, and it will be a bloody mess. We'll march up to that hill over there, and we'll eat their artillery fire all the way across this field. But the important thing is — we'll be able to look at ourselves in the mirror and say we're good soldiers, we did what we were told. And if we're not successful, we can say, well, it was a good plan, but there were contingencies. Then Mr. Lincoln and General Halleck and Secretary Stanton and all their political cronies can pace their offices and fret over what to do next. And you, General, can go back to your home town and tell the families of your men they died doing their duty.

COUCH
The rebs have fortified the high ground up river, and anyway, there are rapids and obstacles to a crossing there. Below Fredericksburg the river is too wide, and now Early's forces are clear down to Port Royal. Fredericksburg is now the only place we can cross. If Burnside doesn't cross here, he might as well resign.

HANCOCK
That wily gray fox has out-manoeuvered our command again. And there's going to be hell to pay.

EXT. FREDERICKSBURG – DAY/TWILIGHT
A MONTAGE of traveling shots. The inhabitants of Fredericksburg leave town, by foot, by cart. They are old and young, women and children and their grandparents, the sick and infirm. Some are veterans of earlier fights, men who have been wounded.

EXT. ROAD, FREDERICKSBURG – DAY/TWILIGHT
A detachment of Confederate soldiers is drawn up by the side of the road, allowing the long line to pass, making room for squeaking carts and richly upholstered carriages.

EXT. TOWN STREETS, FREDERICKSBURG – DAY/TWILIGHT
Other soldiers move through the town. They occupy houses and stores perched along the riverbank. Every window, every small gap in old brickwork, any place a man could fire a rifle, is filled.

177

EXT. STONE WALL, MARYE'S HEIGHTS – DAY/TWILIGHT
Civilians and veterans reach the relative safety of Marye's Heights, passing by the stone wall and the Confederate fortifications.

INT. BEALE HOUSE, BEDROOM – MORNING – DEC 11
Jane Beale is roused from her sleep by the sound of two cannon blasts. She is no sooner out of bed than Martha enters, helping Jane to dress as she speaks.

> **MARTHA**
> Miss Jane, dem Yankees is comin', sure as Jesus. De've got two pontoons nearly 'cross da river. We've got to get you and the chilruns out of here in a hurry.

> **JANE BEALE**
> Martha, don't you be fussin' with me. You get your own family ready. We'll all of us leave together.

> **MARTHA**
> Miss Jane, you know we done talked this over and we's decided to stay on and look after the house. No use sayin' more about it.

> **JANE BEALE**
> Martha, I will not leave you to the mercy of those blue devils.

> **MARTHA**
> Now, you knows dey won't be botherin' no black folks. If we goes wid you dere won't be a forkful of food left in de pantry when we comes back, and we needs to eat same as you.

Suddenly all hell breaks loose, as the Federal guns from Stafford Heights fire volley after volley into the town.

The first shock knocks the women to the floor.

> **JANE BEALE**
> The children!

Only half-dressed, Jane rushes downstairs...

INT. BEALE HOUSE, MAIN FLOOR – MORNING
...with Martha close on her heels. On the main floor she is met by Lucy, Sam and Julian. Shot and shell rain down onto the house. Plaster and splinters of wood fly into the rooms. Everyone falls to the floor. The front door swings open, the Reverend Lacy rushing in, shutting the door behind him.

> **LUCY BEALE**
> Pastor Lacy, we must run to our lines!

> **LACY**
> Too late for that. The streets are raining with iron. Everyone to the basement!

Another shell strikes the Beale house. There is a loud cry, as Sam falls to the floor, holding his chest. Jane and Lacy are at his side at once. Sam moans and writhes in pain. Lacy can't see a wound, so tears open his shirt — where we can see a large purple bruise on Sam's chest, just below the shoulder. Julian discovers a 12-pound solid shot just lying on the floor.

> **LUCY BEALE**
> Look, Mother, a Yankee cannonball.

> **LACY**
> You're a lucky lad, Sam. You were hit by a spent shot. Not so many soldiers as lucky as you.

They help him up as they all...

INT. CELLAR, BEALE HOUSE – DAY
...struggle down the stairs to the cellar.

> **LACY**
> Martha, bring your children!

The concussion of a nearby explosion sends Lacy hurtling down the stairs. Dusting himself off, he is unhurt.

EXT. WHARF AREA, FREDERICKSBURG – MORNING
Confederate soldiers peek out from basement windows and cracks in the brickwork.

EXT. RAPPAHANNOCK RIVER, FREDERICKSBURG – MORNING
The river, first glimpses of the Yankees on the water, one ghostly figure standing in a shallow boat. A scattered volley from the Confederates.

The Yankee falls. Officers shout and point. Their men scamper over the boats, trying to find cover in the wide-open middle of the river.

EXT. WHARF AREA, FREDERICKSBURG – DAY
The Confederates keep firing. WILLIAM BARKSDALE is commander of the Mississippi troops defending the town.

> **BARKSDALE**
> Keep it hot, boys!

INT. CELLAR, BEALE HOUSE, FREDERICKSBURG – DAY
Though it is day, the basement is pitch dark, save for a single candle, held by Lucy. The deafening noise from above continues unabated. Plaster dust drifts down. Lacy reads from his Bible by the light of the candle.

> **LACY**
> "The Lord is my light and my salvation; whom shall I fear? The Lord is the strength of my life; of whom shall I be afraid? When the wicked, even mine enemies and my foes, came upon me to eat up my flesh, they stumbled and fell. Though an host should encamp against me, my heart shall not fear; though war should rise against me, in this will I be confident. For in the time of trouble he will hide me in his pavilion: in the secret of his tabernacle shall he hide me; he shall set me up upon a rock. And now shall mine head be lifted up above mine enemies round about me: therefore

will I offer in his tabernacle sacrifices of joy; I will sing, yea, I will sing praises unto the Lord."

EXT. WHARF AREA, FREDERICKSBURG – DAY
Barksdale looks out from a basement window. Shells burst overhead, shattering the walls of a house. Suddenly there is a lull. He and his men peer down the street, where they see...

EXT. WHARVES, FREDERICKSBURG – DAY
...Blue troops scampering out of the pontoon boats, firing into the town.

EXT. WHARF AREA, FREDERICKSBURG -DAY

BARKSDALE
Let's go, Mississippi. It's house to house now. Make 'em pay for every step.

INT. CELLAR, BEALE HOUSE, FREDERICKSBURG – DAY
No one seems to breathe in the momentary lull in the bombardment. Then the loud sound of banging, followed by footsteps above.

JOHN BEALE (o.s.)
Mother, are you here?

MARTHA
Praise be, it's John!

JANE BEALE
We're down here, in the cellar!

JOHN BEALE (o.s.)
The door is blocked. I'll go around to the yard.

The cellar door is flung open, the sudden light blinding those below.

JOHN BEALE (o.s.)(Cont'd)
Come out, hurry!

EXT. BEALE HOUSE, FREDERICKSBURG – DAY
It's difficult for the family to see as they emerge from the darkness. John is accompanied by two TOWNSPEOPLE.

JOHN BEALE (Cont'd)
There's an ambulance out front. The enemy is crossing the river. We must hurry.

EXT. BEALE HOUSE, FREDERICKSBURG – DAY
Outside they witness the orgy of destruction: felled trees, torn branches, piles of bricks, gaping holes in house walls, collapsed chimneys, and debris strewn everywhere. Smoke drifts in the air. Rebel troops fill the streets, moving up and out of their shelters in the town. John leads them to the waiting ambulance, drawn by a pair of horses. The Beale family enters, leaving Lacy and Martha behind.

JANE BEALE
Martha, I won't leave without you.

MARTHA
I done told you I'm stayin'. Now I'll be here when Mar'se Robert whips dose Yankees.

LACY
Off with you then!

The TEAMSTER snaps his whip and the carriage jerks ahead. In the same instant the bombardment resumes, a shell careening overhead, exploding into a nearby house.

Lacy escorts Martha back to the house as retreating and wounded Confederates move up the street. He joins them, taking a musket from one of the walking wounded.

EXT. TOWN STREETS – FREDERICKSBURG – DAY
The wagon moves as quickly as possible, but is blocked by fallen trees and collapsed walls of brick. The driver turns down a side street to avoid these obstacles. As they approach the next intersection the family looks down toward the river. Just two blocks away are hundreds of Federal troops. The driver snaps his whip, urging his team to maximum effort. Turning back up the hill, they pass more Rebels, firing down the hill as they fall back to the Confederate lines above. There are civilians in the streets as well, all plodding up towards Marye's Heights, away from the river. Women, children and old men are wrapped in blankets, shawls and overcoats.

EXT. FIELDS BELOW MARYE'S HEIGHTS – FREDERICKS-BURG – DAY
Halfway up the hill they are slowed by the congestion of refugees. Jane and her children look back over the town.

EXT. JANE BEALE'S POV, FREDERICKSBURG – DAY
The town is on fire in many places, the old church steeples illuminated with the conflagration. Smoke drifts over the city, temporarily obscuring parts of the town. Across the river on Stafford Heights can be seen the Federal batteries, flashing and belching in an unceasing fury.

EXT. MARYE'S HEIGHTS, FREDERICKSBURG – DAY
The ambulance approaches the Confederate lines, first hundreds, then thousands of soldiers spread in a long line along the hilltops above the town. The regimental flags flap in the smoky breeze.

JANE BEALE
May God be with them. May He strengthen their hearts and their arms for the coming struggle. Oh, give them the victory!

EXT. RAPPAHANNOCK, FREDERICKSBURG – MORNING, DEC 12
Hancock and his division cross over on the pontoon bridges.

EXT. TOWN STREETS OF FREDERICKSBURG – MORNING
Complete mayhem as stores are looted, windows smashed, doors forced open. Household contents are thrown into the street. Furniture and clothing thrown from upper story windows.

EXT. HOUSE, FREDERICKSBURG – MORNING

Soldiers rampage through a private home, slashing paintings with their bayonets, smashing china and porcelain, breaking mirrors and glass, emptying drawers and closets.

EXT. TOWN STREETS, FREDERICKSBURG – MORNING

Soldiers lounge in armchairs in the middle of the street. A group of soldiers gathers round a piano that's been tossed from a front door into the street. A "musician" pounds on the keyboard in a raucous and discordant rendition of "Rally Round the Flag."

Soldiers wear women's clothes and bonnets. Lower grade officers make no efforts to stop the pillage. A soldier strolls down the street with an entire feather bed.

Another throws heaps of leather bound books from windows.

Provost Marshall MARSENA PATRICK rides up with his aides.

> **MARSENA PATRICK**
> This must stop at once! Where are the officers?

Just then a man passes by carrying a carpet on his shoulder.

> **MARSENA PATRICK** *(Cont'd)*
> Drop that at once!

The soldier ignores him. Patrick rides up to the man, striking him with his riding whip. The man drops his booty.

> **MARSENA PATRICK** *(Cont'd)* *(to his aides)*
> Get a message to Couch, to Hancock! This will not be tolerated!
> *(he shouts to the crowd of soldiers)*
> This is an army! Not a rabble!

An officer rounds a corner with elegant drapes slung over his saddle bags.

> **MARSENA PATRICK** *(Cont'd)*
> Have you no shame, man, no honor!
> *(to another aide)*
> Sir, have that officer arrested!

EXT. BEALE HOUSE, FREDERICKSBURG – MORNING

A group of rampaging soldiers approach the front door, immediately pounding on it to force their entrance. The door opens, revealing Martha. She is dressed in a fashionable silk dress. The soldiers are momentarily stopped by this unexpected sight.

> **MARTHA**
> Can I be of service to you fine Northern gentlemen?

> **A LOOTER**
> Is this your master's place?

> **MARTHA**
> This is my place.
> *(she calls behind her)*
> Chil'rens?

Her THREE CHILDREN appear at her side.

> **ANOTHER LOOTER**
> Sorry to bother you, Ma'am.
> *(to the others)*
> Come on, let's go.

Martha heaves a sigh of relief, shooing her children back inside.

EXT. LEE'S HDQS, TELEGRAPH HILL, FEDRICKSBURG – PRE-DAWN, DEC 12

All of Lee's generals are present. There is a table with maps. Aides bring the generals biscuits and coffee.

Jackson is wearing his new uniform.

> **STUART**
> Well, General Jackson, you are a most gallant sight this morning.

> **JACKSON**
> Thank you, General Stuart. Your gift is appreciated. Very kind.

> **LEE**
> General Longstreet, please show us where your troops are positioned.

Longstreet leans over the map.

> **LONGSTREET**
> We're anchored on the north by Anderson's division, up on the bend in the river, then General Ransom's division's in several lines along and below the ridge of Marye's Heights, with Cobb's brigade dug in down on the road, behind that stone wall. To their right is General McLaws, and farther down, in the woods to the right, are Pickett and Hood. General Hood's my right flank, and is connected in those heavy trees with General Jackson's left. Up here, on the heights, are the Washington Artillery, with Colonel Alexander's batteries in support. It is a strong line, General.

> **LEE**
> Very well, General. General Jackson, would you please extend the line for us?

Jackson leans forward slightly, pointing to places on the map.

> **JACKSON**
> General A. P. Hill is on the left, adjoining General Hood. His position's supported here, by General Taliaferro and General Early. To the right flank and behind is D. H. Hill. General Lee...

Jackson pauses, runs his finger along the map.

> **JACKSON** *(Cont'd)*
> ...we've constructed a road, running behind the lines for our entire length. We can move troops as is necessary. If the enemy penetrates our line at any point, the reserves — Taliaferro and Early — can change their position rapidly. If

the enemy makes an attempt to cut our center, or if General Pickett is pressed, we can move to his aid. Our right flank is anchored here.

Jackson points to a straight line, a road that leads away from the river, out to the west.

JACKSON *(Cont'd)*
General Stuart has advised that the enemy has placed his flank on this road, and does not threaten farther southward. Daniel Harvey Hill's positioned to move farther down if the enemy changes his direction.

Lee stares at Jackson, and there is a brief silence.

LEE
Good, very good. General Stuart, are you in a strong position for protecting General Jackson's flank?

STUART
Yes, sir. We're covering the enemy from the river, as far out as our own lines. If the Yankees move down river, or threaten to turn General Jackson's line, we can block his advance until the line is moved.

LEE
Very well.

He looks round at them all.

LEE *(Cont'd)*
Gentlemen, these deployments are sound. The rest is in God's hands.

EXT. CONFEDERATE BATTERIES ABOVE FREDERICKS-BURG – DAWN
The Confederate batteries are set into shallow pits. The men are manning the guns, watching the fog slowly drifting in the growing breeze, a fine, cold mist. Old Penn lifts his field glasses.

EXT. OLD PENN'S POV, FREDERICKSBURG – DAWN
A series of views:

Across the river the far heights can be seen, the flags of the Federal headquarters, the closely spaced guns of the enemy. Now, the fog has settled downward, into the town, and rising above the dense gray are the church spires, the only sign that there is a town there at all.

The town begins to appear, the rooftops of the taller buildings. Also signs of the destruction of the previous day and night, the black skeletons of burnt-out houses.

Now the fog lifts. Through the clearing fog, the vast mass of the blue troops as they start to emerge from the gloom.

Far to the Confederate right flank, Federal regiments form out on the wide plain in front of Jackson's woods. Neat formations are moving out slowly on the clean frost-covered field, the sharp squares of blue spreading out on the stark white.

From Stafford Heights and from their newly emplaced batteries on the south side of the river, the Federals begin a bombardment of the Confederate right flank, Jackson's lines.

EXT. A. P. HILL'S LINES, FREDERICKSBURG – MORNING
The lines of soldiers in their trenches. Their cannon, concealed in the woods, are not firing. Behind the trenches is a roughly constructed road. Jackson rides up with General Hood. They are closely followed by A. P. Hill and Maxey Gregg. Pendleton and Smith follow. Then Hood's aides.

JACKSON
I have often wondered how it is that Texas men, who are the most independent minded individuals in this army of irascibles, ever agreed to serve under the command of a Kentuckian.

HOOD
I have often wondered the same.

JACKSON
Do you expect to live to see the end of this war?

HOOD
I do not know, but I am inclined to think I will. I expect I will be wounded. And you, genr'l?

JACKSON *(taken aback)*
I do not expect to live to see the end of this war. Nor can I say that without victory I would desire to do so.

EXT. HEIGHTS, OPPOSITE FREDERICKSBURG – DAY
The First Division of the Fifth Corps is held in reserve. The Twentieth Maine rests in ranks with the other regiments comprising the Third Brigade. Hundreds of Federal cannon positioned on the heights to their left and right maintain a relentless barrage against the Confederate lines, mostly hidden in the trees more than a mile away.

Chamberlain and his men watch the drama unfold across the river.

CHAMBERLAIN
In the Roman Civil War, Julius Caesar knew he had to march on Rome itself, which no legion was permitted to do. Marcus Lucanus left us a chronicle of what happened.

EXT. CHAMBERLAIN'S POV, FIELDS BELOW MARYE'S HEIGHTS – DAY
The far line of hills circling round the town of Fredericksburg, the river far below, creates the effect of a monumental coliseum.

Chamberlain's voice continues over the ensuing action.

The lead division of General William H. French is given the order to advance. Bugles sound as the lines move forward. The Confederate cannon, some eight hundred yards up the hill, open fire. French's three infantry brigades, moving out one at a time, encounter no massed Confederate musketry until they ascend a gentle bluff, about halfway to the stone wall. The impact of the first volley rips open their front line, staggering the advance. They continue to advance through the now incessant fire to their front, as well as enfilading fire from artillery placed along the left and right of the Confederate line.

The lead division finally reaches the depression a hundred yards in front of the stone wall, where it becomes impossible to advance or retreat. Those who are not felled by lead crouch in behind the small protection afforded by the undulating terrain. French's second and third divisions get stacked up, taking terrific casualties, but succeeding in firing their own volleys as they close on the wall.

> **CHAMBERLAIN** (V.O.)
> "Now swiftly Caesar had surmounted the icy alps and in his mind conceived immense upheavals, coming war. When he reached the water of the little Rubicon, clearly to the leader through the murky night appeared a mighty image of his country in distress, grief in her face, her white hair streaming from her tower-crowned head; with tresses torn and shoulders bare she stood before him and sighing said: 'Where further do you march? Where do you take my standards, warriors? If lawfully you come, if as citizens, this far only is allowed.' Then trembling struck the leader's limbs, his hair grew stiff, and weakness checked his progress, holding his feet at the river's edge. At last he speaks: 'O Thunderer, surveying great Rome's walls from the Tarpeian Rock; O Phrygian house-gods of Iulus' clan and mysteries of Quirinus, who was carried off to heaven; O Jupiter of Latium, seated in lofty Alba, and hearths of Vesta; O Rome, the equal of the highest deity, favour my plans. Not with impious weapons do I pursue you — here am I, Caesar, conqueror by land and sea, your own soldier everywhere, now too if I am permitted. The man who makes me your enemy, it is he will be the guilty one.' Then he broke the barriers of war and through the swollen river quickly took his standards... When Caesar had crossed the flood and reached the opposite bank, on Hesperia's forbidden fields he took his stand and said:

EXT. HEIGHTS OPPOSITE FREDERICKSBURG – DAY

> **CHAMBERLAIN**
> "Here I abandon peace and desecrated law; Fortune, it is you I follow. Farewell to treaties from now on; now war must be our judge!"

Chamberlain surveys his men, the hundreds who will soon go into battle. Then looks back over the vast amphitheater of war across the river.

> **CHAMBERLAIN** (Cont'd)
> "Hail Caesar! We who are about to die salute you."

EXT. FREDERICKSBURG STREETS – DAY
Hancock has been watching, mounted, at the head of his division, which is next in line.

EXT. FIELD BEFORE CANAL – DAY
Zook's Brigade forms at the edge of the town and is immediately under the enemy's guns.

EXT. CANAL, FREDERICKSBURG – DAY
French's division, now retreating, has been cut to pieces. A few stragglers and wounded stumble back over to the relative safety of the canal embankment. Others are pinned in place, unable to move forward or backwards.

EXT. FIELD BEFORE CANAL – DAY
The bugles sound the advance. Zook's Brigade moves forward into the hail of shot and shell from the Confederate artillery.

EXT. CANAL DITCH – DAY
Narrow bridges of thin rails cross the canal ditch, now filled with freezing waist-deep water. The men can only step single file or wade across. The Confederate gunners on the hill have the range and shower them with grape and canister. Federal soldiers are falling into the canal, blown apart by the unseen swarms of hot metal.

SAMUEL KOSCIUSZKO ZOOK brandishes his sword.

EXT. TOWN STREETS FREDERICKSBURG – DAY
Meagher's Irish Brigade, led by MEAGHER and Lt. Colonel MULHOLLAND and JOHN CURTIS CALDWELL'S brigade are massed in formation, standing at ease and leaning against doorways in the streets parallel to the line of battle, in the protection of the city's buildings. The cross streets leading towards Marye's Heights are zones of death, as they afford unobstructed alleys of fire to the Confederates above the town. Incoming Confederate artillery crashes into a wall here, a rooftop there. Shells explode in mid air. The occasional man is struck by an exploding fragment, and falls to the ground. Wounded soldiers from French's division stagger back down the streets, some carried on stretchers.

Nearby, brigade musicians play "The Boys of the Irish Brigade" on concertinas and tin whistles.

Orderlies hurry down the lines carrying bunches of boxwood, green sprigs, which are passed along to every man in the ranks of the Irish Brigade, who fasten them to their caps.

In a clatter of hooves on the cobblestones, Hancock rounds a corner and rides up to the head of the columns.

> **HANCOCK**
> Fall in!

With the order given, Hancock rides back into the fray.

> **MULHOLLAND** (also mounted)
> Fall in, boys!

183

A shell explodes into a nearby house, sending up a cloud of dust and debris.

A wounded man is carried by on a window shutter.

> **MULHOLLAND** (Cont'd)
> Fix bayonets!

Up and down the streets the order is passed as the sound of thousands of bayonets clank into place on their muskets.

EXT. CANAL DITCH, FREDERICKSBURG – DAY
Zook's brigade is falling back to the safety of the ditch, leaving a carpet of blue behind, between the ditch and the stone wall.

EXT. FIELD BELOW MARYE'S HEIGHTS – DAY
Their fifers and drummers play "Upon the Heights of Alma" as the Irish Brigade forms for the assault. They immediately start taking casualties from the artillery barrage.

> **MULHOLLAND**
> Steady, men, steady! You'll soon be forward!

The green flag of Erin is raised. General Meagher is seen raising his sword in the air as the troops pass him by.

> **1ST IRISHMAN**
> Is that to be Meagher's position then?

> **2ND IRISHMAN**
> He's enjoyin' the privilege of a general, protectin' the rear.

> **3RD IRISHMAN**
> He's got a lame knee, for pity's sake.

> **1ST IRISHMAN**
> Fair 'nuf then. Someone's got to keep Burnside company.

> **MULHOLLAND** (standing before the ranks)
> Irish Brigade, advance!

The bugle sounds the advance. Other voices echo the command, "Forward, double-quick, guide center!"

EXT. STONE WALL, McMILLAN'S REGIMENT, FREDERICKSBURG – DAY
McMillan's men stand beneath their own Irish regiment flag.

> **DOOLEY** (in desperation)
> That's the Irish! What are those boys doin' fightin' in blue? Don't they know we're fightin' for our independence? Have they learned nothin' at all at the hands of the English?

> **McMILLAN**
> Meagher's brigade has done as much as the envenomed puritan to rob us of our property, devastate our lands, starve the pleading orphan and the broken-hearted widow, trample in the dust every principle of right and defame our identity as a free people. These brave Irishmen are our brothers, but they've been misled to their fates!

EXT. CANAL DITCH, FREDERICKSBURG – DAY
Leading his division, Hancock rides back and forth, along the canal ditch, exhorting his men.

> **HANCOCK**
> Come on, boys! Give 'em the cold steel!

The Irish Brigade quickly arrives at the ditch, swarming across and briefly catching their breath on the other side, already cluttered with the wounded and repulsed soldiers of French's division and Zook's brigade.

> **HANCOCK** (Cont'd)
> Move out, boys! Move out!

The regiments of the Irish Brigade reform in the protection of the swale, girding themselves for the final effort.

> **MULHOLLAND**
> Steady, men! Steady! Do your duty! At the double quick, forward!

The command is echoed down the line as the entire brigade leaps forward over the crest of the low embankment, charging towards the Confederates at the stone wall.

EXT. STONE WALL, FREDERICKSBURG – DAY

> **McMILLAN** (waving his sword)
> Give it to 'em, boys! Now's the time! Give it to 'em!

A sheet of flame leaps out from the Confederate defenders.

EXT. FIELD BEFORE STONE WALL, FREDERICKSBURG – DAY
As the Irish Brigade moves across the field, other Union wounded who litter the ground cheer and wave them on. Halfway between the ditch and the wall the Irish Brigade begins to falter. Volley after volley is unleashed. One of every three men eventually fall to the ground.

EXT. STONE WALL, FREDERICKSBURG – DAY
Dooley is weeping and crying out in desperate agony as he loads, aims, fires and reloads.

> **DOOLEY**
> You stupid Paddys! You damn stupid idiots! Go to hell, all of you! Go to hell and damnation!

EXT. FIELD BEFORE STONE WALL, FREDERICKSBURG – DAY
Valiantly holding its ground in the withering onslaught, the Irish Brigade halts about thirty yards from the stone wall and delivers a heavy volley into the Confederate line. The forward movement of the brigade now halted, the remaining men stand and continue to fire and reload in place.

EXT. STONE WALL, FREDERICKSBURG – DAY
Another murderous volley from the stone wall.

EXT. FIELD BEFORE STONE WALL, FREDERICKSBURG – DAY
Irishmen collapse onto the bodies of men already fallen from the previous assaults.

EXT. CANAL DITCH, FREDERICKSBURG – DAY
Hancock sees the destruction in his front.

> **HANCOCK** (*to an aide*)
> Caldwell's brigade, forward now!

The aide rides down towards the edge of town, where Hancock's third and remaining brigade is forming for the attack.

EXT. TELEGRAPH HILL, LEE'S POSITION, FREDERICKSBURG – DAY
Lee, Longstreet and their aides observe the battle.

> **LEE**
> General Longstreet, those people are committing more fresh divisions at your lines. Their mounting numbers may overwhelm our defense.

> **LONGSTREET**
> If they put every man they have on either side of the Rappahannock on the field to approach me, just give me plenty of ammunition and I will kill them all before they reach my line.

> **LEE**
> Nevertheless, General, we must be prudent. We must never ignore the unknown, the unpredictable.

> **LONGSTREET**
> Yes sir, I will take the necessary measures.
> (*turning to a courier*)
> Send orders to Ransom's Tar Heels to advance his division. And to General Kershaw to bring up his brigade to support Cobb at the stone wall.

The courier salutes and is off.

EXT. STONE WALL, McMILLAN'S BRIGADE, FREDERICKSBURG – DAY
As the regiments of the Irish Brigade stubbornly fight on, Dooley, still weeping, takes off his hat and begins to cheer. Other soldiers behind him take his example and a cheer moves up and down the Confederate line, in more than begrudging witness of the sheer courage of the fighting Irish.

EXT. FIELD BEFORE STONE WALL, FREDERICKSBURG – DAY
The color sergeant of the 116th Pennsylvania is shot in the leg and falls to one knee, defiantly waving the Stars and Stripes. He is struck by additional minie balls as the flag is riddled with bullets and the flag staff shattered. A lieutenant picks up the colors.

> **MULHOLLAND**
> Lie down and fire!

The Irishmen lie down, loading their muskets on their backs, returning fire.

> **MULHOLLAND** (*Cont'd*)
> Blaze away and stand to it, boys!

But it's more than human beings can take, as heroism borders on suicide.

> **MULHOLLAND** (*Cont'd*)
> Fall back, men, and every man for himself!

Those still standing take tentative backward steps and melt back down the hill, taking cover behind the slight defile halfway back towards the canal ditch.

EXT. MILITARY ROAD, PICKETT'S POSITION, FREDERICKSBURG – DAY
GEORGE EDWARD PICKETT rides along his front, coming into Armistead's lines.

> **PICKETT**
> General Armistead!

> **ARMISTEAD**
> Good afternoon, General Pickett.

> **PICKETT**
> Did you see that last charge by Meagher's brigade?

> **ARMISTEAD**
> Those fellows deserved a better fate. Their bravery is worthy of a better cause.

> **PICKETT**
> My heart stood still as I watched it.

> **ARMISTEAD**
> I would not have believed that mortal men could march into the face of such destruction.

EXT. CANAL DITCH, FREDERICKSBURG – DAY
Hancock rallies the retreating troops from Zook's and Meagher's brigades as Caldwell's brigade reaches the canal ditch, retracing the deathly path of the previous charges.

> **CALDWELL**
> Forward, men! Keep moving! Keep moving!

EXT. TELEGRAPH HILL, FREDERICKSBURG – DAY
Two Confederate siege guns, thirty-pound parrot rifles, pour a deadly enfilading fire into the advancing ranks of Hancock's division. Lee, Longstreet and Old Penn stand nearby.

> **LONGSTREET** (*to a courier*)
> Send this message to General Pickett. Tell him to advance two brigades in support of Ransom's division, Kemper's Virginians and Jenkins' South Carolina. Do you have that Corporal?

> **COURIER**
> Yes sir! Advance Kemper's and Jenkins' to the sunken road!

The courier is barely gone when there is a terrific explosion that knocks all the officers to the ground. They are dazed, but miraculously, no one is hurt. They look to see that one of the two siege guns has exploded at the muzzle. Dead artillerymen lie about the gun.

> **LEE**
> It is not yet our time, gentlemen, not yet our time.

EXT. STAFFORD HEIGHTS, OPPOSITE FREDERICKSBURG – DAY – 4 PM
Chamberlain, the men of the Twentieth Maine and Stockton's brigade watch the grisly spectacle below. The bugle sounds.

> **AMES**
> Third Brigade to the front! Fall in!

The troops sally as the order is repeated down the line.

EXT. MILITARY ROAD, PICKETT'S POSITION, FREDERICKSBURG – DAY
JAMES LAWSON KEMPER stands at the head of his brigade. Pickett rides up with his aides. The fighting to their left front is furious.

> **PICKETT**
> General Kemper, you are ordered by General Longstreet to proceed immediately to your left, in support of McLaws. You are to take two regiments of your brigade to the sunken road behind the stone wall!

> **KEMPER**
> Yes sir, at once!

> **PICKETT**
> Do your duty, General!

Pickett rears his steed and is off at a gallop.

> **KEMPER** (*to his aides*)
> My horse, gentlemen, we're going to where the fight is!

He steps out in front of his men.

> **KEMPER** (*Cont'd*)
> The commanding general has called us into the battle! We move at once!

The men cheer.

> **KEMPER** (*Cont'd*)
> If we can whip the enemy here today, I tell you from what I know, the Confederacy is surely established! Men of Virginia, you who have fought on so many hard won fields, today your country calls on you again to stand between her and the enemy. I know you will do your duty!

The men shout the rebel yell, which is then picked up by the adjoining regiments and carried down the entire front. Kemper's horse is brought up, he mounts, and the brigade moves out.

EXT. PONTOON BRIDGE, FREDERICKSBURG – AFTERNOON
Colonels Ames and Chamberlain ride across the bridge at the head of their column. The bridge sways under the treading feet as shells explode overhead. The entire Third Brigade moves into the town, now under bombardment from the Confederate guns on Telegraph Hill.

EXT. TOWN STREETS, FREDERICKSBURG – AFTERNOON
The Third Brigade marches into the Fredericksburg streets in columns of four. They pass hundreds of wounded and dying veterans of the previous assaults. Now they begin to pass heaps of body parts and piles of amputated limbs, as every house serves as a field hospital. Finally, they are ordered to halt on a side street. General CHARLES GRIFFIN rides up.

From around the corner can be heard the bugle sounding the advance for Griffin's First Brigade, the familiar "Dan, Dan, Dan Butterfield, Butterfield."

> **GRIFFIN** (*under his breath, to Ames*)
> There goes my First Brigade to hell. Alright, get them ready.

> **AMES**
> Attention! Twentieth Maine! Load your muskets! Fix bayonets!

The orders are echoed down the ranks.

> **GRIFFIN**
> Officers of the Third Brigade will dismount!

Ames, Chamberlain and the other officers dismount, tying their horses to whatever fixed objects are at hand.

EXT. FIELD BELOW MARYE'S HEIGHTS – TWILIGHT
Officers and wounded men retreat back to their starting positions, moving through Griffin's First Brigade, Barnes, which now moves up the hill.

EXT. SUNKEN ROAD, FREDERICKSBURG – TWILIGHT
Kemper's regiment moves into position at the stone wall, so that the defending line is now four ranks deep.

EXT. TOWN STREET, FREDERICKSBURG – TWILIGHT
The Twentieth Maine stands at the ready, with fixed bayonets at shoulder arms.

> **GRIFFIN**
> Alright, men, move 'em out!

The bugle sounds as the orders are shouted, "Forward!" The Third Brigade moves forward, four abreast, rounding the street corner which brings them onto the edge of the great killing field.

EXT. FIELD BEFORE CANAL – TWILIGHT
The Twentieth Maine is positioned in the front line as...

> **AMES**
> Twentieth Maine, halt!

The column comes smartly to a halt.

> **AMES** (*Cont'd*)
> Twentieth Maine, left face!

The column turns left in one precise movement.

> **AMES** (*Cont'd*)
> Twentieth Maine, forward, in line of battle, march!

The brigade spills quickly and smoothly into battle formation.

EXT. POV BATTLEFIELD BELOW MARYE'S HEIGHTS – TWILIGHT

For the first time the men of the Twentieth see the awful devastation up close, the field before them a carpet of blue, writhing horses and men, the cries of the wounded piercing the roar of the cannon. Smoke billows across the field.

EXT. FIELD BEFORE CANAL – TWILIGHT

The acrid taste of powder scorches their mouths and burns their eyes. The wounded stream to the rear.

> **KILRAIN** (*under his voice, to Tom*)
> It seems a terrible long distance up that hill.

> **TOM**
> It'll be shortened by those in the front.

> **KILRAIN**
> Beggin' your pardon sir, but the only thing that'll be shortened by those in front is their lives.

> **AMES** (*nearby, to Chamberlain*)
> God help us now. Take care of the right wing!

> **CHAMBERLAIN**
> Yes sir, I'll watch them, sir.

The "Dan Butterfield" bugle call is sounded.

> **KILRAIN** (*under his breath*)
> Hail Caesar, we who are about to die salute you!

Ames steps out in front of the regiment.

> **AMES**
> Twentieth Maine, forward, at the quickstep, march!

The men of the Twentieth Maine step forward as one man, the regimental blue flag flapping in the smoky breeze. The entire brigade lurches forward with them.

The lines move forward, with the sergeants and rank closers in the third line.

EXT. FIELD BEFORE CANAL – TWILIGHT

The shells begin to reach them now. The rhythm of the march is jarred. The ground seems to roll and bounce. Dirt sprays round Chamberlain, pushing him aside with a breath of hot wind. But he does not fall, looks toward the explosion, where there is now a gap in the line.

The noises are growing now, loud hisses, high screams.

EXT. CANAL, FREDERICKSBURG, MOMENTS LATER – TWILIGHT

Chamberlain's regiment is bunched together on the bank of the canal.

> **CHAMBERLAIN** (*calling out a command*)
> Hold up the line, halt!

Chamberlain moves out by himself, closer to the canal, looks at the small fragile planks, the last line of the Second Brigade crossing, forming again on the far side.

The lines of the flanking regiment are lagging a hundred yards behind. Ames is with them, in front, yelling angrily, bringing them on.

> **CHAMBERLAIN** (*Cont'd*)
> Get up here, on the right flank! Step it up!

He steps onto the small bridge, his men following.

Other officers are waving swords, and now the men jump into the water, either side of the bridge. Already lying in the canal are thick masses of blue-coated men.

EXT. CANAL, FREDERICKSBURG – TWILIGHT

At the far end of the canal there is a bright flash. A rebel battery is enfilading them, firing straight down the canal.

EXT. CANAL, FREDERICKSBURG – TWILIGHT

Another great splash of water blows over the small bridge and men below him are suddenly swept away.

Chamberlain is caught up in the heavy flow of men, pushes through, moves out in front waving his sword. Tom and Kilrain hurry to Chamberlain's side.

EXT. CANAL, FREDERICKSBURG – TWILIGHT

The 20th Maine spreads out again, forming the lines, and again they march forward.

> **CHAMBERLAIN**
> Twentieth Maine! Forward! Keep it up.

They are in the thick of it now. The whiz of the musket ball, the hot whoosh of streaking shrapnel.

EXT. HILLS ABOVE FREDERICKSBURG, THE DEPRESSION – TWILIGHT

Chamberlain and his men reach the depression in the ground. In front, on the shallow rise, men in blue are crouching down, some with muskets, firing, reloading, vast numbers that are just bodies.

Beyond is the stone wall.

There is a burst of flame from the wall, another Confederate volley. Around Chamberlain, men fall, and he aims his pistol, fires, and fires again. Tom and Kilrain are at his side, firing as quickly as they can.

TOM (*repeating the re-loading drill, under his breath*)
One, Two, Three, Four...

EXT. STONE WALL, FREDERICKSBURG – TWILIGHT
The four ranks at the wall take turns firing, stepping back, reloading, stepping up, and firing again, in an almost continuous fire.

EXT. FIELD BEFORE STONE WALL, FREDERICKSBURG – TWILIGHT
Just as with the preceding waves of Federal attackers, Griffin's Third Brigade, Stockton's, is stopped and withering away in front of the hellish fire. Kilrain grabs Tom by the arm and pulls him down.

> **TOM**
> What'd you do that for?

> **KILRAIN**
> You'll thank me in the mornin'.

A shot Maine man falls across Kilrain. One eye has been blown away, the other stares Kilrain right in his face.

EXT. FIELD BEFORE STONE WALL, FREDERICKSBURG – TWILIGHT
Ames is at another part of the line. A YOUNG CORPORAL steps up to him and salutes. His left arm has been blown away.

> **YOUNG CORPORAL**
> Request permission to return to the rear, sir.

> **AMES** (*somewhat incredulous*)
> Permission granted.

The corporal turns and nonchalantly walks back down the hill.

EXT. FIELD BEFORE STONE WALL, FREDERICKSBURG – TWILIGHT
Chamberlain is down on one knee, firing, but he's out of bullets. He rolls over onto his back, trying to reload on the ground. A WOUNDED MAINE MAN collapses on top of him. Blood oozes over Chamberlain.

> **WOUNDED MAINE MAN**
> Oh, my mother! Oh, Mother help me!

> **CHAMBERLAIN**
> Is that you, Casey? I've got a hold of you, boy. I'll get you home.

The wounded man groans, twitches, and is dead. Chamberlain gently pushes him off.

EXT. FIELD BEFORE STONE WALL, FREDERICKSBURG – TWILIGHT
Kilrain, keeping prone, removes his blanket roll, placing it above his head, as if to provide protection against the hail of bullets digging up the dirt on all sides.

> **TOM**
> You think a blanket'll stop a bullet?

> **KILRAIN**
> Six layers of Irish wool have blunted the blow of many a claymore, and I'd as soon take my chances with it than without.

EXT. FIELD BEFORE STONE WALL, FREDERICKSBURG – TWILIGHT
The last men left standing before the stone wall are either shot or take cover behind the shallow depression in the ground. Some of the prone men continue to fire from this position, but as loading the musket becomes a lethal proposition, even this return fire is suppressed. Griffin's Third Brigade has been decimated and utterly repulsed.

EXT. TELEGRAPH HILL, FREDERICKSBURG – TWILIGHT
Lee, Longstreet and their aides look out over the whole of the battlefield...

LEE'S POV, MARYE'S HEIGHTS BATTLEFIELD – TWILIGHT
...the smoldering town, the Federal soldiers pinned down before the stone wall, and the piles of blue-uniformed corpses. More than seven thousand dead.

EXT. TELEGRAPH HILL, FREDERICKSBURG – TWILIGHT

> **LEE**
> It is well that war is so terrible. We should grow too fond of it.

INTERMISSION

INT. BEALE HOUSE – FREDERICKSBURG – NIGHT
Loud knocking. Martha, again dressed in her own clothes, opens the door. A SURGEON with two stretcher bearers and a wounded man step inside.

> **SURGEON**
> We're requisitioning your house for use as a hospital.

Martha's attitude is entirely different than her reaction to the looters. She opens wide the door and leads them into the parlor.

> **MARTHA**
> Come inside and out of the cold. Y'all jes come in to the parlor.

Two more wounded men are carried into the house. Martha collects blankets and towels, taking them to the parlor.

> **SURGEON**
> Water, ma'am. Where's your well?

> **MARTHA**
> This way.

EXT. BEALE HOUSE – NIGHT
The streets are filled with the walking wounded and exhausted soldiers, lying in doorways and huddled around fires in the middle of the street. Hancock rides up the street alongside an ambulance, which stops before the Beale house.

HANCOCK
Put these wounded here.

Hancock dismounts as the stretcher bearers carry in two more injured soldiers. He follows them into the house.

INT. BEALE HOUSE – NIGHT
Martha and her children are helping the surgeons as best they can.

HANCOCK
Surgeon, this man is Major Sidney Willard of the 35th Massachusetts.

The bearers lift WILLARD onto the piano-forte. His chest is covered with blood. The surgeon takes a look, closes Willard's coat, and simply shakes his head.

SURGEON
He's been shot twice in the chest. I've no chloroform, General. There's nothing I can do.

HANCOCK
Is there whisky in this house?

Martha nods, then reaches under a floorboard, where she retrieves a bottle of whisky, which she promptly opens and takes to the dying man's lips.

MARTHA
Drink this, child. You'll feel a might better.

Willard takes a sip, coughs. Martha puts a damp towel to his forehead.

MARTHA (Cont'd) (as she tends dying soldier)
Think not, with thyself that thou shalt escape in the king's house, more than all the Jews. For if thou altogether holdest thy peace at this time, then shall there enlargement and deliverance arise to the Jews from another place; but thou and thy father's house shall be destroyed: and who knoweth whether thou art come to the kingdom for such a time as this?

HANCOCK
That's from the Book of Esther.

MARTHA
Esther knew that it was not enough to save herself. That she must save her people as well... I love the folks you have chased out of this house. I have known them all my life. The Beales are good people.
(fixing her eyes on Hancock)
I was born a slave. My own children were born as slaves. What ever you are doing here...what ever must be done for my children to grow up in freedom in a free country — may God bless you for it. Heaven help me, but may God bless you all.

WILLARD'S blood seeps onto the piano keys.

The surgeon is at the next litter, examining a TERRIBLY WOUNDED MAN.

SURGEON
His arms have to come off, both of them.

WOUNDED MAN
Oh God , no, don't take my arms!

Martha rounds up her three children.

MARTHA
Come with me, children, time's come for you to go to bed.

She hustles them out of the room and up the stairs.

INT. BEDROOM, BEALE HOUSE – NIGHT
Martha gets her children into Jane's bedroom and shuts the door. A frightful scream of pain reverberates through the house. She holds her children tight in her arms, covering their ears, trying to shut out the hideous cries.

EXT. HILLS ABOVE FREDERICKSBURG, DEPRESSION – NIGHT
What is left of the Twentieth Maine is lying in groups in the depression, shivering with cold. Many are wounded. We hear the moans, and occasional screams of pain.

Chamberlain is lying down. He raises his head, tries to look round.

GRIFFIN'S AIDE (O.S.)
Colonel Chamberlain, Colonel Chamberlain.

CHAMBERLAIN
Here. Quietly.

GRIFFIN'S AIDE is crawling, trying to keep as low as possible. He approaches Chamberlain.

GRIFFIN'S AIDE
My God, sir. What a terrible place.

He looks round at the heaps of corpses.

GRIFFIN'S AIDE (Cont'd)
Colonel, your orders are to hold this position.

CHAMBERLAIN
Thank you, Captain. We'll do our best. You may return downhill. Keep low.

The Aide crawls away.

Chamberlain begins to shiver, flexes his fingers, wraps himself with his arms, and now shivers more. He raises his head just slightly and looks around him — a great field of black shapes. He begins to move, slides along the hard ground, moves up alongside one of the shapes.

CHAMBERLAIN (Cont'd) (in a low, hoarse voice)
You, there. Are you wounded?

He waits, then reaches out a hand, touches the blue cloth, prods harder, pokes the man's stiff body.

CHAMBERLAIN (*Cont'd*)
Truly sorry, old fellow.

He slides closer, presses his body up against the mass, grabs the man's loose coat, unwraps the body slightly, pulls a flap out over him and slides to another mass a few feet up the rise, prods again, and again waits for a reply, which does not come. Chamberlain slides back down, grabbing the man's foot, pulling him down the hill, and putting him on his other side, pulls another flap of coat out over him, covering his face.

EXT. HILLS ABOVE FREDERICKSBURG, DEPRESSION – NIGHT
Tom crawls up to a man wrapped tightly in a corpse's coat. He strikes a match to examine the face. It is Chamberlain.

CHAMBERLAIN
Damn it, Tom! You scared me half to death!

TOM
Me? I thought you was with the beyond.

INT. HOSPITAL TENT, FREDERICKSBURG – NIGHT
Jane Beale helps soothe the wounded with damp cloths to their foreheads. Lucy Beale enters, confiding to her mother.

LUCY
I was able to secure the aid of a good spyglass and could ascertain beyond all doubt that our house is still standing.

JANE BEALE
I pray God for Martha and her dear ones.

LUCY
But oh, Mother, it is a pitiful sight on the fields below Marye's Heights. I should feel rancor in my heart for those invaders, but all I can feel for them is sorrow.

JANE BEALE
Dear Lucy, when you were but a child in petticoats, I believe the year was 1847, there was a great famine in Ireland. Those fields below the heights were covered with the finest crop of corn ever raised in this section. The greater part of it was sent as a donation to the starving Irish. I cannot help thinking but that it helped to feed some of the poor victims of the Irish Brigade who fell on this very field today.

Nearby, General Maxcy Gregg is badly wounded, lying on a cot. Dr. McGuire is bending over him. Jackson, and Smith, come to the bedside. McGuire shakes his head.

GREGG (*speaking with difficulty*)
General, I wish to apologize for the differences we had ...

Jackson takes Gregg's hand.

JACKSON
The doctor tells me that you have not long to live. Let me ask you to dismiss this matter from your mind and turn your thoughts to God and the world to which you go.

Gregg's eyes fill with tears. Jackson, too, has difficulty in controlling his emotion.

GREGG
You know, General, that I am not a believer.

JACKSON
Then I will believe for the both of us.

EXT. HOSPITAL TENT, FREDERICKSBURG – NIGHT
Jackson, Smith, and McGuire come out. They start to mount their horses. Jackson stops, seems to momentarily lose his breath.

JACKSON
How horrible is war.

McGUIRE
Horrible, yes. But we have been invaded. What can we do?

JACKSON (*grimly, his jaw set*)
Kill them, sir! Kill every last man of them!

EXT. HILLS ABOVE FREDERICKSBURG, DEPRESSION – DAWN
Fine mist. There is a burst of musket fire from the Confederate lines.

Chamberlain wakes suddenly, pulls the corpses' coats off him, tries to look round, carefully, keeping his head down.

He crawls forward, looks toward the Confederate lines.

EXT. POV OF CONFEDERATE LINES – DAWN
They have stopped shooting, and there are signs that they are eating breakfast — smoke from cooking fires.

EXT. HILLS ABOVE FREDERICKSBURG, DEPRESSION – DAWN

KILRAIN (*sniffing the breeze*)
Oh, what I wouldn't give for a cup of "Rio" just now.

Suddenly, there is a flurry of musket fire. Confederates are firing into the flank of the Twentieth Maine.

CHAMBERLAIN
Twentieth Maine! Return fire!

The 20th Maine are being enfiladed. They return fire. Spontaneously, without orders, the troops hurry to pile the many corpses into a breastwork, behind which they take up firing positions.

As Kilrain drags a body to pile on the breastwork, he sees the face. It is Patrick. Kilrain registers who it is. He pauses a moment, and crosses himself. Then continues.

KILRAIN
Ah Patrick, hope ye don't mind. I know yer in Heaven, but yer ain't done yet wit' t'e fight down here, in t'is poor pitiless world. I'd do t'e same for you, me boy, I'd do t'e same for you.

Kilrain notices SECOND MAINE SOLDIER pressing himself from a prone position on his forearms.

> **KILRAIN** *(Cont'd)*
> Keep your head down, soldier.

But Kilrain's call is too late. Although 2nd Maine Soldier has only raised half of his body, while his lower half still lies on the ground, he receives a bullet in the forehead, and dies immediately.

From behind the grisly barricade, the 20th Maine tries to keep up desultory fire on the Confederates.

EXT. HILLS ABOVE FREDERICKSBURG, DEPRESSION – NIGHT

The 20th Maine are still in position, using barricades of corpses to protect them.

GRIFFIN'S AIDE crawls gingerly up to Chamberlain.

> **GRIFFIN'S AIDE**
> Your orders are to withdraw, Colonel. Withdraw to the city.

The night sky is suddenly lit up brilliantly by a display of the aurora borealis. Chamberlain, Tom and the aide are transfixed at the sight.

POV AURORA BOREALIS

EXT. CONFEDERATE LINES, OUTSIDE LEE'S TENT, FREDERICKSBURG – NIGHT

Lee, Jackson, and Longstreet stand watching the brilliant display that fills the sky.

POV AURORA BOREALIS

EXT. TOWN STREET, FREDERICKSBURG – NIGHT

The 20th Maine reach the ruined buildings, and look for places to rest. Chamberlain sits against a wall, exhausted. Ames approaches.

> **AMES**
> Colonel, we are ordered to form a picket line, and cover the army's retreat across the river.

Chamberlain stares at him for a moment, blankly.

> **AMES** *(Cont'd)*
> Colonel Chamberlain, did you hear me?

> **CHAMBERLAIN**
> Yes sir, we're to retreat, sir.

Chamberlain stands, pulls himself together.

> **CHAMBERLAIN** *(Cont'd)*
> Captain Spear, form the regiment, we're moving out.

EXT. LEE'S TENT, TELEGRAPH HILL, FREDERICKSBURG, DEC 15 – PRE-DAWN

Fog. Lee comes out of his tent, stands, wrapping his arms round himself to get warm. Breakfast is being served. Pendleton rides up, dismounts. He walks with a slight limp.

> **PENDLETON**
> Good morning, General. General Jackson offers his respects and reports the enemy's no longer in front of his position, sir.

> **LEE**
> Go on, Mister Pendleton.

> **PENDLETON**
> General, the enemy has withdrawn back across the river. The pontoon bridges are gone, sir, cut loose from the bank.

> **LEE** *(to Taylor)*
> Major, summon General Longstreet. I want to know what's down below us here. I do not wish to wait for the fog to lift. Captain Pendleton, you may return to General Jackson. Please express my appreciation for his diligence. And please remind General Jackson we do not wish to give the enemy an opportunity by exposing our troops to those guns on Stafford Heights. When the fog lifts, any advance will surely receive a concentration of his artillery fire.

> **PENDLETON**
> Yes, sir.

> **LEE**
> Mister Pendleton, I am told you received a wound to your thigh. I trust it is not serious.

> **PENDLETON**
> Thank you for asking, sir. Just a flesh wound. Not serious at all.

Lee smiles, nods. Pendleton salutes and leaves.

EXT. TOWN STREETS, FREDERICKSBURG – DAY

The fog is gone. Lee, Longstreet, Old Penn, Von Borke and Stuart are riding together through the devastated town. In front of them nervous skirmishers move through the streets, probing through the remains of the houses, making sure there are no snipers waiting.

They ride on, round a corner, and see the full impact of the devastation — piles of debris, shattered furniture. Children's toys, doll houses, rocking horses — strewn everywhere with ripped drapes, split open bedding, bed frames, smashed furniture. Clouds of feathers from torn bedding and pillows swirl and float in the air, creating a surreal effect, as if the soldiers are moving through a dream, or inside a sealed glass ball of snowflakes.

Under the horses' hooves the sound of broken glass. They weave their way through piles of collapsed bricks, past mirrors smashed from their frames, paintings ripped and torn, dresses, men's suits, a bridal gown — soaking up muddy water.

And everywhere the corpses of the men in blue left behind.

Lee stops, closes his eyes, lowers his head. As the entourage is stopped in the middle of the ruins, civilians, mostly blacks and elderly whites, come out of the half ruined buildings. Martha and her children stand in front of the Beale house door.

An OLD WHITE MAN hobbles out into the street, barely able to stand with the support of his cane. He addresses Lee.

> **OLD MAN**
> Yankees eve'where, eve'where. Where y'all been? Cain't find ma own house! Gone! Gone! What y'all done wid ma house? Where is it? Where is it? C'n y'all tell me that? Well, c'n ya? C'n ya?

All around is desolation.

EXT. PONTOON BRIDGE – DAY
The Twentieth Maine retreats across the bridge.

EXT. NORTH BANK OF THE RAPPAHANNOCK, NEAR FREDRICKSBURG – DAY
The 20th Maine trudges up a hill.

> **CHAMBERLAIN**
> Twentieth Maine. Halt. Fall out, and rest.

The exhausted men collapse on the ground more or less immediately. Chamberlain sits down with his back against a tree. General JOSEPH HOOKER and his aides ride slowly by. On seeing Chamberlain, he stops.

> **HOOKER**
> You've had a hard chance, Colonel. I am glad to see you out of it.

> **CHAMBERLAIN**
> It was chance, General. Not much intelligent design there.

> **HOOKER**
> God knows I did not put you in.

> **CHAMBERLAIN**
> That was the trouble, General. You should have put us in, sir. We were handed in piecemeal on toasting-forks.

Hooker doesn't take the remark as insubordination. He simply nods, and moves on.

EXT. CONFEDERATE CAMP, NEAR FREDERICKSBURG – NIGHT
Jim Lewis and Washington are finishing constructing a rude coffin. Nearby a group of BLACKS huddles around a campfire humming "Steal Away to Jesus," with a BLACK BANJO PLAYER.

> **JIM LEWIS**
> What you be doin' now your massa dead?

> **WASHINGTON**
> Done already tole you he my boss, not my massa.

> **JIM LEWIS**
> Well, one way or t'otha he gone now.

> **WASHINGTON**
> Nothin' much left for me in Virginny. My brother done run off wi'de Yankees. He in Chambersburg now, up north in Pennsylvania.

> **JIM LEWIS**
> You plannin' on gettin' up dat way?

> **WASHINGTON**
> Once I gets dis body up to his kin in Winchester I sees de way things is.

Jim and Washington lift a shrouded corpse into the coffin.

> **JIM LEWIS**
> Good thing fo you your "boss" get killed in de winter time. Dat's a long way to be carryin' a man in a pine box.

Washington places a sword, sash and hat over the corpse.

> **WASHINGTON**
> White folks be killin' one a'toth'a fo' a while yet. Dey still plenty mad and plenty of 'em. All I knows is dis here rebel give me my freedom papers. He already wid Jesus. I jes takin' him home.

EXT. FEDERAL ENCAMPMENT, STONEMAN'S SWITCH – DAY
The Third Brigade stands in formation. An ADJUTANT reads aloud from a text.

> **ADJUTANT**
> Message to the Army of the Potomac, from the President of the United States. "Men of the army, although you were not successful in the recent battle, the attempt was not an error, nor the failure other than an accident. No soldiers in the annals of war fought more bravely. Condoling with the mourners for the dead, and sympathizing with the severely wounded, I congratulate the army that the numbers of casualties have been comparatively so small."

> **KILRAIN** (*under his breath*)
> Compared to what? The Scots at Culloden? The English at Bunker Hill? The French at Waterloo?

> **ADJUTANT**
> "I tender to you, officers and soldiers, the thanks of the nation." Signed, Abraham Lincoln. Brigade, dismissed!

The men break ranks. Kilrain keeps company with Tom.

> **KILRAIN**
> At this Christmas season, when good fairies fill the air, we can hardly wonder at the sudden miracle which has shown us the Fredericksburg affair in its true light, and given us occasion for national joy instead of national sorrow.

EXT. WOODS, MOSS NECK – DAY
A small Confederate detachment moves through the falling snow,

pulling a caisson, on top of which is a newly felled evergreen of about twelve feet. They ride up to …

EXT. MOSS NECK MANOR – DAY

… A red brick manse in the style of an English country estate. The men lift the tree from the caisson …

INT. MOSS NECK MANOR – DAY, CHRISTMAS, 1862

The evergreen stands resplendent, decorated for Christmas. A fire roars in the hearth. Twelve officers are present, including Lee, Longstreet, Jackson, Stuart, Pendleton, Smith, Taylor, Major Von Borke, William Nelson Pendleton, Colonels CHARLES VENABLE and CHARLES FAULKNER, Majors John Pelham and Charles Marshall, Capt. JOHN ESTEN COOKE, and Lt. GEORGE PETERKIN.

Roberta Corbin, the hostess, sits near the fireplace between her two relations, her five-year-old daughter Jane and her unmarried sister-in-law Catherine, now 23. Catherine has caught the eye of Sandie Pendleton. With Jane Beale looking on, Lucy Beale plays "Angels Watch Over Me" at the piano. Sam and Julian Beale are also present. Jackson admires the decorations on the tree. Little Jane Corbin goes to him.

> **JANE**
> General Jackson. Do you know what these decorations signify?
>
> **JACKSON**
> I was wondering if someone would tell me.
>
> **JANE**
> This is Santa's sled. And this is his staff, made of candy. This is a gingerbread snowflake and this a paper chain of angels.
>
> **JACKSON**
> How old are you, Jane?
>
> **JANE**
> I'm five years old. How old are you?
>
> **JACKSON**
> I'm thirty-eight.
>
> **JANE**
> My father is thirty-eight. He is a soldier like you. I haven't seen him for more than a year.
>
> **JACKSON**
> I've not met him. But I am told he is a very good man. A very brave man. I'm sure he misses you very much, as I miss my daughter.
>
> **JANE**
> When did you last see your daughter?
>
> **JACKSON**
> I've never seen her. She was born just days ago. I want to see her more than anything in the world. I want to see her as much as your father wants to see you.

JANE
You see that star at the top of the tree?

JACKSON
The star of Bethlehem. The star that showed the wise men how they could find the baby Jesus.

JANE
Mother says that star will show Daddy how to find his way back home.

JACKSON (*his voice cracking*)
Your mother is a very wise and a very good person. Your daddy will come home. All the daddies will come home.

Lucy Beale has finished her solo, to the applause of the guests.

ROBERTA CORBIN
We Southern women have been called upon for more manly duties since our husbands have gone off to war. So permit me to stand in for Mister Corbin, who, if he were here, would propose this toast:

She lifts her glass; all rise. She addresses each man as she speaks his name.

ROBERTA CORBIN (*Cont'd*)
"So a health to Stonewall Jackson,
To Longstreet, brave as steel;
To Stuart with the fearless soul,
A knight from plume to heel.
And last to Lee, our General,
Beneath whose flag we go,
To test the edge of Southern steel
On a vulgar, brutal foe.
Though all the hounds of ruin howl,
Our nation shall be free.
For the Red Cross flag is borne aloft,
By the stalwart hand of Lee!"

The group applauds. Lee steps forward, with a slight bow to Roberta Corbin.

LEE
It is a fine toast, Mrs. Corbin. But woefully incomplete. Gentlemen, let us lift our glasses to our Southern women, without whose fortitude and courage, without whose endurance and sacrifice not a man among us could stay the course or defend the cause.

The men exclaim "Hear, hear," and all sip their drinks.

JANE BEALE
Now, it's time for a carol. Come up, everyone must sing!

Jane Corbin takes Jackson by the hand, leading him to the piano.

JANE
Carols are my favorite!

JACKSON
But I can't sing.

Roberta Corbin has overheard his last remark.

ROBERTA CORBIN
Of course you can sing, Mister Jackson. You can breathe, can't you? Just let your breath flow gently over your vocal chords and nature does the rest.

STUART
I'm afraid General Jackson's voice is more suited to the battle-field than the parlor! You may take my word on it, Mrs. Corbin.

The officers have a good laugh at Jackson's expense. He turns red as a beet.

JACKSON (*stammering*)
If it's singing you want, my adjutant Mister Pendleton is your man. We've made our way through the hymnal together, and he always takes up where I leave off.

Catherine opens the book of carols, offering it to Sandie Pendleton, who is smitten by her attention.

CATHERINE
Well then, Mister Pendleton, since the general has appointed you cappelmeister, what shall we sing?

PENDLETON (*leafing through the pages*)
"Silent Night."

Lucy begins the introduction on the piano, as the group clusters around her. Jackson lifts Jane Corbin in his arms. They all sing the carol.

EXT. CONFEDERATE CAMP, WINTER QUARTERS, NEAR FEDRICKSBURG – DUSK
The music of the carol continues as snow falls over the thousands of mud huts, log shacks and campfires of the Confederate army.

EXT. FEDERAL CAMP, WINTER QUARTERS, STONEMAN'S SWITCH – DUSK
The music of the carol continues as snow falls over the encampment of the Army of the Potomac. A low, dull haze of pine smoke rests over the scene, fed by the burning fuel of thousands of interior fires from the city of makeshift dwellings.

CHAMBERLAIN (*V.O.*)
Dearest Fanny, The bugle has just sounded, Third Brigade, extinguish lights. It makes me happy to think of you and my dear little ones at home, all nestled together...

INT. CHAMBERLAIN'S TENT, STONEMAN'S SWITCH – NIGHT
Chamberlain is writing a letter by candle light,

CHAMBERLAIN
...I know that it is all well and bright with her whose sweet face shines in my heart. Come and let me kiss your dear lips, precious wife. Let our hearts worship together God's

love and wisdom and mercy. Yes, all is well — well with us, darling — well if we can only meet at last, as I pray God we may, never to part again.

INT. CHAMBERLAIN HOUSE, BRUNSWICK, MAINE – NIGHT
Fanny reads the letter.

EXT. JACKSON'S HDQS, MOSS NECK MANOR, WINTER '63 – DAY
Three Confederates, hands bound, are marched by under guard. Sandie Pendleton enters the headquarters.

INT. JACKSON'S HDQS, MOSS NECK MANOR – DAY

> **PENDLETON**
> Sir, the men have rounded up three deserters.

> **JACKSON**
> Establish the courts-martial. Have them arraigned. See that they are given a fair hearing.

> **PENDLETON**
> Yes sir. I thought you should know, sir, they all belong to the Stonewall Brigade.

Jackson flinches, as though he'd been viciously slapped. He catches his breath.

> **JACKSON**
> Do your duty, soldier.

Pendleton is about to leave.

> **JACKSON** *(Cont'd)*
> Mister Pendleton. If these men are innocent, they will go free. But if they are guilty of desertion, and the courts-martial condemns them to death, it must be so.

> **PENDLETON**
> Yes, sir. Of course, sir.

> **JACKSON**
> If the Republicans lose their little war, they are voted out in their next election. They return to their homes in New York and Massachusetts and Illinois fat with their war profits. If we lose, we lose our country, we lose our independence. We lose it all. Our soldiers are brave. They have endured hardships none of them could ever have imagined. Desertion is not a solitary crime. It is a crime against the tens of thousands of veterans who are huddled together in the harsh cold of this winter. Against all those who have sacrificed. Against all those who have fallen. Against all the women and children we've left alone to fend for themselves. I regard the crime of desertion as a sin against the army of the Lord. Duty is ours. The consequences are God's.

EXT. CONFEDERATE ENCAMPMENT, NEAR FEDRICKSBURG, WINTER 1863 – DAY
Under a gray sky on a blisteringly cold day, an entire division is assembled in a three-sided formation. The Stonewall Brigade faces the open side. The fifers and drummers play "The Rogue's March." Three men, hands tied behind their backs, stand facing the brigade. One of the condemned is George Jenkins of the 4th Virginia Regiment. Immediately behind them are three freshly dug graves. Each man is blindfolded.

> **A LIEUTENANT**
> The Courts-Martial of the Army of Northern Virginia has found you guilty of desertion and sentences you to death by firing squad.

> **A CAPTAIN**
> Firing squad, forward march!

Twelve riflemen from the center of the Stonewall Brigade march forward to within twenty paces of the condemned.

> **A CAPTAIN** *(Cont'd)*
> Squad, halt!

Jackson, Pendleton and Smith can be seen standing just beyond the formation.

> **A CAPTAIN** *(Cont'd)*
> Ready, aim, fire!

The three condemned men topple into the open graves. We see Jackson, his jaw locked, betraying no emotion.

EXT. PICKET LINE, RAPPAHANNOCK RIVER, NEAR FREDERICKSBURG – DAY
Deep winter. Snow thick on the ground. Pogue, McClintock and other soldiers warm their hands around a fire. Someone is singing quietly in the background, from campfires across the river. Pogue sighs deeply, then rolls a tobacco leaf, strolls over to the water's edge.

> **POGUE**
> Hey, Billy Yank!

The singing stops.

> **POGUE** *(Cont'd)*
> That's a might' nice song!

> **FEDERAL SOLDIER** *(V.O.)*
> I'm pleased you find it so agreeable!

> **POGUE**
> I'd like it even more with some coffee to wash it down. You want some 'baccy?

A FEDERAL SOLDIER emerges from the woods on the far side of the river.

> **FEDERAL SOLDIER**
> Sure, Johnny. Have you got a lame horse?

> **POGUE**
> What would you be wantin' to trade for a lame horse?

FEDERAL SOLDIER
Would you take General Burnside?

Muffled laughter from the Yankee side of the river.

POGUE
Guess I'll keep the horse-hide. Come an' git yer 'baccy.

Here the river is fordable, strewn with large boulders. Pogue and the Yank leave their muskets on their respective banks and stride out...

EXT. RAPPAHANNOCK RIVER, NEAR FREDERICKSBURG – DAY

... to the middle of the river, where they meet on a large shelf of rock. Pogue hands the tobacco to the Yankee, who hands Pogue a steaming tin cup of coffee. The Yankee lights up. One drinks, the other smokes, both savoring the exotic delight in the middle of the icy river. Without shaking hands, without a further word, with only a hesitant smile, Pogue hands back the cup and they each return their own way.

INT. JACKSON'S HDQS, MOSS NECK MANOR – DAY

Jackson is sitting at a small table covered with a pile of reports. He stares at a blank page, holds a pencil tightly, starts to write, stops. Picks up his personal Bible, leafs through.

Smith enters. Jackson looks up, relieved at any interruption to report-writing.

JACKSON
Did you know the Bible gives models for official battle reports?

SMITH
No, sir.

JACKSON
Nevertheless, there are such. Look at the narrative of Joshua's battles with the Amalakites. It has clearness, brevity, modesty; and it traces the victory to the right source — the blessing of God.

SMITH
Has it helped you with your reports, sir?

We hear a child's giggle. Through the flaps comes a small pink hand, then more, a tiny face, a beaming smile. Jackson kneels down, surprises the little girl — Jane — with a quick grab, pulls her up and into the tent, and she bursts into loud and happy laughter. He holds the child up above him, toward the top of the tent. She reaches for the hat on his chair, and he sets her down.

JACKSON
No, child, you can't have my hat. It's much too large for you.

He removes it, sees the strip of gold braid wound around the hat, pulls, and it comes loose in his hand. He tosses the hat aside, wraps the gold braid around the girl's head and ties it up around the fine golden hair.

JACKSON *(Cont'd)*
Well, now, I believe that suits a young girl better than an old soldier.

She laughs again, touching the braid.

JACKSON *(Cont'd)*
Now, I was just about to go for some lemonade. I would very much like the company of one beautiful little lady.

She nods, smiling brightly.

JACKSON *(Cont'd)*
Mister Smith, you may continue writing the report. Consult First and Second Samuel, and First and Second Kings. They will be of help to you.

...and he leads her out of the tent, leaving Smith with the paperwork.

EXT. CONFEDERATE ENCAMPMENT, NEAR FREDERICKS-BURG – DAY

A makeshift stage has been set up. Thousands of soldiers are crowded around a "USO style" camp show in progress. In the first row of spectators are Jackson, Hood and his TEXANS, Colonel PATTON, Pendleton, Smith, McGuire, Paxton and Von Borcke.

PATTON
We owe your Texas boys a debt of gratitude for putting on these shows.

HOOD
Colonel Patton, any man that cain't handle a guitar or a fiddle ain't fit to carry a musket.

HARRY MacCARTHY and LOTTIE ESTELLE do their 'personations of President and Mrs. Lincoln to the roar of the soldiers.

LOTTIE
And now, my gallant friends, my own dear beau will sing a verse of his original creation, and invites you to all j'ine in on the chorus. "The Bonnie Blue Flag!"

The crowd roars their approval, amid Texas "yeehas" and rebel yells. The minstrel band strikes up the introduction. Blue flags are lifted in the audience.

HARRY MacCARTHY
We are a band of brothers/And native to the soil/Fighting for our liberty/Through famine, war and toil/And when our rights were threaten'd/The cry rose near and far, "Hurrah for the Bonnie Blue Flag/That bears a single star."

AUDIENCE
Hurrah! Hurrah! for Southern rights, hurrah! Hurrah! for the Bonnie Blue Flag that bears a single star!

HARRY MacCARTHY
As long as the Union was faithful to her trust/Like friends and brethren were we, and just/But now, when Northern treachery attempts our rights to mar/We hoist on high the Bonnie Blue Flag that bears a single star.

AUDIENCE
Hurrah! Hurrah! for Southern rights, hurrah! Hurrah! for the Bonnie Blue Flag that bears a single star!

INT. CHAMBERLAIN'S TENT, STONEMAN'S SWITCH – DAY
Chamberlain is trimming his whiskers before a small pocket mirror. Tom enters with a newspaper.

TOM
Mornin', Lawrence.

CHAMBERLAIN
Any mail?

TOM
Nope. But I did manage to get a copy of the *New York Tribune*.

CHAMBERLAIN
What are they saying about us now?

TOM
Not much about us, that is, the army here in Stoneman's Switch. But there sure is a fuss over Lincoln's Emancipation Proclamation. Says here enlistments are down, desertions are up.

CHAMBERLAIN
Any grumbling among the men?

TOM
Well, not in our regiment. But there are some wonderin' out loud why they're supposed to be riskin' their lives for the darkies.

CHAMBERLAIN
Tom, you know my position. I signed up to preserve the Union. But I think the president did the right thing. What's the use of a uniting the country by force and leaving slavery in place?

TOM
It's gonna get them Johnny Rebs mighty riled up. It looks to them like old man Lincoln's inciting the slaves to rise up against them.

CHAMBERLAIN
And why shouldn't they? Freeing the slaves wasn't a war aim when all this began. But war changes things. Sorts things out. Things get clarified.

TOM
I don't know, Lawrence. Not everyone feels like we do about the darkies, especially when it comes to fightin' and dyin'.

CHAMBERLAIN
Do me a favor, Tom. Don't call me Lawrence, and don't call Negroes darkies. That's a patronizing expression from which we must free ourselves. Come outside. I want to show you something.

Chamberlain leads his brother out of the tent...

EXT. FEDERAL CAMP, STONEMAN'S SWITCH – DAY
...and up a small hill to a vantage point overlooking the encampment.

EXT. POV FEDERAL CAMP – DAY
Thousands of tents and makeshift huts.

EXT. FEDERAL CAMP, STONEMAN'S SWITCH – DAY

CHAMBERLAIN
All these thousands of men, many of them not much more than boys. Each one of them is some mother's son, some sister's brother, some daughter's father. Each one is a whole person loved and cherished in some home far away. Many of them will never return. An army is power. Its entire purpose is to coerce others. This kind of power must not be used carelessly or recklessly. This kind of power can do great harm. We've seen more suffering than any men should ever see, and if there's going to be an end to it, it must be an end that justifies the cost.

Chamberlain looks out...

EXT. POV WINTER WILDERNESS -DAY
...across the empty vastness, away from the Federal encampment.

EXT. FEDERAL CAMP, STONEMAN'S SWITCH – DAY

CHAMBERLAIN
Somewhere out there is the Confederate army. They claim they are fighting for their independence, for their freedom. I cannot question their integrity. I believe they are wrong, but I cannot question it. But I do question a system that defends its own freedom while it denies it to others — to an entire race of men. I will admit it Tom, war is a scourge. But so is slavery. It is the systematic coercion of one group of men over another. It is as old as the Book of Genesis and has existed in every corner of the globe. But that is no excuse for us to tolerate it here, when we find it before our very eyes, in our own country.

He puts an arm around his brother.

CHAMBERLAIN (*Cont'd*)
As God is my witness, there is no one I hold in my heart dearer than you. But if your life, or mine, is part of the price to end this curse and free the Negro, then let God's will be done.

EXT. PORCH, MOSS NECK MANOR (SPRING) – DAY
Catherine Corbin is stirring a pitcher of lemonade as Sandie Pendleton squeezes lemons. Jackson and Jane wait, the little girl reaching her hand high to hold his.

CATHERINE
My, General, we do appreciate the gift. Where do you get all these lemons?

JACKSON
It's a kind Providence that provides kindly. And Miss Corbin, those Yankees haven't closed our rail lines to the South.

She hands glasses to Jackson, Pendleton and Jane.

PENDLETON (*lifting his glass in a toast*)
Here's to the sultry, balmy South!

JACKSON
And here's to your engagement, Miss Corbin. May Mister Pendleton be as good a husband as he is a soldier.

Jackson lifts little Jane into his arms. They all toast and drink from their glasses. Then, wiping at wet chins, as if repeating a ritual, Jane and Jackson close their eyes.

JACKSON & JANE
Mmmmmmmmmmmmm!

CATHERINE
I swear, General, if you spoil your own child like that ... you'll have your hands fuller than a bushel basket in June.

EXT. PLANTATION HOUSE YARD, MOSS NECK – DAY
Jackson saunters out off the porch, carrying Jane on his shoulders. He makes the sounds of a horse, whinnying and snorting, as he hops about the yard, Jane giggling the whole time. Catherine and Pendleton have followed on the porch.

Not far away, Smith and SOLDIERS stare in utter amazement.

EXT. PLANTATION HOUSE YARD, MOSS NECK – DAY (MARCH 16)
Jackson's troops are drawn up in line, ready to march out. The tents are all struck.

Pendleton and Catherine are on the porch, taking their leave. Jackson steps up to Roberta Corbin.

JACKSON
Thank you, Mrs. Corbin, for your many kindnesses. Our cause and our country are in your debt.

ROBERTA CORBIN
I only regret, General, that we could not do more. Please visit us again, when this cruel war is over.

JACKSON
If you please, I'd like to say good-bye to your daughter. I shall miss her.

ROBERTA CORBIN
Certainly, General. She's not feeling well today. All the children have come down with a fever. Please, come in.

Jackson follows her into the house.

INT. CHILD'S BEDROOM, MOSS NECK MANOR – DAY
Jane Corbin is lying in bed. Jackson comes in, kneels down beside her. Roberta Corbin stands beside him.

JACKSON
Well, now, what's this? How can I play with my friend if she insists on staying in bed?

She can only faintly smile. He sees the look in her eyes, feels her forehead.

JACKSON (*Cont'd*)
I'll have my doctor, Dr. McGuire, attend to her. I'll send him immediately.

Roberta Corbin nods, grateful. He kisses Jane on her forehead.

EXT. JACKSON'S CAMP, NEAR FREDERICKSBURG – EVENING
Jackson and his staff come out of the mess tent.

SMITH (*to Harman*)
Fresh meat, what a change.

HARMAN
A live steer is as rare around these parts as a peacock in a poultry pen.

Pendleton and Doctor McGuire ride up, and dismount.

The smile fades from Jackson's face. He looks fiercely at McGuire.

McGUIRE (*in a low voice, to Jackson*)
It was scarlet fever. The children are all right. They'll be fine. Except... I'm terribly sorry, General. The little girl, Jane... did not survive. She died, sir.

Jackson stares at him, does not speak.

Abruptly, Jackson marches away from the tents, out into the field. Alone, Jackson sits on a tree stump. He puts his head in his hands and begins to sob.

Pendleton stays a short distance away. McGuire puts a hand on his arm.

PENDLETON
What is it? He's never cried before. Not for all the blood and all the death. Not for his young students from VMI, not for his friends, not for anyone.

McGuire nods quietly.

McGUIRE
Not so, Mister Pendleton. I think he's crying for them all.

They watch from a distance, in silence, as Jackson pours out his grief.

EXT. GUINEY RAILWAY STATION – DAY
Jackson rides in as the train arrives. A brass band plays "Dixie."

The crowd cheers at the first sight of Anna, who is carrying their baby JULIA. She is accompanied by her brother, JOSEPH G. MORRISON, and Hattie. Jackson sees his child for the first time.

INT. BEDROOM, YERBY HOUSE (BELVOIR) – DAY

Jackson and Anna enter their room. Jackson hurriedly throws off his overcoat, and takes the baby in his arms.

> **JACKSON**
> She's too pretty to look like me.

> **ANNA JACKSON**
> Nonsense, Thomas. She is very like you — she rises early and loves to be held in my arms.

Jackson smiles as he continues to caress the baby.

> **ANNA JACKSON** (Cont'd)
> I've never seen you look so well, Thomas. You're handsomer than ever.

EXT. GROVER'S THEATER, WASHINGTON CITY – EVENING (APRIL 11)

Posters affixed to the theater walls: "The Youngest Star In the World," "The Pride of the American People," "J. Wilkes Booth as Macbeth."

> **MARY TODD LINCOLN** (V.O.)
> Mr. Booth is in the city for the entire month. He is playing in Hamlet, Katherine and Petrucio, The Merchant of Venice, Richard the Third and Macbeth.

> **MORTON** (V.O.)
> What is your favorite, Mr. President?

> **LINCOLN** (V.O.)
> I think nothing equals Macbeth. I have read it many times.

A handsome carriage pulls up to the front. President and Mrs. Lincoln, accompanied by Senator OLIVER P. MORTON, descend the carriage and stroll to the entrance. THEATERGOERS notice the celebrities and politely applaud.

> **LINCOLN** (Cont'd)
> I am most curious to see Mister Booth's rendition.

> **MORTON**
> Indeed, I am told Booth does the death scene spectacularly. Very physical, wilder than his brother Edwin.

> **LINCOLN**
> That is one reproach I have of Shakespeare's heroes.

> **MARY TODD LINCOLN**
> What reproach is that, dear?

> **LINCOLN**
> They all make long speeches when they are killed.

Senator Morton and Mrs. Lincoln laugh at this remark, as they are ushered into the theater.

INT. GROVER'S THEATER, WASHINGTON CITY – EVENING

Booth is onstage in the role of Macbeth. Lincoln sits with his wife and the senator in the presidential box near the stage.

Booth appears to be staring directly at Lincoln as he declaims his soliloquy.

> **BOOTH** (as Macbeth)
> Is this a dagger which I see before me, The handle toward my hand? Come, let me clutch thee. I have thee not, and yet I see thee still. Art thou not, fatal vision, sensible To feeling as to sight? or art thou but A dagger of the mind, a false creation, Proceeding from the heat-oppressed brain? I see thee yet, in form as palpable As this which now I draw. Thou marshall'st be the way that I was going; And such an instrument I was to use. Mine eyes are made the fools o' the other senses, or else worth all the rest; I see thee still, And on thy blade and dudgeon gouts of blood, Which was not so before. There's no such thing: It is the bloody business which informs Thus to mine eyes...Whiles I threat, he lives: Words to the heat of deeds too cold breath gives.
> (a bell rings)
> I go, and it is done; the bell invites me. Hear it not, Duncan; for it is a knell That summons thee to heaven or to hell.

INT. GROVER'S THEATER, BACKSTAGE – EVENING

Booth and Harrison are removing their make-up. The STAGE MANAGER enters, all smiles.

> **STAGE MANAGER**
> Well, Mister Booth. Another triumph. The President and Mrs. Lincoln wish to see you.

Booth turns to the Stage Manager, with insolence.

> **BOOTH**
> You may tell that tyrant, that destroyer of civilian liberties, that warmonger — that I am indisposed!

The Stage Manager is stunned and immobile. Booth takes a deep breath.

> **BOOTH** (Cont'd)
> Better still, tell him nothing. Say that I'd already gone.

The stage manager, still rattled, nods and leaves the room.

> **HARRISON** (with a sense of irony)
> Golly gee, Booth. An endorsement from the President of the United States could be a big thing for your career.

Booth simply scowls.

INT. PARLOR, YERBY HOUSE – DAY

The baptism of Jackson's daughter Julia. Jackson holds the baby in his arms. Anna stands next to him. Then her brother Joseph Morrison, the members of the YERBY HOUSEHOLD, Jim Lewis, and Jackson's staff.

Chaplain Lacy takes the baby from Jackson's arms, and baptizes her.

> **LACY**
> Julia Laura, I baptize thee in the name of the Father, and of the Son, and of the Holy Ghost. Amen

We see the delight on Jackson's face, as he gently takes Julia back from Lacy.

INT. ANOTHER ROOM, YERBY HOUSE – DAY
Anna Jackson and Morrison watch a photographer, Mr. MINNIS, setting up his camera, ready to take a portrait. Pendleton enters.

> **ANNA JACKSON**
> He won't agree.

> **PENDLETON**
> Mr. Minnis, would you tell him you were sent from Richmond to take General Lee's photograph, but that General Lee declined, unless General Jackson's photograph was taken first.

> **MINNIS**
> Certainly, Captain Pendleton.

Jackson appears, holding Julia.

> **JACKSON**
> No photographs.

> **MINNIS**
> Sir, I was sent from Richmond to take a photograph of General Lee. But the General refused to have his photograph taken unless I took your photograph first.

> **PENDLETON**
> Sir, General Lee was most insistent on the importance of your photograph.

> **JACKSON**
> I cannot refuse General Lee's request. Where do you wish me to stand?

Handing the baby to Anna, he sits in the chair provided.

Minnis takes the photograph.

INT. BEDROOM, YERBY HOUSE (BELVOIR) – DAWN
The Jacksons are in bed, asleep. Little Julia is asleep in her crib. There is a tapping on the bedroom door.

> **JIM LEWIS** (O.S.)
> Mar'se Jackson, dere's an officer come to see you, sah. He need to see you now, sah.

Jackson is quickly awake. He snatches up his clothes, kisses Anna softly, then steps over to the crib. Tenderly, so as not to awake her, he ever so gently kisses his child.

EXT. LEE'S HDQS, CHANCELLORSVILLE – EVENING
SUPER TITLE: The Wilderness, May 1st, 1863

Lee and Jackson are seated on cracker boxes. They lean over another box which serves as a map table, illuminated by the nearby campfire. They speak in low voices.

> **LEE**
> General, from what we've observed, Hooker has moved five corps, maybe seventy thousand men. They are digging in around Chancellor mansion. Sedgwick has another forty thousand spread out along the Stafford Heights on the north bank of the Rappahannock in front of General Early at Fredericksburg. There are possibly thirty thousand more back along the river, north of here, that we have not yet located. We're not in a position of strength here. We owe a great deal to the unexplainable, to the mystery of General Hooker. He's allowed us to manoeuvre freely between two parts of an army that's more than twice our strength. I'm concerned. We do not yet understand his plan.
>
> He may yet be planning a move toward Gordonsville, move around below us, to cut us off from Richmond. We must not forget about General Sedgwick, on the river. Sedgwick shows no signs of moving, but that could change. They're anchored against the river, up here. Their line's continuous, down below Chancellorsville, then curves along here.

> **JACKSON**
> Yes, we observed — their lines curve around these open clearings, then toward the west.

> **LEE**
> Then what, General? D'you know where their right flank is?

> **JACKSON**
> No. Not yet.

> **LEE**
> We must know, General. If he marches in that direction, he could threaten our flank, or be gone toward Gordonsville before we can react.

Horses arrive at a gallop. A small squad of cavalry and the tall dark plume on Stuart's hat. He jumps from his horse.

> **STUART**
> General, sir.

He strides over and points to the map.

> **STUART** (Cont'd)
> Out here, to the west — along the turnpike here — their right flank is in the air. It's the one place they're not digging in. Clearly, they do not expect any pressure there.

Lee glances at Jackson, leans closer to the map.

> **LEE**
> Who's on their flank?

> **STUART**
> The Eleventh Corps, Oliver Howard.

Lee continues to look at the map, reaches a hand out.

> **LEE**
> Are there any roads, down this way, below the turnpike?

STUART
Yes, sir, indeed there are. Good roads.
(*pointing*)
That's Catherine's Furnace, and there's a road — wait —

He pulls a stub of a pencil from his pocket, draws a ragged line.

STUART (*Cont'd*)
Here, there's a road, over this way.

JACKSON
Then we will hit them there. We can move around their flank.

He looks up at Lee.

JACKSON (*Cont'd*)
And they will have nowhere to go but back across the river, or we will destroy them.

LEE
Those roads — that's ten, eleven miles, General. And we'd be too close to their lines. They'll observe any movement. We must find another road, farther down. Do we have someone here, someone we can trust, who knows the area?

JACKSON
Mr. Pendleton, find Chaplain Lacy.

Lacy is standing near by, unnoticed by the generals. Lacy comes towards them.

LACY
Begging your pardon, General, but I'm here, sir.

Jackson turns, moves back toward the map and Lacy follows.

JACKSON
General, this is my chaplain, the Reverend Tucker Lacy. He has family in this area, sir.

LEE
Reverend, it would be very helpful if you could find us a safe route around the enemy.

Lacy leans over slightly.

LACY
Well, sir, there —

He points to a spot marked Catherine's Furnace.

LACY (*Cont'd*)
I know a family, the Wellfords. I'd suggest a visit to them. We may find ourselves a guide.

JACKSON
Please go there at once, Mr. Lacy. Find us someone who can tell us how we might proceed.

LEE (*smiling*)
Then we've decided, General, that this mission will be yours.

I would not have it any other way.

INT. JACKSON'S TENT, CHANCELLORSVILLE – EVENING
Jim Lewis is tidying up Jackson's things. Then he starts packing a haversack.

Von Borcke looks into the tent.

VON BORCKE
Where's General Jackson, Jim?

JIM LEWIS
He done gone to see his officers, sir.

VON BORCKE (*commenting on the packing*)
How come you know so much about what the general is thinking, Jim? None of us do.

JIM LEWIS
Sir, Massa Jackson never tell me nuttin'. But de way I knows is dis. Massa say his prayers twice a day, mornin' and night. But if he gets out o' bed two or three times in da night to pray, you see I just packs de haversack, for I knows dey's a move on hand, and hell to pay in de mo'nin'.

EXT. LEE'S HDQS, CHANCELLORSVILLE – NIGHT
All around are sleeping soldiers. Everyone is asleep except for Jackson and Lee, who are sitting at the two boxes, by a small fire. They are looking over a hand-drawn map. Nearby stands the WELLFORD boy.

JACKSON
There is another road, a road that will take us well below the Federal lines. The Wellford boy has explained it to me. He knows the route. He'll ride with us. There. We'll march to that point, where this road rejoins the turnpike. Then we'll turn east and attack the flank. It's a greater distance, perhaps twelve, thirteen miles altogether. But the boys can do it. They've never let us down.

LEE
Very well, General. How many troops will you require?

JACKSON
Well, General, my whole corps.

Lee flexes his stiff hands.

LEE
And what will you leave me?

JACKSON
Why, the divisions of Anderson and McLaws.

LEE (*thoughtfully*)
You leave me twelve thousand men against Hooker's seventy thousand. If Hooker pushes out of his trenches, he could destroy not only the plan, but possibly the army. And there's still Sedgewick along the river. How long will he sit staring at Marye's hill?

Jackson stares the cold stare. His blood is up.

> **LEE** *(Cont'd) (decisively)*
> We've divided the army before. We must retain the advantage of surprise. We must outflank the flankers, General. We must beat them at their own game. Take your entire corps, General Jackson, and destroy the enemy.

Jackson salutes …

> **LEE** *(Cont'd)*
> God be with you.

…and leaves.

EXT. CONFEDERATE CAMP, CHANCELLORSVILLE – PRE-DAWN

Men are in silent preparation. Jackson finds Smith.

> **JACKSON** *(in a low voice)*
> Mr. Smith, instructions to the ranks. There is to be no noise, no talking. All stragglers will be bayoneted. No muskets loaded until we are deployed for battle. Everything depends on the element of surprise.

> **SMITH**
> Yes sir, I'll convey the orders, sir. No stragglers, sir.

He salutes and is off.

EXT. CONFEDERATE CAMP, CHANCELLORSVILLE – PRE-DAWN

A group of soldiers in the Stonewall Brigade are settling down. The group includes Pogue and McClintock. A CORPORAL hands out rations.

> **CORPORAL**
> Three days, lads. Three days' rations.

> **POGUE**
> Three days' fightin' then. Three days fightin' and marchin'.

The Corporal hands rations to Stout, who shakes his head.

> **McCLINTOCK**
> None for me, Corporal.

There is a pause. Everyone is astonished. Who would conceivably refuse rations?

> **McCLINTOCK** *(Cont'd)*
> Boys, my days are numbered. My time has come. Ah, you may laugh; my time has come. I've got a twenty dollar gold piece in my pocket that I've carried through the war, and a silver watch that my father sent me through the lines. Please take 'em off when I'm dead. Give 'em to my captain to give to my father when he gets back home. Here's my clothing and blanket. Anyone who wishes may have 'em. My rations I do not wish at all. My gun and cartridge-box I expect to die with.

EXT. CONFEDERATE CAMP, CHANCELLORSVILLE – PRE-DAWN

Nearby Reverend Lacy is waiting with Pendleton, Smith, Morrison, Colston and Rodes. As soon as Jackson joins them, they bow their heads.

> **LACY**
> Dear Lord, Heavenly Father, you who know all things. We face again a mighty foe, a vast host, an enemy more than twice our number. But you have taught us to fear not. To trust in you. When the Philistines came before them, the people of Israel feared the giant Goliath. Their army was in terror. No one had the courage to stand against the mighty warrior. Then You brought forth David, a mere boy.

EXT. MONTAGE JACKSON'S POSITIONS, CHANCELLORSVILLE – PRE-DAWN

The soldiers make their final preparations before battle. Many wear improvised rags for shoes. Their clothes are in tatters. They load their cartridge boxes. They fix bayonets. There is no talking. Then they are formed into columns of four. Jackson, with a hard, fixed stare, rides alongside the troops. Colston and Rodes give a silent command and the "foot cavalry" moves out, silently, quickly, resolutely. There is grim determination etched into the face of every man. Lacy's voice continues over these preparations and the flank march.

> **LACY** *(V.O.)*
> And Saul armed David with his armour, and he put an helmet of brass upon his head: also he armed him with a coat of mail. And David girded his sword upon his armour, and he assayed to go…

EXT. TURNPIKE, CHANCELLORSVILLE – LATE AFTERNOON

A clump of bushes. Jackson, with a couple of aides, and YOUNG WELLFORD, their guide, push through.

EXT. JACKSON'S P.O.V. CHANCELLORSVILLE – LATE AFTERNOON

The Federal lines, Howard's men, sitting round fires, smoking, playing cards. Others preparing meals.

EXT. TURNPIKE, CHANCELLORSVILLE – LATE AFTERNOON

Jackson's aides hold his horse. He mounts.

His corps is drawn up in column, on the road. The commander of this division is Rodes. COLSTON'S OFFICER rides up.

> **JACKSON**
> General Rodes, you will deploy your men on either side of the turnpike, brigade front. How soon will General Colston's men be up?

> **COLSTON'S OFFICER**
> We're right behind, General.

Jackson reaches into his pocket, pulls out a small pencil, a rough piece of crumpled paper, holds the paper flat against his saddle and scribbles a brief message.

> **JACKSON** (V.O.)
> I hope as soon as practicable to attack. I trust that an ever kind Providence will bless us with great success...

He motions to a courier to come forward. Jackson gives him the note.

> **JACKSON** (Cont'd)
> Take this to General Lee.

The courier is off.

> **JACKSON** (Cont'd) (to Rodes and Colston)
> Well, gentlemen. It seems the Virginia Military Institute will be heard from today! Deploy your brigades!

Rodes and Colston salute, and are off.

EXT. JACKSON'S POSITIONS, CHANCELLORSVILLE – LATE AFTERNOON

First Rodes' division, and then Colston's, spread out in lines on each side of the road. They move forward into the dense woods.

EXT. JACKSON'S POSITIONS, CHANCELLORSVILLE – LATE AFTERNOON

Jackson mounts and watches. It is getting late in the day. He casts a long shadow down the road.

Jackson looks sharply behind him, sees Pendleton.

> **JACKSON**
> Is Hill coming up?

> **PENDLETON**
> General Hill will be up with his lead brigade very soon. They're not more than a mile behind. His last two brigades are well back, sir.

EXT. JACKSON'S POSITIONS, CHANCELLORSVILLE – LATE AFTERNOON

Jackson spurs his horse, moving down the road following Rodes' troops.

Jackson reaches the line of men, leans over and tries to see out through the thick brush.

EXT. JACKSON'S POV, CHANCELLORSVILLE – LATE AFTERNOON

The line disappears in both directions, the men slowly moving forward with small noises, the officers keeping them in line.

There are muffled curses and nervous laughter, as the men struggle with the tangled brush.

EXT. JACKSON'S POSITIONS, CHANCELLORSVILLE – LATE AFTERNOON

Jackson looks down the road, lifts his field glasses, stares ahead and sees two small black eyes, the silent stare of Howard's cannons.

He lowers the glasses, reaches into his pocket and pulls out a small gold watch. We see the time, five-fifteen.

> **JACKSON**
> Two hours of daylight. Are you ready, General Rodes?

Rodes simply nods.

> **JACKSON** (Cont'd)
> You can go forward, sir.

Rodes gestures. A bugle sounds.

EXT. JACKSON'S POSITIONS, CHANCELLORSVILLE – LATE AFTERNOON

Out in front the first line begins to crash through the tangle of briars and thickets. From the entire force comes the sound, the high, screaming rebel yell.

Ten thousand men — a solid line a mile wide pushing and clawing through the brush — emerge into the first clearing in one great mass of motion.

EXT. HOWARD'S LINES, CHANCELLORSVILLE – LATE AFTERNOON

Federal soldiers spill plates of hot food, snatch up weapons, but do not form up.

Jackson's men halt, raise their muskets in one sweeping motion, and fire a massive volley along the whole length of the line. Jackson himself rides just behind the front line.

Fleeing Federals are cut down by the bullets.

The Federals continue to run, passing untouched stands of muskets, campfires and tents and wagons.

The pace of the Confederate advance increases.

Devens' division, retreating in chaos, stampedes past the trenches of the next division in line. These men turn, form a line of fire, and send a volley at the gray wave. But they are panicked, and their aim is poor. The gray tide quickly rolls over them.

There are more trenches now, more substantial earthworks. Jackson's force occupies them quickly.

EXT. JACKSON'S FLANK, CHANCELLORSVILLE – DAY

Jackson rides up onto a long mound of dirt. Rodes' division is ahead of him, continuing to press on. Colston's first line is coming up to him.

> **JACKSON** (yelling)
> Press on! Forward!

Colston's men go over the embankment, fighting their way through felled trees.

There is some shooting from small pockets of men in blue, who stand to fight. But these small groups are quickly overrun. They die, or flee, or are captured.

Jackson pushes on, rides through the earthworks.

EXT. FEDERAL LINES, FURTHER IN, CHANCELLORSVILLE – EVENING

There are yet more trenches. The Federals are now at last seriously returning fire from within thick brush. Confederate troops are falling.

Jackson rides up to where his lines are thinning.

> JACKSON
> Form the lines! Keep it up!

There are more volleys, from both sides, and men fall in front of Jackson.

EXT. FEDERAL CAMP, CHANCELLORSVILLE – DAY

Across the road there is a glimpse of blue, hidden by the brush, and a roar of muskets blows into the line behind Jackson. He turns back, sees a dozen men, a neat straight line, still pointing their muskets forward, and the men are all down, having fallen together.

Now there is a sharp blast from the Confederates toward the brush, screams, and blue soldiers stumble out toward the road — blue coats with new stains of red. The gray line moves on by, keeps going.

EXT. FEDERAL CAMP, CHANCELLORSVILLE – DAY

Colston's second line is passing by Jackson now. Suddenly there is a cheer, echoing down through the roar of the guns and the rising smoke. It spreads, grows into the high scream, a new chorus of the rebel yell.

> JACKSON
> Keep it up! Move forward! Stay together!

The smoke is heavier now, shells ripping the air, bursting in the road, tearing through the brush.

EXT. FEDERAL BATTERIES, CHANCELLORSVILLE – DAY

Federal batteries are firing, and his lines begin to shatter.

EXT. FEDERAL CAMP, CHANCELLORSVILLE – DAY

Jackson turns to the side, rides along a thick patch of the dense woods, sees a small group of men with an officer standing, unsure.

> JACKSON
> Get them together, press them on!

The officer looks stunned.

> JACKSON (Cont'd) (yelling to the officer)
> Get them into line!

In a sudden blast the officer and men are gone.

Jackson jerks at his horse, moves back into the clearing, to the road, begins to follow the line again.

EXT. FEDERAL CAMP, CHANCELLORSVILLE – DAY

The Federal troops are still falling back.

EXT. JACKSON'S FLANK, CHANCELLORSVILLE -DAY

Jackson spurs his horse, moves forward. There is a vast spread of debris, shattered guns and wagons, and the broken bodies of men.

EXT. FEDERAL CAMP, CHANCELLORSVILLE – DAY

In a grove of trees, there are blue soldiers, crouching, aiming. A volley rips...

EXT. FEDERAL CAMP, CHANCELLORSVILLE – DAY

...past Jackson, strikes men behind him. Men are falling on all sides, shot by muskets, or cannon fire.

EXT. WOODS, CHANCELLORSVILLE – LATE AFTERNOON

Out of the smoke come Pogue and McClintock. They collapse exhausted behind a large bolder, catching their breath.

> POGUE
> Oh, that's hot. I knew you'd be alright, you dang fool.

But before he can reply, McClintock is hit by shrapnel, his guts spilling out over the ground.

> McCLINTOCK (screaming)
> Oh, oh, God!

He is dead as he hits the ground, his gold coin clutched in his left hand.

EXT. COLSTON'S LINES, CHANCELLORSVILLE – LATE AFTERNOON

A line of Colston's men are moving into a grove. There are volleys from both sides, a thick mass of smoke spreading out everywhere. Jackson strains to see, raises his pistol, ready, then sees the blue bodies, swept from their cover.

Colston's men move forward. There is ONE BLUE SOLDIER, only a boy, still standing, facing the oncoming gray line. He is trying to reload, but Colston's men are on him. The boy tries to raise his rifle. There is a flash of steel, the quick rip of the bayonet, and the boy is down.

EXT. HOWARD'S POSITION, CHANCELLORSVILLE – LATE AFTERNOON

Howard is mounted, brandishing the Stars and Stripes, which he holds clamped to his body with the stump of his previously amputated arm. His one hand brandishes a pistol. He is shouting at his troops, who run by him, taking no notice.

> HOWARD
> Stop, for God's sake, turn and fight!

But they just keep on running.

EXT. CHANCELLOR HOUSE – EVENING

Hooker is on the porch, surrounded by his staff and other officers.

Hancock rides up at the gallop. He pulls up hard, jumps down. On the road behind them there is a sound, the clatter of wheels.

A horse appears, at a fast gallop, pulling an empty wagon,

without a driver. The wagon moves past. An OFFICER ON THE PORCH is looking in the direction where the wagon came from.

OFFICER ON THE PORCH (*shouting*)
Good God! Here they come!

Down the road, across the clearing on both sides, comes a ragged mass of troops, no coats, no hats, without guns. There is the rattle of another wagon, then many more, still without drivers, terrified horses, pulled along by a growing tide of running men.

Beyond the house, in a wide clearing, is a line of resting troops, a reserve division. Now orders are flying, the men scrambling into formation. Hooker shouts from the porch.

HOOKER
Move into line, move around, move into line! Give them the bayonet!

Hancock grabs his horse, jumps up and spurs the big animal out into the road.

HANCOCK
These aren't Rebs! These are our men!

We hear guns now, scattered cannon, but mostly muskets. There are more wagons, men on horses, and the mad stampede is moving past the mansion. The line of fresh troops swings around, moving toward the road, trying to stop the panicked mob.

From the thicket below the road more men appear, torn uniforms, still running. Hancock raises his sword, swings it down hard, hits a man flat across the shoulder, knocking him down. The man looks at him with raw terror.

HANCOCK (*Cont'd*)
Get up! Stop running!

The man is back on his feet, seeming to understand. But then another rush, and the man is caught up and gone again. Hancock turns his horse, rides quickly down the road, fighting through the running troops, moves past, tries to get out in front.

EXT. JACKSON'S ADVANCE, CHANCELLORSVILLE – EVENING
Woods and clearings. The area is full of Jackson's troops. Shells are bursting round them, but are not doing much damage. The full moon has risen.

Colston's officer rides up.

COLSTON'S OFFICER
Form the company!

Jackson rides up. Colston's officer turns to meet him.

COLSTON'S OFFICER (*Cont'd*)
We have stopped, sir! Can't see! The lines are tangled, we're mixed in with Rodes' men. It's confusion, sir! We need Hill to come up. Hill's men can move on by us!

JACKSON
Inform general Colston, try to re-form your men. I'll tell General Hill to push on! We must not stop! They're running. They'll keep running if we press them.

More troops are arriving. Jackson turns his horse, rides back toward the oncoming lines of A. P. Hill. Hill salutes.

JACKSON (*Cont'd*)
Keep them moving, General. Keep the pressure up. We've broken their flank. We can crush them now, cut them off. We must not give them time to organize. Take your division forward, then press on to the north, toward the river. Move toward United States Ford. They must not escape!

A. P. HILL
General, it's dark. We don't know the ground.

Jackson turns around, looks, as his own staff come together. Among them is Captain Boswell, the engineer.

JACKSON
Boswell, stay with General Hill. Find a way through the woods to the northeast. Find the rear of the enemy's position. We will cut them off!

Boswell salutes Jackson, and moves out with Hill.

Jackson turns away, and rides forward down the dark road.

EXT. ROAD THROUGH THE WOODS, CHANCELLORSVILLE – EVENING
Jackson and his staff ride forward. He holds up his hand, waves them back, tries to listen.

The shelling has stopped. Scattered musket fire echoes through the trees.

An aide comes up with young Wellford, who knows the woods.

JACKSON
Is there a road that way, toward the United States Ford?

WELLFORD
No, sir, not here. There's some old trails, but farther up, there's the Bullock Road. Some trails off of that.

Jackson nods impatiently.

JACKSON
Show me! Now. We must not waste time!

The boy moves forward. Jackson follows, his staff in tow.

EXT. TRAIL, FURTHER DOWN, CHANCELLORSVILLE – NIGHT
It is a narrow trail. Young Wellford appears, walking. Jackson rides at a walk beside him. The staff come behind.

They move slowly in the growing moonlight. Jackson stops often, strains to hear.

There are sounds of troops ahead, digging in: the clear sound of axes, the chopping of trees.

JACKSON (*almost a whisper*)
Digging in, that's Federals. But sound carries at night. They could be a ways off.

The boy watches Jackson, who motions, and they begin to move along the trail again.

From behind them comes the deafening blast of a big gun, a Confederate one.

Then, from in front comes the Federals' answer, several bright flashes. Dirt flies up, and there are screams from the wounded behind them.

EXT. TRAIL, CHANCELLORSVILLE – NIGHT
Jackson reaches behind the saddle for the black rubber overcoat, pulls it quietly over his shoulders, and they keep moving.

There is a burst of fire from their front – from the Federal troops.

Lieutenant Morrison touches Jackson's shoulder.

MORRISON (*in an anxious whisper*)
Sir, we are beyond our lines. This is no place for you, sir.

Jackson stops the horse, raises his hand, halting the group.

JACKSON
You're right. It can't go the way I'd hoped. It will have to be in the morning. We'll return to the road.

He turns the horse, begins to move quickly now, and the others follow.

EXT. WOODS, CHANCELLORSVILLE – NIGHT
Jackson and his aides ride in the moonlight.

1ST NORTH CAROLINA SOLDIER (*O.S.*)
Who's that? Halt!

2ND NORTH CAROLINA SOLDIER (*O.S.*)
It's cavalry! Fire!

There is a quick sheet of flame, and someone is shot.

Morrison rides toward the hidden soldiers.

MORRISON
No, stop firing! You're firing on your own men!

2ND NORTH CAROLINA SOLDIER (*O.S.*)
It is a lie! Pour it to them!

The moonlight silhouettes the men on horseback. Jackson is hit in the right hand and left shoulder. His horse lunges, terrified, jumps and jerks.

Morrison grabs the reins that Jackson has dropped.

Jackson is sliding, tries to reach for the saddle, cannot grab with his hand, slides down the side of the horse and falls hard to the ground.

There is more yelling now. Horsemen are galloping toward them on the trail. It is A. P. Hill and his staff.

A. P. HILL
Hold your fire! These are your own men here!

His staff ride quickly toward the line of hidden troops.

Hill comes forward, sees bodies, wounded men and dying horses. He dismounts.

He sees the dark form of Jackson on the ground, and the dark form of Morrison kneeling.

A. P. HILL (*Cont'd*)
Oh God! What have they done?

He sees the face of young Morrison, streaked with tears.

A. P. HILL (*Cont'd*)
Who is this?

In the moonlight, Hill recognizes Jackson.

A. P. HILL (*Cont'd*)
Oh God. General, are you hurt?

JACKSON
I'm afraid so. I'm hit in the shoulder — and... here.

He raises his right hand, turns it in the faint light, tries to see what has happened.

Now there are more shots from the direction of the Federal lines.

A. P. HILL (*to one of his aides*)
Get a litter! We need a litter!

HILL'S AIDE hesitates, stares at the blood flowing from Jackson's shoulder, soaking into his uniform.

A. P. HILL (*Cont'd*)
Move!

The aide looks at Hill, then turns and is gone.

A. P. HILL (*Cont'd*)
We must leave here, General. Can you walk?

Others gather. A tourniquet is wrapped high around Jackson's left arm.

Jackson bends his knees, tries to stand. Hands around him pull him up.

They begin to move quickly down the trail. Jackson tries to run, held up by the hands round him.

Soldiers run up the trail toward them, carrying a litter.

Jackson stares at the litter, tries to continue on his feet. But the hands pull him down, lay him down on the litter.

Smith leans over close to his face.

SMITH
General, are you in pain? Can I give you something? Here — take this, it will help.

He puts a small bottle to Jackson's mouth, who takes a swig.

A. P. HILL
I will try to keep this from the knowledge of the troops.

JACKSON
Thank you.

Jackson is lifted up. The four bearers hurry off, half running.

EXT. WOODS, CHANCELLORSVILLE – NIGHT
A sudden roar of fire, bursts of light, exploding shells.

The litter bearers drop down, lie flat. Overhead, limbs and small branches fly into pieces, wood and dirt rain over them.

Smith covers Jackson with his body, shielding him from the debris.

The shelling stops. The bearers rise in unison, pick up the litter, and hurry off.

EXT. TRAIL, ANOTHER SECTION, CHANCELLORSVILLE – NIGHT
The group appear again, the litter carried at a run. Musket fire, and one of the litter bearers suddenly grunts and crumples, dropping the litter.

Jackson rolls off to the side, lands hard.

Others pick him up, place him back on the litter, and move off.

INT. CONFEDERATE FIELD HOSPITAL, CHANCEL-LORSVILLE – NIGHT
Jackson is lying on a cot, Dr. McGuire at his side, holding a tourniquet on his upper arm. Jackson opens his eyes. Jim Lewis has a wet towel, with which he wipes Jackson's face. Morrison and Smith stand nearby.

McGUIRE
Welcome back, General. Can you hear me?

JACKSON
I am glad to see you. I am badly injured, doctor. I fear I am dying.

McGuire brings a cup up to his mouth.

McGUIRE
Drink this, sir, whisky and morphine.

Jackson swallows the drink. He holds up his right hand, sees that it is bandaged.

McGUIRE *(Cont'd)*
General, your right hand is minor. The ball lodged under the skin. It's the other wounds...

He pauses.

McGUIRE *(Cont'd)*
We need to examine your wounds. We will administer chloroform to make it painless. If we find that the condition warrants amputation, may we proceed at once?

JACKSON
Yes, certainly, Doctor McGuire. Do for me whatever you think right.

A surgeon's aide fashions a piece of cloth into the shape of a cup, into which he pours a half-ounce of chloroform. McGuire takes the cloth, holding it two inches from Jackson's nose and mouth.

McGUIRE
Breathe deeply, General.

Jackson inhales, once, twice, three times... He begins to visibly relax as the all consuming pain drifts away.

JACKSON
What an infinite blessing... blessing... blessing...

And he lapses into unconsciousness.

EXT. CHANCELLOR HOUSE – DAY
A chaos of Federal bodies. The house is destroyed by shell-fire. Confederate troops and guns move forward.

Lee sits on Traveller, watching.

There are shouts and cheers from the men as they pass: "We whipped 'em good." "Them blue-bellies still runnin', Gen'rl."

TAYLOR
Doesn't seem right General Jackson isn't here to see this.

LEE
No, Major. It does not seem right at all. But it is the will of God.

He pauses.

LEE *(Cont'd)*
He has lost his left arm. I have lost my right.

INT. FIELD HOSPITAL TENT, CHANCELLORSVILLE – NIGHT
Jackson is in bed. McGuire is examining the shoulder of Jackson's amputated arm. Jim Lewis and Smith stand vigil.

McGUIRE
General, very good. It should heal nicely. How's the hand?

Jackson raises the clump of bandages, turns it, moves the fingers.

JACKSON
It seems fine, Doctor.

McGUIRE
It was not a bad wound. Should heal completely. Be sore for a while, but you'll have full movement in a week or two. We'll move to Guiney Station where we can take better care of you.

Smith moves toward the bed, bends down on one knee.

SMITH
General? How are you feeling, sir?

JACKSON
Don't concern yourself about me, Mr. Smith. But tell me, how are we faring?

SMITH
General, the enemy's gone, across the river. We've secured the high ground around Chancellorsville. General Stuart did well by you, sir. And the Stonewall Brigade...right in the middle of it, sir. "Remember Jackson" they shouted. I heard that all day. They were fighting for Stonewall.

JACKSON
That's just like them. Just like them. They are a noble set of men. The name of Stonewall belongs to that brigade, not to me.

SMITH
But General Paxton, sir — he was killed early in the action, sir.

JACKSON (*disbelieving*)
Paxton? Paxton?

This news takes his breath away. He closes his eyes.

SMITH
General, I have the ball. Dr. McGuire allowed me to keep the musket ball he took from your hand, sir. It's a round smoothbore, sir. It has to be one of ours.

JACKSON
Yes. I heard. They thought I was asleep. It could not be helped. There's no blame in war. We must all forgive.

EXT. GUINEY RAILWAY STATION – DAY
A train has just arrived. Soldiers and officers stand around a coffin.

Accompanied by Hattie and Morrison, Anna Jackson descends a passenger car, holding her baby. Smith and McGuire are there to greet her.

McGUIRE
Hello, Mrs. Jackson.

Tears welling in her eyes, she motions to the coffin.

ANNA JACKSON
So, am I allowed to visit my husband before he's buried?

McGUIRE (*puzzled*)
Buried? He's not ...

He registers the men and the coffin.

McGUIRE (*Cont'd*)
Oh my... no, no, ma'am, that's the body of General Paxton, Frank Paxton. His body's being moved, taken back to his home in Lexington.

She stares at the box.

ANNA JACKSON
I knew Mr. Paxton — General Paxton. He's our neighbor.

His wife — she cried when he left. I suppose she knew something like this would happen.

She is calm now, looks at McGuire, waits.

McGUIRE
We removed his left arm, patched his right hand — it's healing well, I'm very pleased. But there's a new problem. I believe he is developing pneumonia.

ANNA JACKSON
May I see him, Doctor?

McGUIRE
Certainly. He's weak, I've given him medicine to help him sleep. He is in some pain. The medicine makes him drift away, in and out.

Morrison helps Anna and Hattie into a waiting carriage.

EXT. CHANDLER HOUSE, GUINEY STATION – DAY
The carriage is parked out front. Soldiers mill around.

INT. CHANDLER HOUSE, GUINEY STATION – DAY
Jackson is lying in bed. McGuire carries a glass of lemonade. Anna Jackson follows behind.

McGUIRE
General, we have a treat for you, something you may have been missing.

Jackson lifts his head, sees the glass.

JACKSON
Another medicine? Very well, Doctor.

McGUIRE
No — well, not mine, actually. But it should do you some good.

He holds the glass, lowers it to Jackson's mouth.

Jackson takes a short drink.

JACKSON
Ahhhgggg, it's so sweet. Too much sugar. Always the problem with my esposita's...

McGuire is smiling. Jackson suddenly realizes Anna is there. She leans over and kisses him.

JACKSON (*Cont'd*)
I am very glad to see you looking so bright.

McGuire backs away and leaves.

Anna Jackson stares down at her husband's clear blue eyes, sees how weak he is, cannot hide her sorrow.

JACKSON (*Cont'd*)
My darling, you must cheer up and not wear a long face. I love cheerfulness and brightness in a sickroom.

Anna's smile is the needed tonic.

JACKSON *(Cont'd)*
Esposita... esposita... I know you would gladly give your life for me, but I am perfectly resigned. Do not be sad. I hope I may yet recover. Pray for me, but always remember in your prayers to use the petition, "Thy will be done."

INT. WASHINGTON THEATER, WASHINGTON CITY , EVENING – MAY 8
SUPER TITLE: Washington Theater, May 8

The play is Julius Caesar. Booth plays Brutus, Harrison plays Cinna. In the audience are Chamberlain and Fanny.

"CAESAR"
Et tu, Brute!

Brutus stabs him.

"CAESAR" *(Cont'd)*
Then fall Caesar.

He falls to the stage, dead.

HARRISON *(as CINNA)*
Liberty! Freedom! Tyranny is dead!

INT. GREEN ROOM, WASHINGTON THEATER – NIGHT
It is immediately after the play. Booth, Harrison, "Caesar" and the other actors are there, still in costume. Members of the audience are present, including the Chamberlains.

"CAESAR"
Mr. Booth, Mr. Harrison. May I present Colonel Chamberlain and his wife.

Hand-shakes all round.

CHAMBERLAIN
May I congratulate you, all of you, on a most moving interpretation.

"CAESAR"
But this is only a play. We have heard of you, Colonel, and how you stood on the bridge of the Rappahannock, like Horatius, while hundreds fled in panic round you. How can our playing compare with what you have seen, what you have done?

CHAMBERLAIN
Remember, gentlemen, I am not a soldier by nature. I am a teacher of rhetoric, and my master, as yours, is Shakespeare.

Chamberlain has an immensely charismatic presence. The actors have recognized this as soon as he walked into the room.

BOOTH
And did you enjoy the play, Mrs. Chamberlain?

FANNY *(with her dazzling smile)*
Immensely. Tell me, Mr. Booth. Do you regard yourself as the hero or the villain of Shakespeare's play?

The actors suddenly realize that Fanny is not only attractive, she is also learned.

BOOTH
Well...

He is not quite sure how to answer.

HARRISON
An actor, Mrs. Chamberlain, must always regard the role which he is playing as that of a hero, even if that role be no more than a simple foot soldier who only speaks one line.

BOOTH
Yes. It is for the audience to decide who is hero, who is villain. We simply play the parts allotted to us.

HARRISON
How do you think of us, Mrs. Chamberlain — Cinna and Brutus? As heroes or villains?

FANNY
Well, "The noblest Roman of them all." You cannot be villains in Shakespeare's eyes, though Dante makes you the worst villains in the history of the world after Judas Iscariot. No, you are not villains to Shakespeare. But, I wonder, are you heroes?

She looks round the company, and smiles again.

FANNY *(Cont'd)*
I have spoken too much.

A polite muttering of "No, no" from several of the actors.

FANNY *(Cont'd)*
My beloved husband has been granted a few days of furlough in Washington. Everything about these days delights me utterly. Do not expect me to talk intelligently about your play, or anything else. My eyes, my heart, my whole being, is dancing uncontrollably with joy at being together with the man I love. Thank you for enriching my stay here with those immortal words. Thank you.

She pauses, looks round the company.

CHAMBERLAIN
Come, Fanny, we must leave the players to rest after their exertions.

Fanny takes Chamberlain's hand. He looks at her with love and admiration, and bows to the actors. The Chamberlains leave the room.

Booth and Harrison are left standing together. The other actors move off into different groups.

BOOTH *(to Harrison)*
What a Caesar, Harrison. What a Caesar.

HARRISON
Too young for Caesar. Henry the Fifth.

BOOTH
Henry the Fifth, of course. That voice, shouting, "Once more unto the breech!" Oh yes. Henry the Fifth.

HARRISON
A teacher and a soldier. And a better actor than either of us. But he's chosen the right role in the right play, and he will be applauded long after we're forgotten.

BOOTH
All we can do, Harrison, is as I said to Mrs. Chamberlain. All we can do is play the roles allotted to us.

HARRISON
If a teacher of rhetoric can become a soldier, so can an actor. I've known for some time I could not go on like this. And now ... If the Yankee cause can sway the heart of a man like that, then we need every soldier we can muster. Booth, I'm quitting the stage. I have to go. I loathe and detest his cause. But were I to be killed by a man like that, I would regard it an honor. Yes sir, an honor.

BOOTH
You were always inclined to melodrama, Harrison. What makes you think you will be better as a soldier than as an actor? Stay here. Your place is here. Why should we think that what we do is less than what the soldiers do? We may be mere actors. But think of the words we are helping to keep alive. Who can remember the names of Queen Elizabeth's generals and politicians? Who can ever forget the name of Shakespeare?

INT. JACKSON'S ROOM, CHANDLER HOUSE – DAY
McGuire stares at the bottles of medications and opiates, at his surgeon's instruments laid out on a black leather pouch, shining steel blades, tongs, small, pointed scissors. He folds the pouch, rolls it up, carefully ties it closed with the small attached ribbon. Pendleton sits near the bed, where Jackson lies asleep.

JACKSON (in delirium)
Order A. P. Hill. Prepare for action! Pass the infantry to the front!

McGuire comes close to the bed.

JACKSON (Cont'd)
Tell Major Hawks to send forward provision for the troops.

Jackson's breathing is in short, quick, rasps. His eyes open. He can see Pendleton and McGuire.

PENDLETON
General, sir. The whole army is praying for you.

JACKSON
They are very kind. Very kind.

He lapses back to unconsciousness.

INT. JACKSON'S ROOM, CHANDLER HOUSE – DAY
It is later. Anna sits by the bed, holding little Julia in her arms. The only sounds come from Jackson — his breathing, high and quick and rasping.

Jackson's eyes open and he stares up, far away.

Hearing the gurgling sounds of his baby, he notices Anna and his daughter.

JACKSON
My little darling, sweet Julia... little comforter, little comforter...

Jackson begins to drift away again, his eyes turning dimly toward the ceiling.

Anna glances at McGuire, who stands at the door. She goes to him.

INT. CHANDLER HOUSE HALLWAY – DAY

ANNA JACKSON
Is it certain, Doctor?

He nods, resigned.

ANNA JACKSON (Cont'd)
Does he know?

McGuire shakes his head.

McGUIRE
I have not told him.

ANNA JACKSON
Then I will. He must know. He must be prepared.

EXT. CHANDLER HOUSE, GUINEY STATION – DAY
Soldiers stand outside the house in prayer, part of the silent vigil.

INT. JACKSON'S ROOM, CHANDLER HOUSE, LATER – DAY
Anna, Lieutenant Morrison are seated by the bed, singing quietly the hymn "Lead Us Heavenly Father, Lead Us."

As they sing, Jackson seems to revive a little. He opens his eyes.

ANNA JACKSON
My darling, today is Sunday. Do you know the doctor says you must very soon be in Heaven?

Jackson drifts off again. Anna touches him to wake him up again.

ANNA JACKSON (Cont'd)
Do you not feel willing to acquiesce in God's allotment, if He wills you to go today?

Jackson struggles to bring himself awake.

JACKSON (almost inaudibly)
I prefer it.
(more distinctly)
I prefer it.

ANNA JACKSON
Well, before this day closes, you will be with the blessed Savior in His glory.

JACKSON
I will be an infinite gainer to be translated.

There is a pause. The clock ticks on the mantelpiece. He relapses into unconsciousness.

INT. LEE'S HDQS – DAY
Reverend Lacy enters the tent.

LEE
What is the news, Reverend?

LACY
General Lee, I must report that his case appears hopeless. His wounds are healing, but he is dying of pneumonia.

LEE
Surely General Jackson must recover. God will not take him from us. Not now that we need him so much.

LACY
Will you see him, sir?

LEE (*shakes his head "no," fighting hard to hide his feelings*)
When you return, I trust you will find him better. When a suitable occasion offers, tell him that I prayed for him last night as I never prayed, I believe, for myself.

Lee can speak no more. Lacy understands, and leaves.

INT. JACKSON'S ROOM, CHANDLER HOUSE, LATER – DAY
In the room are Anna Jackson, Morrison, McGuire, Smith, Pendleton, Lacy and Jim Lewis. They stand round the bed, watching.

Jackson lies with his eyes closed.

Silence, broken only by the ticking clock on the mantelpiece. To the delirious Jackson the ticks grow in volume and rapidity.

They become muskets firing, the sounds of shot and shell.

Jackson opens his eyes. They burn with intensity.

JACKSON
Push up the columns! Hasten the columns! Pendleton, you take charge of that line! Where's Smith? Tell him to push up the column! Move up the batteries! General Stuart, no quarter to the violators of our homes and hearth! General Lee, we must take the war to the enemy! Advance, my brave boys, advance!

The last vestiges of mortal strength leave him. A deep relaxation permeates his body. He smiles as he sees his boyhood home.

JACKSON (*Cont'd*)
Let us cross over the river, and rest under the shade of the trees.

Jackson dies. There follows a long silence. Then, as eerily as it occurred at Bunker Hill in the Shenandoah Valley, the sound of the rebel yell grows like a murmuring wind outside the small house. It rises in intensity, the sound of thousands of wailing souls.

EXT. VIRGINIA MILITARY INSTITUTE, LEXINGTON – DAY
SUPER TITLE: Virginia Military Institute, May 15, 1863

Led by cadets with reversed arms and muffled drums, a horse drawn caisson carries Jackson's casket ... past lilacs and early spring flowers, across the quad where the entire corps of cadets stands at attention ... to the main classroom building. The coffin is taken inside ...

INT. VIRGINIA MILITARY INSTITUTE, LEXINGTON, VIRGINIA – DAY
... up the stairs into Jackson's old lecture hall, unchanged after two years, where it is placed before an honor guard of cadets. Outside can be heard the booming of the guns.

THE END

217

An ANTIETAM FILMWORKS Production

of a RON MAXWELL Film

In Association with
Esparza/Katz Productions
Rehme Productions
IncMace Neufeld Productions

GODS and GENERALS

Casting by . . . . JOY TODD, C.S.A.
Music Supervision . . . . .DAVID FRANCO
Music Composed by . . . . . .JOHN FRIZZELL
RANDY EDELMAN
Visual Effects Producer . .THOMAS G. SMITH
Production Designer . . . . .MICHAEL HANAN
Editor . . . . .CORKY EHLERS
Director of Photography
KEES VAN OOSTRUM, A.S.C.
Executive Producers . . . . .ROBERT KATZ
ROBERT REHME
MOCTESUMA ESPARZA
MACE NEUFELD
Co-Executive Producer . .RONALD G. SMITH
Co-Producer . . . . .NICK GRILLO
Executive Producer . . . . .TED TURNER
Associate Executive Producer
ROBERT J. WUSSLER
Produced by . . . . . . .RONALD F. MAXWELL
Based on the book by . . . . .JEFF SHAARA
Written for the screen and directed by
RONALD F. MAXWELL

Unit Production Manager D. SCOTT EASTON
First Assistant Director DONALD P.H. EATON
Second Assistant Director . .LYNN WEGENKA
Second Second Assistant Director
JON MALLARD
Add'l Second Assistant Director
TARA NICOLE WEYR
DGA Trainee . .DANIEL HAMILTON-LOWE

Cast (in alphabetical order)
DONZALEIGH ABERNATHY . . . . Martha
MARK ALDRICH . . . . .Adjutant
GEORGE ALLEN . . . . Confederate Officer
KEITH ALLISON . . . . . . Capt. James J. White
ROYCE APPLEGATE . . . . Gen. James Kemper
JEREMY BECK . . . . .Rob Lee
RICHARD BEKINS . . . . .Gen. Oliver Howard
BRUCE BOXLEITNER Gen. James Longstreet
BO BRINKMAN . . . . .Major Walter Taylor
WARREN BURTON   Governor Oliver Morton
MAC BUTLER . . . . Gen. Joseph Hooker
ROBERT C. BYRD . . . . . Confederate General
SHANE CALLAHAN . . . . Bowdoin Student
BILLY CAMPBELL . . . . . Gen. George Pickett
DAVID CARPENTER Rev. Beverly Tucker Lacy
JOHN CASTLE . . . . Old Penn
JIM CHOATE . . . . Gen. Bernard Bee
MARTIN CLARK . . . . Dr. George Junkin
CHRIS CLAWSON . . . . Charles Beale
CHRIS CONNOR . . . . John Wilkes Booth
KEVIN CONWAY . . . . Sgt. Buster Kilrain

SCOTT COOPER . . . . Lt. Joseph Morrison
DEVIN CROMWELL . . . Cadet Charlie Norris
RYAN CUTRONA . . . . . Gen. Marsena Patrick
JEFF DANIELS . . . . Lt. Col. Joshua
Lawrence Chamberlain
SCOTT DAVIDSON . . . . Sam Beale
MIA DILLON . . . . .Jane Beale
JUSTIN DRAY . . . . George Jenkins
ROBERT DUVALL . . . . . . Gen. Robert E. Lee
ROBERT EASTON . . . . John Janney
FRANKIE FAISON . . . . .Jim Lewis
MILES FISHER . . . . John Beale
KEITH FLIPPEN . . . . Maj. Gilmore
BOURKE FLOYD . . . . . Longstreet's Courier
DAVID FOSTER . . . . Capt. Ricketts
DENNIS E. FRYE . . . . Griffin's Aide
JOSEPH FUQUA . . . . Col. J. E. B. Stuart
JAMES GARRETT   Gen. John Curtis Caldwell
KAREN GOBERMAN . . . . Lucy Beale
ALEXANDER GORDON   Martha's Older Son
PATRICK GORMAN . . . . Gen. John Bell Hood
PHIL GRAMM . . . . Virginia Delegate
BO GREIGH . . . . Pvt. Pogue
FRED GRIFFITH . . . . Gen. Robert Rodes
KAREN HOCHSTETTER . . . Roberta Corbin
JAMES HORAN . . . . Col. Cummings
CON HORGAN . . . . Pvt. Dooley
C. THOMAS HOWEL Sgt. Thomas Chamberlain
COOPER HUCKABEE . . . . .Harrison
BEN HULAN . . . . A Lieutenant
SAM HULSEY . . . . Julian Beale
ALEX HYDE WHITE Gen. Ambrose E. Burnside
LYDIA JORDAN . . . . Jane Corbin
MICHELLE JORDAN . . . . . .Stage Door Belle
CHRISTIAN KAUFFMAN . . Abraham Lincoln
LES KINSOLVING . . . Gen. William Barksdale
DAMON KIRSCHE . . . . Harry McCarthy
LEW KNOPP . . . . Jackson's Courier
ROSEMARY KNOWER . . . Mary Todd Lincoln
STEPHEN LANG . . . . Gen. Stonewall Jackson
JAMES THOMAS LAWLER . .Another Looter
MATT LETSCHER . . . . . Col. Adelbert Ames
MATT LINDQUIST Johann Heros Von Borcke
MARTY LODGE . . . ."Caesar"
JEREMY LONDON Alexander "Sandie" Pendleton
DOUG LORY . . . . 2nd Irishman
BRIAN MALLON Gen. Winfield Scott Hancock
DAN MANNING . . . . Maj. John Harman
EDWARD MARKEY . . . . Irish Brigade Officer
TOM BOYD MASON Old Man in Fredericksburg
JONATHAN MAXWELL . . . . Capt. Ellis Spear
OLIVIA MAXWELL . . . . .Stage Door Belle
MALACHY MCCOURT . . . . . . Francis P. Blair
TERRY MCCREA . . . . A Captain
ANDREW MCOMBER II . . . . Young Corporal
ROSEMARY MEACHAM . . . . Hattie
MARQUIS MOODY . . . . Martha's Younger Son
PETER NEOFOTIS . . . . Wounded Maine Man
MARK NICHOLS . . Surgeon in Fredericksburg
CARSTEN NORGAARD Gen. Darius Nash Couch
TIM O'HARE . . . . . . Lt. Col. Clair Mulholland
JAMES PARKES . . . . . .Gen. George McClellan
CHRIS POTOCKI . . . . .Stage Manager
SEAN PRATT . . . Dr. Hunter Holmes McGuire
JASMYN PROCTOR . . . . . . Martha's Daughter

JOHN PROSKY . . . . Gen. Lewis Armistead
KYLE PRUE . . . . Wounded Maine Soldier
W. JOSEPH QUAM . . . . .1st Irishman
TED REBICH . . . . Looter #3
BROOKE RILEY . . . . .Stage Door Belle
KALI ROCHA . . . . Anna Morrison Jackson
DANA ROHRABACHER . . 20th Maine Officer
TIM RUDDY . . . . Pvt. McMillan
WILLIAM SANDERSON . . . . . Gen. A. P. Hill
NOEL SCHWAB . . . . Colston's Officer
MORGAN SHEPPARD . . . . Gen. Isaac Trimble
THOMAS SILICOTT . . . . .Washington
CHRISTIE LYNN SMITH . . Catherine Corbin
MICHAEL SORVINO . . . . Federal Soldier
MIRA SORVINO . . . . Fanny Chamberlain
STEPHEN SPACEK . Capt. James Power Smith
DANA STACKPOLE . . . . Lottie Estelle
MATTHEW STALEY . . . . Lieutenant Boswell
DAVID STIFEL . . . . Rev. David S. Jenkins
JAMES PATRICK STUART . . . . . Gen. Edward
Porter Alexander
STEPHEN LEONARD SULLIVAN Federal Soldier
BUCK TAYLOR . . . . Gen. Maxcy Gregg
TYLER TRUMBO . . . . Young Wellford
R.E. TURNER . . . . Col. Tazewell Patton
CHRISTOPHER CRUTCHFIELD
WALKER . . . . A Looter
TRENT WALKER . . . . Pvt. McClintock
SCOTT WATKINS . . . . . Gen. Raleigh Colston

Stunt Coordinator . . . . Chris Howell
Stunt Co-Coordinator . . . . Jason Rodriguez
Stunt Performers . . . . . Seth Arnett, Brian Avery,
David Barrett, John Brimley, Richard Bucher,
Gil Combs, Dale Gibson, Tad Griffith, Jim Hart,
Freddie Hice, Shawn Howell, Bobby Jauregui,
Casey O'Neill, Scott Rogers, Mike Watson,
Stanton Barrett, Gene Harrison, Brian Duffy,
Mark Norby, Sean Graham, Victor Quintero,
Phil Colutta, Gene Walker, Chris Branham,
David Burton, Monte Simmons, Rick Barker,
Jason Russo, Jim Pratt, Eric Norris,
Mark Rodriguez, Troy Brown, Todd Forsberg,
Brian Brown, Ryan Brown
Stunt Students . . . . Eric Miranda, David Martin
Associate Producers . . . . Suzanne Arden,
Dennis Frye, Jeff Shaara
for Ted Turner: Frank Janke, Barbara Johnson,
Tina Knight, Chris Molnar, Mimi Wilson
Production Executive . . . . Lynda Clarke
Producer's Personal Assistant . . . Jennifer Slatkin
Consultant to the Producer . . . . Charles J. Mott
Mr. Maxwell's Assistant . . . . . . Michael Atlan
Set Production Staff AssistantJason "Oak" Ritchie
Apprentice . . . . Sam Phillips
Director VP of Development L. Virginia Browne
Historical Coordinator/Set Historian Patrick Falci
Historical Character Research . . . . . . Leo Aylen
Historical Advisors
James I. Robertson, Jr.–*Virginia Tech*
Ervin Jordan–*University of Virginia*
Gabor Boritt–*Civil War Institute, Gettysburg College*
Craig Symonds–*US Naval Academy, Annapolis*
A. Wilson Greene–*Pamplin Historical Park*
Marc Snell–*Civil War Study Center, Shepherd College*

Keith Gibson–*Virginia Military Institute*
David Madden–*LSU*
Dennis Frye
Brian Pohanka
Ed Bearss
Dialect Coach . . . . Robert Easton
Casting Associate . . . . Craig Campobasso, C.S.A.
Extras Casting Central Casting–Washington, DC
Carol Ness, Dagmar Wittmer, Kristine Brooks
Reenactor Manager . . . . Dennis E. Frye
Reenactor Technical Advisor . . . . Dana Heim
Reenactor Technical Advisor . . . . John Bert
Assistant Reenactor Technical Advisor John Goode
Reenactor Artillery Commander Andy Franklin
Reenactor Logistics Manager . . . . Don Warlick
Assistant Reenactor Logistics Manager Bob Tolar
Assistant Reenactor Logistics Manager Kelly Irwin
Reenactor Logistics Assistant . . . . Jan Tolar
Reenactor Office Coordinator . . Monica Hopes
Reenactor Production Staff Assistant Melissa Arch
Reenactor Production Staff Assistant Rita Arch
Reenactor Security . . . . . John Baker, Tudd Dean
Donnie Griffin, Dave Tipler
Key Location Manager . . . . Tom Trigo
Location Manager . . . . John Crowder
Assistant Location Managers . . . . . Joe Cacciotti,
Chris Rock, Stephanie Miller
Location Accountant . . . . Dawn Blacksten
Location Production Staff Assistants . . . .
Raquel Dawn Trigo, Peter Frank
Art Director . . . . Gregory Bolton
Assistant Art Directors . . . . . . Daniel Jennings,
Hugo Santiago
Set Designers . . Patty Klawonn, Jonathan Short,
Martin G. Hubbard, Stan Tropp
Model Builder . . . . C. Scott Baker
Story Board Artists Bot Roda, Timothy Braniff
Art Department Coordinator . . . . Cheree Welsh
Production Staff Assistant . . . . . . Angela DeVore
Set Decorator . . . . Casey Hallenbeck
Leadman . . . . Monti Santilli Rainbolt
Buyer . . . . Carl Cantanese
On-Set Dresser . . . . Andrea Levine
Swing Jamie Bishop, Terry Clark, Lisa Dietrich,
Jeffrey Pratt Gordon, Cliff Euban,
Clark Hospelhorn, Thomas Martin,
Tommy McCutcheon, John Millard,
Angela M. Ratliff, Taylor S. Reese,
Kenny Sheehan, Michael Sabo, Rebecca Shpak,
E. Parker Webb, R. Scott Trieschman,
Mike Reybould, Rick Reeder
Drapery Foreman . . . . Alan Porter
Set Dressing Assistant . . . . Andrew Zeller
Property Master . . . . Kelly G. Farrah
Assistant Property Master . . . . . . Dr. Ray Giron
Assistant Property . . . . Cynthia Giron,
Andrew Brenner
A Camera Operator . . . . Tom Weston
A Camera First Assistant . . . . Clyde Bryan
A Camera Second Assistant . . . Suzanne Trucks
B Camera Operator . . . . Tom Shaughnessy
B Camera First Assistant . . . . Chris Schenck
B Camera Second Assistant . . . Matthew Haskins
Still Photographer . . . . Van Redin
Loader . . . . John R. Hamilton

Gaffers . . . . Bill O'Leary, Brian Gunter
Best Boys . . . . . . Stephen Crowley, Joe Grimaldi
Electricians . . . . Don Aros, Todd H. Ranson,
Russell Wicks, Lewis Sadler
Generator Operator . . Kevin "Vinnie" Campbell
Rigging Gaffer . . . . Jay Douglas Kemp
Best Boy Rigging Electric . . . . . . Robert Spencer
Rigging Electric . . . . Chris Thompson,
Aaron Johnson
Key Grip . . . . Eddie Evans
Best Boy Grip . . . . Tom Barrett
Dolly Grip . . . . Rich Kerekes
Company Grips . . . . Franc Boone, John Kimmer,
Rick Strodel, Kent Eanes, Michael Gearhardt,
Greg Martin, Chris Young
Key Rigging Grip . . . . Charlie Harris
Best Boy Rigging . . . . Michael I. Flinn
Rigging Grips . . . . Chip Ingram, Tim Cote,
Daron Hallowell, Brian Leach
Sound Mixer . . . . Steven Halbert
Boom Operator . . . . Javier Hernandez
Cable Person . . . . Ivan Hawkes
Video Assist . . . . William "Rusty" Gardner
Script Supervisor . . . . Ray Quiroz
Key Makeup . . . . Patty Androff
Assistant Makeup . . . . Rachel Kick,
Janeen Davis-Schreyer
Key Hair . . . . Taylor Knight
Assistant Hair . . . Vanessa Davis, Rosalee Riggle
Mr. Duvall's Hair & Makeup   Manlio Rocchetti
Special FX Makeup   Joe Hurt, Corey Castellano
Special Effects Coordinator . . . . Matt Vogel
First Unit Key . . . . Durk Tyndall
Second Unit Key . . . . Bill Traynor
SPFX Technicians . . Jim Bilz, Thomas Fife, Jim
McPherson . . . . Gary Piklington, Michael Clark,
Harold McConnel, Tom Turnbull, Robert Spore,
Mitch Medford, J.W. McCormick, Hank Attbury,
Rob Vaughan, Jason Ivey, Bill Catania,
William "Bo" Seidel, Mike Tunstall, Tom Scruggs,
Ralph Pivirotto, Ray Tasillo, Barry Davis
Publicity Coordinator . . . . Vic Heutschy
Historical Photographer . . . . Rob Gibson
Production Supervisor . . . . Elpe Villard
Production Coordinator . . . . Gina D'Orazio
Assistant Production Coordinator   Paula Piepho
Production Secretary . . . . Ed Tapia
Travel Coordinator . . . . Monica Goldstein
Ass't to Mssrs. Reheme & Grillo Damon O'Daniel
Set PasStaff Assistants   Greg Dunn, Scott Rorie,
Jonas Spaccarotelli, Brian Avery Galligan,
Stephanie Lovell
Office PasStaff Assistants . . . . . . Kate Meushaw,
Bekki Hunter, Norm Knoerlein, Stas May
Production Accountant . . . . Frank Ellison
First Assistant Accountant . . . . Nancy Klein
Second Assistant Accountant . . . . Sandra Dixon
Payroll Accountants . . . . . . Taffy Schweickhardt,
Timberlee Kislan
Assistant Accountant . . . . Dawson Nolley
Accounting Clerk . . . . . . Cameron McPherson
Construction Auditor . . . . Johnnie Jenkins
Accounting Assistant . . . . Sara Campbell
Construction Coordinator . . . . Bill Iiams
Construction Coordinator (B&O) Michael E. Davis

Construction Foremen . . . . . . Mark Rasmussen,
David Beach
Construction Gangboss . . . . Scott C. Dunn
Propmaker Foremen . . . . Michael Crowe,
Chris Iiams, Samuel H. Brinson, Joe Fama
Labor Foreman . . . . Jamie Soria
Plaster Foreman . . . . Alfred Alvarado
Propmakers . . . . Dames D. Boisseau Jr.
Shane L. Buzby, John Harris Chandler,
Thomas P. Cowen, F. Dale Davis,
Edward G. "Ted" Nolan, Eric Paulson,
Steven Blake, Wesley M. Goodwin,
Ronald J. Napier Jr., Christopher D. Soutwick,
Ron Taylor, John Weiffenback, Daniel J. Yeager,
Joel A. Walton, Walter R. Wright Jr.
Head Greensperson . . . . Mark David Kersey
Greens Foreman . . . . Gordon McVay
Greenspersons James Fulgham, Tommy Grimes,
John Tartaglino, Ronald Sachs, Craig M. Taylor
Lead Paint Foreman . . . . Gary Clark
Lead Painter (B&O) . . . . Susanna Glatty
Painter Gangboss . . . . Ralph Sarabia
Painters . . . . Rafael Lopez, David Eubank,
Wayne L. Miller Jr., Tracey Shusta
Scenic Painters . . Cherie Bowers, Susanna Glatty
Bobby Raber, Willy Richardson, Claire Sharp
Standby Painter . . . . Steve Kerlagon
Carpenters . . . . Dandro Fralinger,
Eric "Ric" Gruber, Randy G. Herbert,
Howard Leigh Jones, John Struss, Jeffrey A. Zook
Toolman . . . . Dan Mark Rasmussen
Plasterers . Michael Alvarado, David L. Falconer
Construction Utility . . . . Dale V. Swavely
Special Construction . . . . James Bingham
Costume Designer . . . . Richard LaMotte
Costume Supervisor . . . . Tom Dawson
Costume Shop Supervisor
Catharine Fletcher Incaprera
Key Set Costumers . . . . . Toby Michael Bronson,
Deborah Latham Binkley
Costumers . . . . James Broomall, Bud Clark,
Brian Callahan, Carl Z. Cunette III,
Linda Boyland, Michael Castellano
Head Tailor . . . . Irvin Gates
Head Cutter / Fitter . . . . . . Robert E. Moore III
Cutter / Fitter . . Maria Vaughan, Marsha Barton
Set Tailor . . . . Mary Wolfson
Tailors . . . . . . Vicente Aguilar, Jo-Sherryl Amos,
Mary Frances Miles, Robert J. Surratt,
Kathie Pierson, Diann Savoy, Pauline Yon
Seamstress . . . . Janet Melody, Janelle Jordan
Wardrobe Staff Assistant . . . Christiana Stetzman
Ayn Vaughan
Cap Costumes . . . . Greg Starbuck
Transportation Coordinator . . . . . . Dan Romero
Transportation Captains . . . . Vic Cuccia,
Michael Luckeroth
Transportation Co-Captains Michael Sean Ryan,
Gerry Titus
Drivers . . . . Robert Dean Winton, Roy A. Grace,
Robert S. Wilhelm Sr., Douglas Walk,
Randolph "Duke" Grant Jr., Lee Jennings,
Kenneth Ziegler Jr., Dan Deprest, Jim Petti,
David Wang, Tom Whelpley, Richard B. Cochin,
Albert "Big Al" Hamilton Sr., Sal Raimond,

Drivers . . . . . James Hubbard, Daniel A. Hirsch, Dave Higdon, Frank G. Metts Sr., Charles "Lenny" Davis, Ira Ayers, Charles B. Plantholt Sr., Stephen Elgert, Frank R. Matkins, Michael Baker, Walter "Pete" Wright, David A. White Jr., James "Jimbo" Hulson Jr., Charles "CJ" Johnson, Ronald Bruce Holtman, Daniel W. Taylor III, William "Billy" Hubbard, Kevin Smith, Robert L. Willumsen, Jennifer Weiland, Patricia "Tinker" Pickens, Jacob Wade Stout, Vincent J. Guariglia, Byron Bobo, David "Hoot" Gipson, Walter Garret, Robert Kurt Brubaker, Richard Lee Cox, John Wayne Kirschke, John C. Watkins, Tom Braatz, Randy Luna, Steve Mitchell, Ronn R. Cain, Gathia "GG" Gillespie, Steve Pollock, George "Woody" Samuels, Walt Miller, William "Bill" Gibson, Charles B. Artley

Head Wrangler . . . . Doug Sloan
Wrangler Gangboss . . . . . Billy L. "Butch" Frank
Second Unit Gangboss . . . . C.J. Staats
Wranglers . . . . Rob Cain, Jim Rostron
Cody Haynes, Jeff Talbert, Joseph M. Radvany, Gil Dean, Marvin F. Schroeder, Ryon Marshall, Charles T. "Tom" Ward, Mike Taft, Paul Ward, Karl Luthin, D.V.M. Lawrence Wesson, Chris Rohlfing, Charley Ward, Charley Sloan
Caterer . . . . Hanna Brothers
Craft Service . . . . Amy Panzer, Donna Kurtinecz Julie Briggs
Set Safety . . . . Peter Marziale, Gary Samuels
American Humane Society . . . . Tayna Obeso

SECOND UNIT
2nd Unit Director/ Cinematographer
William Wages
2nd Unit First Assistant Director . . . Robert Rooy
2nd Unit Second Assistant Director
Joe Incaprera
2nd Unit Add'l Second Assistant Director
Xanthus Valan
A Camera Operator . . . . Chris Moseley
Jeremy Callaway
A Camera First Assistant . . . . . . Lee Blasingame
A Camera Second Assistant   Jacqueline J. Nivens
B Camera Operator . . . . Tom Loizeux
B Camera First Assistant . . . . . Robert Robinson
B Camera Second Assistant . . . . . Wayne Arnold
Camera Loader . . . . Sean Sutphin
Key Grip . . . . Rodney G. French
Jesse Wayne Parker
Best Boy Grip . . . . . . Mark Hutchins, Joe Kurtz
Dolly Grip . . . . John Mang
Hair Stylist . . . . Jo Jo Gutherie Stevens
Shirley Baker
Makeup . . . . Teresa Foschee, Leslie Devlin
Set Dresser . . . . Tommy McCutcheon
Property Master . . . . Steve George
Assistant Property Master . . . . . R. Mark Hughes
Script Supervisor . . . . Lee Bigelow
Sound Mixer . . . . C. Peter Thomas
Boom Operator . . . . Lorenzo Milan
Video Assist . . . . Chaz Laughon

Key Costumer . . . . Drew Fuller
Costumer . . . . Sammy Steward
Craft Service . . . . Bill Kassman, John Ryan
Set PasStaff Assistants . . . . Ruben Rios
Drew Vandervelde, Erin Meehan, Tim Blockburger, Stas May
Transportation Captain . . . . Tom Mawyer
Transportation Co-Captain . . . . Bo Jenkins
Drivers . . . Bobby Jones, Norman "Dick" Taylor W. Carroll Mashall Jr., William "Buddah" Benner, Ted B. Glenn, Riley J. Ordoyne, Greg Patterson, Gerald A. Nuckols, Richard Bursado, Robert W. Proffitt, Robert W. Phillips . . . . George Grenier, Bruce Zamzow, Luther R. Huff

POST PRODUCTION
Post Production Supervisor
Donald "Corky" Ehlers
1st Ass't Editor & Additional Editing Marc Pollon
Second Assistant Editor . . . . Susan Ehlers
Music Editor . . . . Lisa Jaime
Assistant Music Editor . . . . Robb Boyd
Post Production Staff Assistant   Philip Tatler IV
Supervising Sound Editor J. Stanley Johnston, C.A.S.
Bob Newlan, David Hankins
Re-Recording Mixers . . Melissa S. Hofmann, C.A.S.
J Stanley Johnston, C.A.S.
Additional Re-recording Gary J. Coppola, C.A.S.
Pete Elia, C.A.S.
ADR Mixers . . . . Ron Bedrosian
Robert Deschaine, C.A.S., Paul Zydel
Foley Mixers . . . . . Nerses Gezalyn, James Howe
Re-recording Assistants . . . . . Eric Flickinger
Christopher Sidor, Mark Harris, Chris Ostler, Aaron Levy
Engineering . . . . Pat Stoltz, Gary Simpson
Steve Hollenbeck, Bill Ritter, Dave Turkow, Jim Albert, Bill Johnston

Re-Recorded at Todd-AO Studios West
Assistant Sound Supervisor . . . . Robert Morrisey
Dialogue Editors . . . . Ralph Osborn, Jane Boegel
Helen Luttrell
ADR Editor . . . . Patrick Hogan
Effects Editor . . . . . . Brian Thomas Nist, MPSE
Bruce Tanis, Jeff Sawyer, Andrew Ellerd, Mike Babcock
Foley Supervisors . . . . Larry Mann, David Cohn
Foley Editors . . . Richard Burton, Jeremy Grody
Marc Glassman
Foley Walkers . . . Jeffrey Wilhoit, Chris Moriana
James Moriana, Catherine Harper
Assistant Sound Editors . . . . Mary Morrisey
Mark Tracy, Nathan Hankins, Tom Bognar, Jay Clinton, Andrew Bock
Sound Administrators . . . . George Borgh
Casey Barclay, Sara Hankins
Group by . . . . LA Mad Dogs
Group Historical Consultant . . . . Carl Klink

MUSIC
Score Conducted by . . . . Nick Ingman
Orchestra Contractor . . . . Isobel Griffiths
Orchestra Leader . . . . Gavyn Wright
Orchestrator . . . . Andrew Kinney

Orchestrations . . . . Jeff Atmajian, Frank Bennett, Bruce Babcock, Robert Elhai, Don Nemitz, Lolita Ritmanis, Carl Rydlund
Music Scoring Coordinator . . . . Jon McBride
Supervising Copyists . . . . Ross O. deRoche
Audrey deRoche
Recorded at . . . . . Air Lyndhurst Studios, London
Recordist . . . . Jake Jackson
Score Recorded and Mixed by . . . Rick Winquest
Digital Audio Engineer . . . . Tom Trafalski
Mixed at . . . . The Village Recorder, Los Angeles
Assistant Engineer . . . . Okhee Kim
Engineer for Randy Edelman . . . . Elton Ahi
Assistant to Music Supervisor . . . Jari Villanueva
Historical Music Research . . . . Pat Gibson

Uilleann Pipes & Tin Whistle Solos by Paddy Moloney

Fiddle Solos by Mark O'Connor

" 'CROSS THE GREEN MOUNTAIN"
Written and Performed by Bob Dylan
Courtesy of Columbia Records

"GOING HOME"
Music and Lyrics by Mary Fahl, Byron Isaacs and Glenn H. Patscha. Performed by Mary Fahl
Violin solo by Mark O'Connor
Courtesy of Sony Classical/Odyssey Records

"ROGUES MARCH"
Music by D. Emmett & G. Bruce
Performed by The Confederate Guard Fife & Drums

"ANGELS WATCH OVER ME"
Traditional

"THE BONNIE BLUE FLAG"
Written by Harry McCarthy
Performed by 2nd Carolina String Band with David Kincaid & John Whelan

"SILENT NIGHT"
Music by Franz X. Gruber, Lyrics by Joseph Mohr

"SONG FOR THE IRISH BRIGADE"
(aka "Martinmas Time")
Performed by David Kincaid, John Whelan & Group, Traditional, Arranged by David Kincaid

"DIXIE"
Music By D. Emmett. Performed by The 28th Pennsylvania Regimental Band

"UPON THE HEIGHTS OF ALMA"
Performed by Camp Chase Fife & Drums, Tom Kuhn, Director

"McLEOD'S REEL"
Performed by 2nd Carolina String Band with David Kincaid & John Whelan

"SILENT NIGHT"
Music by F.X. Gruber / Lyrics by J. Mohr

VISUAL EFFECTS
Visual Effects Coordinator . . . . Justin Paul Ritter
Visual Effects Cinematographer . . . . Tim Angulo
Visual Effects 1st Ass't Camera . . . Boots Shelton
Visual Effects 2nd Ass't Camera . . . Beth Horton
Visual Effects Key Grip . . . . Ted Spiegler
Visual Effects Best Boy Grip . . . . Rod Fitzgerald

TOYBOX
Senior Inferno Artist . . . . Randy Egan
Inferno Artist . . . . Erik Nordby
    Brian Wawzonek
3D Animator . . . . Doug Oddy
    Benjamin J. Wylie
    Jon Bon Dionne
Visual Effects Coordinator . . . . Christopher Elke
Visual Effects Producer . . . . Lorraine Rozon
Technicolor Creative Services - Hollywood
Executive Producer . . . . Steve Rundell
Digital Matte Painter . . . . Bob Scifo
Digital Composite Artists . . . . . . Adam Howard,
    Eric Myers, Everett Webber,
    Kenny Kinble, Ron Barr
Model Builder . . . . Jon Boneske
I/O Data Managers . . . . Mark Sahaugun
    Dave Alonzo
    Alex Levy
Project Manager Visual Effects . . . . . .Eva Prelle
    MetroLight Studios, Inc.
Executive Producer . . . . Dobbie G. Schiff
Head of Production . . . . John Follmer
VFX Supervisor . . . . .John Townley
Producer . . . . Matt Hullum
CG Supervisor . . . . Chris Ryan
3D Animator . . . . Jerry Weil
Con Pederson . . . .
Compositing Supervisor . . . . Jeremy Burns
Compositor . . . . . Heather McPhee, So-ok Kim,
    Judith Bell, Randy Brown, Walt Cameron,
    Shannon McGee
Rotoscope Artist . . . Elissa Bello, Carlos Morales
Production Coordinator . . . . Jenny Arata
Chief Technology Officer . . . . Brian Krusic
Systems Administration . . . . Michael Whang
System Support . . . . Richard Choi
Production Support . . . . . . Reynaldo Mollinedo
Administrative Assistant . . . . Natalie Carroll
Executive in Charge of Production
    James W. Kristoff

PERPETUAL MOTION PICTURES
Visual Effects Supervisor . . . . . Richard Malzahn
Visual Effects Producer . . . . . Kimberly Sylvester

Efilm Digital Laboratory
Project Manager . . . . Terra Bliss
PM Assistant . . . . Loan Phan
Editorial Supervisor . . . . Kacie Haggerty
Post-Production Audio Services . . . . .Todd-AO
    Vine Street Studios, Miles O' Fun,
    Westwind Media, Sound One
Digital Color by . . . . TECHNIQUE™,
    a Technicolor Business
Executive Producers Evan Edelist, Peter Sternlicht
Digital Intermediate Producer . . . . Tim Belcher

Color Management . . . . Joshua Pines
    Raymond Yeung, Ph.D.
Colorist . . . . Rich Montez
Color Consultant . . . . Dana Ross
Chief Technology Officer . . . . Bob Blanks
Imaging Supervisor . . . . Chris Kutcka
Imaging Technicians . . . . Alex Hernandez,
    Steve Hodge
Digital Restoratio Marco Aiello, LaNelle Mason
Data Management . . . . .Brian Kun, Brian Shows
    George Zidd
Editorial . . . . .Uri Katoni, Jennifer Lee,
Production Technology . . . . Michael Tosti
System Administration Julio Juarez, Ariel Oclarino
Production Coordinator . . . . . Jennifer Coleman

POST-PRODUCTION VIDEO SERVICES
Digital Motion Picture Laboratory Services
    LaserPacific
Digital Cinema Preview Services . . . .LaserPacific
High-Definition Service Coordinator . . . .
. . . . .Nancy Fuller
Digital Projection Consultant . . . . .Terry Brown
Avid Editing Systems and Support .Byrne Bobbitt

Technicolor Creative Visual Services –Hollywood
Executive in Charge . . . . Rich Ellis
Project Manager Editorial Services Devin Sterling

Projectionists . . .Karl O. Gilbert, Mark Holland,
    Frank Barron, Michael Clem, Donald W. Perdue

NEGATIVE CUTTING
Executive Cutting Services
Film Optical .F-Stop
Titles by . . . . .Scarlet Letters
Processing, Printing & Video Dailies . . . . .CFI
Main Titles Design . . . . .Ronald F. Maxwell

THANKS TO

The Commonwealth of Virginia
Virginia Film Commission
The Virginia Military Institute
Washington and Lee University
The towns of Lexington, Staunton & Winchester
Virginia Highlands Film Commission
Silver Brook Farm, Middlebrook

The Governments and Citizens of Hagerstown
& Washington County, MD
Maryland Film Commission
Department of Natural Resources
State of Maryland
Austin Flook farm, Boonsboro

Harpers Ferry National Historic Park
West Virginia Film Commission
The towns of Harpers Ferry, Charles Town &
Martinsburg, WV

Bob Arch, Ted Baehr, Bob Ernst, Dan Ostroff,
Pam Gleason, Bruce Poole, Mike Callas,
Brad Siegel, Stephen Unger, Olivia Maxwell,
Mark McAffee, Cecelia Mason, Michael Wicklein

SPECIAL THANKS TO
Gamila Fakhry-Smith

...and a special acknowledgment of appreciation for the thousands of military and civilian re-enactors who gave generously of their time, learning and devotion to living history and the remembrance of the generation that fought and endured the Civil War. Their voluntary participation enhanced the authenticity of the film. On their behalf, Ted Turner Pictures has helped to inaugurate and has contributed funds to a trust for the preservation of Civil War era sites.

PC video game of *Gods and Generals* published by
Activision, developed by AniVision.

www.godsandgenerals.com
www.ronmaxwell.com
www.tedturnerpictures.com

Original Motion Picture Soundtrack on
SONY Records

Completion Guaranty provided by
International Film Guarantors, Inc.

Production Legal Services by Weissmann Wolff
Bergman Coleman Grodin & Evall LLP

Legal Services by O'Melveny & Myers LLP
Lawson Davis Pickren & Seydel LLP

American Humane Association monitored the
animal action. No animal was harmed in the
making of this film.   (AHA 00337)

Made In America

This Film is Dedicated to the Memory of
John F. Maxwell 1922 – 2001
and Royce Applegate 1939 – 2003

ACKNOWLEDGMENT OF PERMISSIONS: We are grateful to the publishers and other copyright holders named below for permission to reprint artwork and excerpts from these previously published works. Artwork and excerpts appear on the pages listed.

ART: **Page 1:** Courtesy of the Library of Congress, Geography and Map Division, reproduction number G3884.M25S5 1861 .C65 CW 564. Lith. by A. Hoen & Co., Baltimore. **24:** "His Supreme Moment," by Mort Künstler, © Mort Künstler, Inc. www.mkunstler.com. **25:** "War Is So Terrible," by Mort Künstler, © Mort Künstler, Inc. www.mkunstler.com. **34:** Courtesy of the National Archives Records Administration. **48:** Copyright National Portrait Gallery, Smithsonian Institution, Washington, D.C./Art Resource, NY. Photo by H.B. Hull. **49:** Courtesy of Missouri e-Communications. **53:** Courtesy of the Maine Memory Network. **56 (top):** Copyright National Portrait Gallery, Smithsonian Institution, Washington, D.C./Art Resource, NY. Photo by Edward Caledon Bruce. **56 (bottom):** Courtesy of Missouri e-Communications. **58:** Courtesy of the Stonewall Jackson Foundation, Lexington, Virginia. **60:** James C. Frasca Collection. Photo by Haseltine of Portland, Maine. **64:** Courtesy of Missouri e-Communications. **69 (bottom left):** Courtesy of the Virginia Military Institute. **83 (top):** Courtesy of the Ohio Historical Society, Library of Congress, Civil War Stereoviews Collection, call number SC5227. This stereoview is No. 2597 of the "War Views" section of the series entitled "Photographic History: The War for the Union," published by E. & H.T. Anthony & Col, American and Foreign Stereoscopic Emporium, New York. **83 (bottom):** Courtesy of the Ohio Historical Society, Library of Congress, Civil War Stereoviews Collection, call number SC5227. This stereoview is No. 2594 of the "War Views" section of the series entitled "Photographic History: The War for the Union," published by E. & H.T. Anthony & Col, American and Foreign Stereoscopic Emporium, New York. **90 (all three bottom posters):** Courtesy of the New York Historical Society. **94 (bottom):** Courtesy of Missouri e-Communications. **96 (top):** Library of Congress, Prints & Photographs Division, reproduction number LC-DIG-cwpb-00815 DLC. Photo by Timothy H. O'Sullivan, August 1863. **97 (top):** National Museum of American History, Smithsonian Institution. Photo by David Miller. **98:** Courtesy of HarpWeek, LLC. **99:** Library of Congress, Prints & Photographs Division, reproduction number LC-DIG-cwpb-03915 DLC. Photo by Timothy H. O'Sullivan, August 1863. **100 (bottom):** Courtesy of the University of Oklahoma Press. **101 (top):** Library of Congress, Prints & Photographs Division, reproduction number 42160. Photo by Timothy H. O'Sullivan, 1863. **101 (bottom left):** Cooper-Hewitt, National Design Museum, Smithsonian Institution. Winslow Homer (American, 1836-1910), *Young Soldier: Separate Study of Soldier Giving Water to a Wounded Companion*, 1861. Oil, gouache, black crayon on canvas. 360 x 175 mm (14 7/8 x 6 7/8 in.) Gift of Charles Savage Homer, Jr., 1912-12-110. Photo Ken Pelka. **101 (bottom right):** Cooper-Hewitt, National Design Museum, Smithsonian Institution. Winslow Homer (American, 1836-1910), *Wounded Soldier Being Given a Drink from a Canteen*, 1864. Charcoal, white chalk on green paper. 365 x 500 mm (14 3/8 x 19 11/16 in.). Gift of Charles Savage Homer, Jr., 1912-12-100. **102:** Library of Congress, Prints & Photographs Division, reproduction number LC-DIG-cwpb-03847 DLC. Photo by Timothy H. O'Sullivan, August 1863. **103 (top):** Library of Congress, Prints & Photographs Division, reproduction number LC-DIG-cwpb-01097 DLC. Photo by Alexander Gardner, September 1862. **103 (bottom):** Library of Congress, Prints & Photographs Division, reproduction number LC-DIG-cwpb-0 DLC. July 22, 1861. **104 (bottom):** Courtesy of Missouri e-Communications. **105 (bottom):** Courtesy of the National Postal Museum, Smithsonian Institution. **113 (bottom):** Courtesy of the National Archives Records Administration. **116 (top):** Courtesy of Missouri e-Communications. **117 (top):** Courtesy of the National Archives Records Administration. **117 (bottom):** Courtesy of Missouri e-Communications. **125:** Painting by Don Troiani, www.historicalprints.com. **126:** Courtesy of Missouri e-Communications. **131:** Courtesy of the Library of Congress, Geography and Map Division, reproduction number G3884.C36S5 1863 .M3 Vault: CW 528. **138 (top):** Historic American Sheet Music, "The Bonnie Blue Flag," Conf. Music #7, Duke University Rare Book, Manuscript, and Special Collections Library. **138 (bottom):** Historic American Sheet Music, "The Bonnie Flag with the Stripes and Stars," Music B1001, Duke University Rare Book, Manuscript, and Special Collections Library. **140 (left):** Historic American Sheet Music, "Our National War Songs," Music W926M, Duke University Rare Book, Manuscript, and Special Collections Library.

EXCERPTS: **49:** Richard Taylor, *Deconstruction and Reconstruction: Personal Experiences of the Late War* (J. S. Sanders & Co.). **52:** From *The Killer Angels* by Michael Shaara, copyright © 1974 by Michael Shaara. Used by permission of David McKay Company, a division of Random House, Inc. **58:** Kagan & Associates, *Great Battles of the Civil War: An Illustrated History of Courage Under Fire* (Oxmoor House, Inc.). **97:** Edited by Ella Jane Bruen and Brian M. Fitzgibbons, *Through Ordinary Eyes: The Civil War Correspondence of Rufus Robbins, Private, 7th Regiment, Massachusetts Volunteers* (Praeger Publishers). **103:** *Humphry's Journal.* **105:** John William DeForest, *A Volunteer's Adventures: A Union Captain's Record of the Civil War* (Yale University Press).

The publisher has made every effort to contact copyright holders; any errors or omissions are inadvertent and will be corrected upon notice in future reprintings.

ACKNOWLEDGMENTS

Publisher Esther Margolis of Newmarket Press wishes to thank the following for their special contributions to this book:

At Person to Person Films, the *Gods and Generals* production office: Michael Atlan, who kept the book project in front of Ron Maxwell during a hectic post-production schedule, L. Virginia Browne, and Marc Pollan. At Ted Turner Pictures: President Robert Wussler, Suzanne Arden, Tina Knight, and Peter McPartlin. Unit publicist Vic Heutschy, and unit photographer Van Redin for his superb photographs of the production. At Warner Bros: Mick Mayhew, Marc Cohen, Drew Giordano, Ernie Johnston, Ron Chan, Dawn Taubin and Debbie Miller. Associate producer Dennis E. Frye and historians James I. Robertson, Jr. and Frank A. O'Reilly for their invaluable essays. Production designer Michael Z. Hanan, costume designer Richard La Motte, storyboard artist Bot Roda, dialect coach Robert Easton, casting director Joy Todd, special effects producer Thomas G. Smith, makeup artist Patty Androff, and cast members Donzaleigh Abernathy, Kali Rocha, and Mia Dillon for providing information and materials about their roles in the production. Artist Mort Künstler and historical photographer Rob Gibson, for their generous cooperation and permission to reproduce their work in connection with *Gods and Generals*. Please visit www.mortkunstler.com and www.civilwarphotography.com. Contributing writers Nancy Friedman and Antonia Felix; book designers Timothy Shaner and Christopher Measom of Night & Day Design; project editor Diana Landau of Parlandau Communications; and Keith Hollaman, Shannon Berning, Frank DeMaio, Tom Perry, and Kelli Taylor at Newmarket Press. Special thanks to Ted Turner for his vision in making this film. We are grateful to Jeff Shaara for his support of this book and for his moving foreword. Our deepest thanks go to director, producer, and screenwriter Ron Maxwell for his passionate commitment to the making of *Gods and Generals* and his generous contributions to this book.

Original Motion Picture Soundtrack available on Sony Classical.